Large Print 791.457 Arm
Armstrong, Jennifer Keishin.
Seinfeldia : how a show about
nothing changed everything

SEINFELDIA

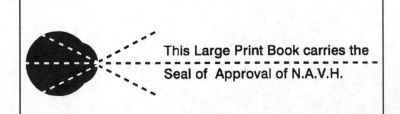

This Large Print Book carries the
Seal of Approval of N.A.V.H.

SEINFELDIA

HOW A SHOW ABOUT NOTHING
CHANGED EVERYTHING

JENNIFER KEISHIN ARMSTRONG

THORNDIKE PRESS
A part of Gale, Cengage Learning

GALE
CENGAGE Learning·

Farmington Hills, Mich • San Francisco • New York • Waterville, Maine
Meriden, Conn • Mason, Ohio • Chicago

GALE
CENGAGE Learning®

LIBRARY OF CONGRESS CATALOGING-IN-PUBLICATION DATA

Names: Armstrong, Jennifer Keishin, author.
Title: Seinfeldia : how a show about nothing changed everything / by Jennifer
    Keishin Armstrong.
Description: Large print edition. | Waterville, Maine : Thorndike Press, 2016. |
    Series: Thorndike Press large print popular and narrative nonfiction | Includes
    bibliographical references.
Identifiers: LCCN 2016020174 | ISBN 9781410490711 (hardcover) | ISBN 1410490718
    (hardcover)
Subjects: LCSH: Seinfeld (Television program) | Large type books.
Classification: LCC PN1992.77.S4285 A86 2016 | DDC 791.45/72—dc23
LC record available at https://lccn.loc.gov/2016020174

Published in 2016 by arrangement with Simon & Schuster, Inc.

Seinfeld is something I learned to do because I was given the opportunity. Then the show spiraled off into this whole other entity that I knew I had to serve because it had its own desire to be something.

— Jerry Seinfeld

CONTENTS

7

NOTE ON
REPORTING METHODS

The following narrative's scenes from the years *Seinfeld* was on the air are re-created with the help of dozens of personal interviews with those who were present, as well as accounts from newspapers, books, magazines, recorded interviews, and other research materials. I privileged uncut, recorded, archival interviews over other secondary sources. I've indicated within the text, when necessary, who is doing the recounting. Scenes were checked by multiple sources when possible; dialogue comes from the accounts of those who were present. Full notes on specific sourcing are available at the end of the book.

INTRODUCTION:
THE BASEBALL GAME

Three women in big hair and flowered dresses — plus another in jeans — convulsed on the grass near third base. Earth, Wind & Fire's "Shining Star" pumped through the speakers of the Brooklyn Cyclones' minor league stadium for the world's most herky-jerky dance-off. Only one woman could be crowned the Best Elaine. They writhed and spasmed as if their lives depended on it. And this was exactly what the sold-out crowd of 7,500 spectators had come for. The baseball game was beside the point.

On July 5, 2014, the team's stadium — nestled within Coney Island's boardwalk and hot dog stands — became its own carnivalesque attraction. A banner at the entrance to the field rebranded it "Vandelay Industries Park" for the day. The first three thousand fans through the gate got bobblehead dolls that looked like former Mets player Keith Hernandez. This meant showing up at least three hours early. There were reports of people later selling them for up to $60 to other desperate fans. (A year later they were selling for up to $100 via online auction sites.)

Inside, a lanky seventy-one-year-old with a backward baseball cap over his gray curls hocked ASSMAN license plates and MASTER OF MY DOMAIN sweatshirts. Among the many who threw out "first" pitches: an importer/exporter, postal workers, architects, a latex salesman, and a New York resident named George Costanza. If you do not understand why this procession of individuals was chosen, you did not belong at this game.

This bizarre parade of nonsensical characters and references made plenty of sense to those who had clamored for the tickets. It was *Seinfeld* appreciation night, and it was packed with activities that brought the show's trademark bouillabaisse of cultural references and inside jokes to life. The aspiring Elaines were reenacting the 1996 episode in which Elaine — the only woman among the four main characters, and the only one with any clear career ambition — loses the respect of her employees when she dances absurdly at a work function. Vandelay Industries is the company that George, the balding schlub with a deficit of ambition, pretends to work for. Keith Hernandez famously played himself in a 1992 episode, becoming a sore point between Jerry, the show's main character, and Elaine, who ends up dating Jerry's longtime idol.

Never mind that this show went off the air sixteen years earlier. The game sold out weeks in advance, and the vast majority of the crowd was not there for baseball. Few people left even as the score shot farther and farther out of the Cyclones' favor, ending up at an 18–2 blowout. That's because almost every nonbaseball moment was filled with something far more fun: a Junior Mint toss, a cereal-eating contest, a marble-rye fishing race, a pick-or-scratch contest. In a presumable coincidence, the women's restrooms ran low on toilet paper. Some fans reenacted the "Can you spare a square?" *Seinfeld* moment, whether they wanted to or not, giggling knowingly.

Fans carried giant cutouts of Seinfeld's and Hernandez's faces. One guy dressed like Kramer, with a bushy wig and a pipe. Another wore a jersey with the name KOKO on the back, an obscure reference to George's least-favorite office nickname. Several puffy shirts of the kind Jerry once reluctantly wore appeared throughout the crowd, and on the team's seagull mascot.

Emily Donati, who had traveled nearly a hundred miles from Philadelphia to be there, had VANDELAY INDUSTRIES business cards printed up, with the fake e-mail address importer@exporter.gov and the tagline . . . AND YOU WANT ME TO BE YOUR LATEX SALESMAN! She passed them out to appreciative fellow fans throughout the day.

Fans preferred talking *Seinfeld* with one another to watching the increasingly horrific game. By the fifth inning (score: 16–0), they were mostly concerned about how much longer they'd have to wait before the end of the game so they could participate in the promised postgame extravaganza: Every fan who wished to could run the bases, and people named Jerry got to go first.

This particularly consumed Jerry Kallarakkal. He'd gone to get a wristband that would allow him to the front of the line, but the woman hadn't even asked him for an ID. And they'd run out of wristbands, so she gave him a stick-on name tag that said JERRY. What kind of operation was this? Surely there would be hundreds of fake Jerrys out on that field after the game.

Then again, the boundaries between "real" and "fake" had dissolved long before this incident.

Seinfeld has a special kind of magic.

The Cyclones' *Seinfeld* gambit was so successful that five months later, a minor-league hockey team, the Condors, of Bakersfield, California, had its own *Seinfeld*-themed night, with the players wearing puffy shirt–style jerseys. And the Cyclones planned another *Seinfeld* night for summer 2015, packed with still more references: Kramer's Technicolor Dreamcoat jerseys, a muffin-top-popping competition, a trash-eating competition . . .

Like those who filled the Cyclones' stadium in 2014, almost every fan thinks he or she is the biggest *Seinfeld* fan. Like those 7,500 fans, many *Seinfeld* acolytes share an urge to express their fandom in some grand, public way; specifically, to interact in real life with the fictional world it created. *Seinfeld* created more ways to do that, more portals between its fictional world and reality, than the average show. Knowing Elaine's dance, or the Keith Hernandez joke, or the "master of my domain" joke, is like knowing a secret password — a very widely known secret password — among the show's fans. Coming to "Vandelay Industries Park" that day allowed those 7,500 fans not only to reach out to other fans but also to interact with the very object of their fandom. They could meet the Soup Nazi or the "real Kramer." They could *be* George or Jerry or Elaine or Kramer. They could, in fact, be all of them in the same day.

When it comes to all things *Seinfeld,* such strange intermingling of fiction and reality has long been status quo. Such was the power of this show — and its staying power in constant reruns — that its characters, settings, jokes, and catchphrases continue to intrude on our daily reality twenty years later. Fans may wake up on any given day in the 2010s to find that someone has made *Seinfeld* emojis; or a 3-D rendering of Jerry's apartment that anyone with an Oculus Rift can electronically "walk" through; or an online game that allows them to drop Junior Mints into a surgery patient, as once happened on a particularly bizarre *Seinfeld* episode. They can go to a college campus celebration of Festivus, the fictional holiday *Seinfeld* introduced, and even turn on the TV to find an earnest Fox News host debating the merits of Festivus as if our country's future depended on it. They can attend a med school class in which students solemnly diagnose *Seinfeld* characters' mental illnesses. In fact, almost from the beginning,

16

Seinfeld has generated a special dimension of existence, somewhere between the show itself and real life, that I've come to call "Seinfeldia."

It is a place that the show's creators, Larry David and Jerry Seinfeld, constructed themselves, even if they didn't realize it at the time, when they blurred the boundaries between their fictions and reality like no show before *Seinfeld* did. (Is the comedian named Jerry Seinfeld on the show the same as the comedian named Jerry Seinfeld who plays him? Are the real New York places depicted on *Seinfeld* as filled with crazy characters and antics as they are on television? Is *Seinfeld* the "show about nothing" that Jerry and his friend George pitch to fictional NBC executives in the show's fourth season?) Seinfeldia is a place that now carries on, as vital as ever, without its original architects, thanks to incessant syndicated reruns that continue to gain new generations of fans and a religious fan base bent on ritually resurrecting the show's touchstone moments via cocktail-party quote recitations.

This show that officially ended in 1998 still, almost two decades later, draws crowds to bus tours of its sites and ultracompetitive trivia contests about its minutiae. In 2014,

17

the most anticipated Super Bowl commercial featured Jerry and George chatting at a coffee shop as if no time had passed.

Seinfeld has continued to survive in the most exciting — and precarious — time in television since the medium's invention. By now, the show has been off the air almost twice as long as it was on the air, and yet it lives on like no other television series. Thus it continues to bring in millions of dollars in syndication fees and advertising revenue every year — $3.1 billion total between its 1998 finale and 2014. In 2015, streaming video service Hulu won an intense bidding war for rights to the show, offering a reported $160 million to bring it to a new generation of viewers.

The history of *Seinfeld* is not complete, and may never be. It is the story of two men whose sitcom — full of minute observations and despicable characters — snuck through the network system to become a hit that changed TV's most cherished rules; from then on, antiheroes would rise to prominence, unique voices would invade the airwaves, and the creative forces behind shows would often gain as much power and fame as the faces in front of the cameras.

Seinfeld's story is the story of the rise of fan culture, and Internet communion among those fans, starting from the web's nascent days. It is the story of television gaining respect as an art form and the subject of serious academic study. It is the story of one show that has defied the odds again and again, then a few more times still, to remain a vibrant force in everyday life, in ways mundane and strange alike. It is a story still playing out every day here in Seinfeldia. But it is, of course, a story that starts with that of its founders, Larry David and Jerry Seinfeld, and the people who helped them build it. This is that story.

1
THE ORIGIN STORY

Jerry Seinfeld ventured into a Korean deli one night in November 1988 with fellow comic Larry David after both had performed, as usual, at the Catch a Rising Star comedy club on the Upper East Side of New York City. Seinfeld needed David's help with what could be the biggest opportunity of his career so far, and this turned out to be the perfect place to discuss it.

They had come to Lee's Market on First Avenue and Seventy-Eighth Street, maybe for some snacks, maybe for material. The mundane tasks of life and comic gold often merged into one for them. Sure enough, they soon were making fun of the products they found among the fluorescent-lit aisles. Korean jelly, for instance: Why, exactly, did it have to come in a jelly form? Was there also, perhaps, a foam or a spray? The strange foods on the steam table: Who ate those?

"This is the kind of discussion you don't see on TV," David said.

Seinfeld had told David a bit of news over the course of the evening: NBC was interested in doing a show with him. Some executive had brought him in for a meeting and everything. Seinfeld didn't have any ideas for television. He just wanted to be himself and do his comedy. He felt David might be a good brainstorming partner.

Seinfeld and David had a common sensibility, in part because of their similar backgrounds: Both had grown up in the New York area and were raised Jewish. Both seized on observational humor for their acts. They had their differences, too, that balanced each other nicely: Seinfeld was thirty-four and on the rise thanks to his genial, inoffensive approach to comedy and his intense drive to succeed. David was far more caustic and sensitive to the slightest audience infractions (not listening, not laughing at the right moments, not laughing enough). He was older, forty-one, and struggling on the stand-up circuit because of his propensity to antagonize his audiences out of a rather explosive brand of insecurity.

Seinfeld had dark hair blown dry into the classic '80s pouf, while David maintained a magnificent Jew-fro, dented a bit in the middle by his receding hairline. Seinfeld's delivery often ascended to a high-pitched warble; David favored a guttural grumble that could become a yell without warning.

They'd first become friends in the bar of Catch a Rising Star in the late '70s when Seinfeld started out as a comic. From then on, they couldn't stop talking. They loved to fixate on tiny life annoyances, in their conversations and their comedy. Soon they started helping each other with their acts and became friendly outside of work.

Seinfeld had gotten big laughs by reading David's stand-up material at a birthday party for mutual friend Carol Leifer — one of the few women among their band (or any band) of New York comedians. David, nearly broke, had given Leifer some jokes as a birthday "gift." Too drunk to read them aloud, she handed them off to Seinfeld; he killed, which suggested some creative potential between the two men.

As a result, it made sense for Seinfeld to approach David with this TV "problem" he now had. David also remained the only "writer" Seinfeld knew, someone who had, as Seinfeld said, "actually typed something out on a piece of paper" when he churned out bits for sketch shows like *Fridays* and

Saturday Night Live.

Seinfeld was smart to consult David on this TV thing. David did have a vision, if not a particularly grand one. "This," David said as they bantered in Lee's Market, "is what the show should be." Seinfeld was intrigued.

The next night, after their comedy sets at the Improv in Midtown, David and Seinfeld went to the Westway Diner around the corner, at Forty-Fourth Street and Ninth Avenue. At about midnight, they settled into a booth and riffed on the possibilities: What about a special that simply depicted where comics get their material? Jerry could play himself in that, for sure. Cameras could document him going through his day, having conversations like the one at the market the night before; he'd later put those insights into his act, which audiences would see at the end of the special. As they brainstormed, Seinfeld had one cup of coffee, then two. He usually didn't drink coffee at all. They were onto something.

Seinfeld liked the idea enough to take it to NBC. The network signed off on it, suggesting a ninety-minute special called *Seinfeld's Stand-Up Diary* that would air in *Saturday Night Live*'s time slot during an off week. As he thought about it, though, Seinfeld worried about filling an entire ninety minutes; thirty minutes, on the other hand, he could do.

By the time he and David had written a thirty-minute script, in February 1989, they realized they had a sitcom on their hands instead of a special. Jerry and a Larry-like guy could serve as the two main characters, who would discuss the minutiae of their lives and turn it into comedy — like Harold Pinter or Samuel Beckett for television. "Two guys talking," Seinfeld said. "This was the idea."

To that setup, they added a neighbor. David told Seinfeld about his own eccentric neighbor, Kenny Kramer — a jobless schemer with whom David shared a car, a TV, and one pair of black slacks in case either had a special occasion. He would be the basis for the third character. They set the first scene in a fictional coffee shop like the one where they'd hatched their idea, and called it Pete's Luncheonette.

Seinfeldia's founding father and namesake got his first inkling that he was funny at age eight. Little Jerry Seinfeld was sitting on a stoop with a friend in his middle-class town on Long Island, eating milk and cookies. Jerry — usually a dorky, shy kid — said something funny enough to cause his friend to spit milk and cookies back into Jerry's face and hair. Jerry thought, *I would like to do this professionally.*

Seinfeld was born in Brooklyn but grew up in Massapequa. He spent his childhood watching *Laugh-In, Batman, The Honeymooners,* and *Get Smart.* ("When I heard that they were going to do a sitcom with a secret agent who was funny, the back of my head blew off," he later said.) His parents, Betty and Kal, made humor a priority in their home. His father, a sign merchant, told jokes often. Even his business's name was a joke: Kal Signfeld Signs.

As Jerry came into his own sense of humor, his performances grew more elaborate than mere jokes on the stoop. At Birch Lane Elementary School, he planned and starred in a skit for a class fair with his friend Lawrence McCue. Jerry played President Kennedy, and Lawrence played a reporter who asked him questions — essentially, set up his jokes. They were the only ones at the fair who did a comedy routine. When Jerry graduated to Massapequa High School in 1968, he grew obsessed with two things: cars and the comedian Bill Cosby. He dabbled in acting, playing Julius Caesar in his tenth-grade English class. But comedy remained his focus. He saw even geometry class as training for comedy; a good joke, he felt, had the same rigorous internal logic as a theorem proof. The only difference was the silly twist at the end of a joke.

When a long-haired Jerry Seinfeld attended Queens College, he acted in school productions and hung around the New York comedy clubs, wearing white sneakers like his idols Joe Namath and Cosby (circa the comedian's time on the '60s show *I Spy*). As he waited to get up the nerve to pursue stand-up as a profession, he used his attendance at Manhattan comedy clubs as a kind of independent study. He analyzed comics' approach to their material and even wrote a forty-page paper on the subject.

He started to know the players: He eavesdropped, for instance, on Larry David talking to another comedian. David happened to be leaning on Seinfeld's car, a 1973 Fiat 128 SL, in front of the Improv one day in 1975, the first time Seinfeld ever saw his future writing partner. Seinfeld was impressed with these guys' dedication to the profession. He didn't dare speak to them yet.

After he graduated in 1976 as an honor student, Seinfeld applied his sense of discipline to becoming a stand-up, approaching it methodically. His first appearance on a professional stage as a comedian was at Catch a Rising Star in 1976, at age twenty-two. He'd practiced his routine with a bar of soap until he had every word memorized. Comedian Elayne Boosler introduced him, and he took the stage. Once he got there, though, he couldn't remember a word. He stood there for several long seconds, not saying a thing. Finally, he remembered the subjects he'd planned to talk about, so, without anything else to say, he listed them to the audience: "the beach, driving, parents." People laughed, thinking this *was* his act, some high-concept performance art. Eventually he managed to fill three minutes with bits of material until he escaped the spotlight.

"That's Jerry Seinfeld," Boosler quipped to the audience when it ended, "the king of the segue."

For four years, Seinfeld walked around the city night after night to hit clubs. He'd go eighteen months in a row without one night off. He tape-recorded his routines, then analyzed them to improve by the next night. He also fell in love with *The Mary Tyler Moore Show,* which became a favorite among New York City comics in the '80s because its syndicated reruns aired after

Late Night with David Letterman, dovetailing with the time they got home from work. They talked about the previous night's episode when they saw one another at clubs, sometimes making dirty jokes about Mary and Rhoda.

In 1979, after three years on the circuit, Seinfeld got what could have been a big break. He was cast as a recurring character on the hit sitcom *Benson,* a mail delivery guy named Frankie who did comedy routines no one wanted to hear. (The five-foot-eleven-inch comedian would bound into *Benson*'s living-room set with an attempted catchphrase: "Give a cheer, Frankie's here!") After three episodes, however, he showed up for a read-through and found no script waiting with his name on it. When he asked what was going on, an assistant director pulled him aside to tell him: He'd been fired.

Still, by the early '80s, Seinfeld was secure in his position on the comedy circuit. He knew his brand. As he told teenage interviewer Judd Apatow, who hosted a show called *Club Comedy* on the Syosset High School radio station on Long Island, it took time to develop the skills that led to great observational jokes. "It's one thing to see something," Seinfeld said, "and another thing to do something with it."

He would start with something that struck him as funny — it could be something as small as a silly word — and then work on it until he conveyed what he found *so* funny about it to his audience. The first line of a joke always had to be funny. Then he went from there, from funny thought to funny thought with the fewest possible unfunny thoughts in between, until it got to the absolute biggest laugh at the end. He was focused only on making people laugh, nothing else. "Funny is the world I live in," he later said. "You're funny, I'm interested. You're not funny, I'm not interested."

By the time he chatted with young Apatow in the early '80s, he was playing clubs in New York, Atlantic City, and elsewhere. Apatow asked him, "Where do you go from here? How much farther can you get?"

"There's a lot you can do," Seinfeld said. "You can do a sitcom, which is something a lot of people don't want to be associated with. I'm going to do some acting. But stand-up is what I am. The acting will be to improve my visibility." When Apatow asked what "success" meant to Seinfeld, the comedian had a clear and simple answer: "To be considered one of the best stand-up comics."

Around the same time as his interview with Apatow, Seinfeld hit the big time: his first appearance on *The Tonight Show Starring Johnny Carson* in 1981. For him it was "the Olympics, the Super Bowl, and the World Series all rolled into one," he later said. He edited his usual twenty-minute set down to its best five minutes, then practiced it at clubs five or six times a night, repeating it probably two hundred times before his big debut. He jogged to get into top physical condition. He played tapes of the *Superman* theme to psych himself up.

Kal Seinfeld made a sign that he placed on his van the week before his son's appearance. In black letters over orange and green paint, it said: JERRY SEINFELD OF MASSAPEQUA WILL BE ON CARSON SPECIAL. Kal also took out an ad in the local paper to announce the occasion.

The actual performance flew by for Jerry like a downhill roller coaster. He riffed on complex turn lanes, the 1,400-pound man in *The Guinness Book of World Records,* and weather reports: "They show you the satellite photo. This is real helpful, a photograph of the earth from ten thousand miles away. Can you tell if you should take a sweater or not from that shot?" Better yet, he earned laughs in all the right places, some spontaneous applause, and an "OK" sign from Carson himself.

The appearance would lead to several more on Carson's show as well as *Late Night with David Letterman.* Seinfeld later called being on Carson "the difference between thinking you're a comedian and really being one." Seinfeld would not have to do any more embarrassing bit parts on sitcoms.

In 1984, though, he did go back to acting, as he'd predicted when speaking to Apatow. This time, his prospects looked a little better. There he was, a lanky young man with a whoosh of dark hair, slick as ever in a black suit, black tie, and white shirt as he sat behind a network-executive desk in a Showtime movie that satirized the TV business, *The Ratings Game.* "The networks aren't buying Italians, Jews, Puerto Ricans this season," he says as he swigs milk and eats chocolate cookies. "They're buying gays, alcoholics, child molesters."

A few years later came one more chance in television. In 1988, a new production company named Castle Rock considered casting Seinfeld in a sitcom pilot called *Past Imperfect* for ABC. Ultimately, the network rejected him because of his lack of acting experience, and the part went to another stand-up, Howie Mandel, but the pilot never aired.

Seinfeld segued back into full-time stand-up, doing up to three hundred appearances per year across the country. He had regular spots on *The Tonight Show.* He had a comfortable life and didn't seem concerned with fame.

As it turned out, however, those last two experiences in television — his Showtime role and his almost-pilot — were prophetic. *The Ratings Game* included Seinfeld's future *Seinfeld* costar, Michael Richards; Seinfeld's line anticipated how NBC execcutives would later object to his own sitcom creation — the part about the Jews, at least. And his relationship with Castle Rock would prove critical when it came time to produce his own sitcom.

Larry David was what's known as a comic's comic, an acquired taste, "which means I sucked," he often said. One bit, indicative of his style, zeroed in on the confusing rules of when to use the familiar *tu* for "you" in romance languages. "Caesar used the *tu* form with Brutus even after Brutus stabbed him," he said, "which I think is going too far." Other riffs had him putting himself on trial for masturbation and playing the part of Hitler enjoying a magician's act. Even his appearance seemed a willful attempt to spurn mainstream audiences: He favored an army jacket and emphasized his receding hairline by letting the sides grow into great poufs that his friend Richard Lewis once described as "a combination of Bozo and Einstein. . . . Talk about walking to the beat of your own drum. I mean, this guy was *born* in a snare drum."

In the early '80s, David found a place to channel his unusual talents, ABC's attempt at a *Saturday Night Live*–like sketch show filmed in Los Angeles called *Fridays*. There, he, too, worked with Michael Richards, one of the show's core cast members and another baffling comic.

Fridays' debut was received by critics and viewers with indifference for the most part. Some affiliates, however, refused to air it after seeing stomach-churning sketches like "Diner of the Living Dead" (in which patrons chew on corpses' body parts) and "Women Who Spit" (in which female talk show guests . . . spit). In its second season, the series started to find its footing, impressing some critics with its pointed political satire, like a skit featuring a Ronald Reagan impersonator in the role of Frank, the alien transvestite in *The Rocky Horror Picture*

Show, and another with Popeye fighting fascism.

David played a major part in one of the show's signature political send-ups, a riff on Bing Crosby and Bob Hope's series of silly, musical travel movies (*Road to Singapore, Road to Zanzibar,* etc.). The sketch skewered President Ronald Reagan's El Salvador policy, with the bumbling stars affably engaging in hijinks in the military-governed state. David did a solid Crosby, and Richards appeared as an El Salvadoran soldier. "Boy, I gotta figure out a way to get my buddy boy out of there," David burbled as the soldiers mistook Bob Hope for the American sent to teach them how to use the machine guns.

In other ingenious sketches, David played a childhood friend of Libyan dictator Muammar Gaddafi; a temp hired to fill in for the Secretary of State on one occasion and Gloria Steinem on another; and half of a couple who lives their life in front of a sitcom studio audience in their apartment.

But David hated being recognizable because it made him susceptible to public criticism of his work. With his first steady gig at *Fridays,* he bought himself a Fiat convertible. Ten minutes out of the dealership, with the top down, he pulled up at a light and someone at a nearby bus stop yelled out, "Your show stinks!" He put the top up and, at least the way he later told the story, never put it down again.

Fridays ended after three seasons, in 1982. *Saturday Night Live*'s executive producer, Dick Ebersol, offered jobs to everyone who'd worked on the show. Only David and fellow writer Rich Hall took Ebersol up on it.

In David's one season on the writing staff of *Saturday Night Live,* 1984–85, he got just one sketch onto the show. It aired in the time slot few ever saw: 12:50 A.M. He quit in a rage, then regretted it and showed up back at work as if nothing had happened. He would file this experience away — and many other indignities large and small — to use as a plotline in the show he and Seinfeld would eventually create together, reinventing the medium that had once humiliated him.

A few years later, David was finished with writing for sketch and variety shows. MTV executive Joe Davola had noticed his work on *Fridays* and liked it so much that he asked David in for a meeting on a comedy/game show hybrid he produced called *Remote Control.* "I appreciate it," Davola recalls David saying, "but this is not where

I want to go with my career." Instead, David wrote a screenplay called *Prognosis Negative,* which never got produced.

Meanwhile, Seinfeld had already made several smart choices in his fledgling career, and among them was to sign with manager George Shapiro.

Shapiro was inspired to go into show business like his uncle, *Dick Van Dyke Show* creator Carl Reiner. Shapiro's charm — kind eyes, a warm smile, and a hint of a New York accent — made him particularly suited to being a talent manager, endearing himself to both performers and executives. He had spent the early years of his career at the William Morris talent agency in New York. There, he'd helped put together TV comedies such as *The Steve Allen Show, That Girl,* and *Gomer Pyle.* Now, as a talent manager for young comedian Jerry Seinfeld, he may have been simply doing his job when he told NBC executives that his client belonged on their network. But he was also speaking from decades of experience during TV's formative years.

Shapiro sent regular letters to NBC's entertainment president, Brandon Tartikoff, and its head of development, Warren Littlefield, every time Seinfeld had a good performance on *The Tonight Show* or *Late Night.*

In 1988, he made his strongest epistolary plea as Seinfeld prepared for his first concert broadcast at Town Hall in New York City. "Call me a crazy guy," Shapiro wrote to Tartikoff, "but I feel that Jerry Seinfeld will soon be doing a series on NBC." He closed by inviting Tartikoff to attend the Town Hall event. No one from the network came, but Tartikoff invited Seinfeld and Shapiro in for a meeting.

Seinfeld didn't know his manager had badgered NBC about him. He was still unaware when he and Shapiro headed to NBC's Los Angeles offices on November 2, 1988, to discuss the possibility of a network project with Tartikoff, Littlefield, and the head of late-night programming and specials, Rick Ludwin. Seinfeld hadn't the first idea what he'd do on television — his main career plan was to be a stand-up comedian for as long as he could.

He was also a little annoyed at this meeting screwing up his whole afternoon. He'd become a comedian partly to have his days free from 10:00 A.M. to 6:00 P.M. This meeting was at 5:15 P.M., cutting right into his free time, but he sucked it up and went anyway.

"What would you like to do in television?" Ludwin, a milky-skinned, bespectacled executive, asked. "Would you like to host a late-night show? Would you like to do prime-time specials?"

"The only thing I had in mind was having a meeting like this," Seinfeld said, half joking. A fancy meeting with network executives had crossed his mind as a symbol of success in comedy, but he'd never thought beyond that. He told the executives he'd want to play himself in anything he did, but that was all he knew for sure.

A few months later, Seinfeld had joined forces with Larry David on the script, starting with their fateful discussion in the diner. Once they had come up with what they believed was a solid sitcom proposal, Seinfeld had to return to pitch it to the network executives. For a real, ongoing sitcom, they'd also need a studio to finance production, and Shapiro hooked them up with Castle Rock Entertainment, which Carl Reiner's son, *All in the Family* star and movie director Rob Reiner, had just cofounded. The studio had also considered Seinfeld for the *Past Imperfect* pilot. Now they signed on with Seinfeld's possible new project, given that the network had just agreed to air it. Why not? The deal was done with NBC. The studio simply had to finance it, which was easy with a recent investment they'd gotten from Columbia Pictures. The network had already promised to put the show on the air, which guaranteed at least some return for the studio.

Several Castle Rock executives sat in as David and Seinfeld outlined the new sitcom concept to NBC in entertainment president Brandon Tartikoff's office.

The comedian charmed the room, got some laughs. Tartikoff signed on with a bit of a shrug. It would require a small development deal. He and his executives liked Seinfeld's humor. They, too, thought: *Why not?* "George," Tartikoff said to Shapiro, "now you don't have to send me any more letters." They weren't sure about this Larry David guy, some struggling comic who had never written a sitcom script, much less produced a show. But they went along with his involvement for the moment since it seemed to be what Seinfeld wanted.

The executives had one suggestion: They envisioned the show as a multicamera production — that is, a traditional sitcom shot in front of a studio audience, like *I Love Lucy* and most other TV comedies since the 1950s — rather than a one-camera show, shot more like a film, as the comedians had pitched it. David hated this change. "No, no, no, no, no," he said, "this is not the show." Silence descended. "If you think we're going to change it, we're not."

Seinfeld proved the more diplomatic of the two, as he would in many instances to come. He said he and his partner would talk about it.

Once David and Seinfeld left the meeting, David remembered the $25,000 he was being paid for the pilot. David agreed to the change. He would at least make his twenty-five grand and move on.

Soon came another test of the budding relationship between Seinfeld and NBC, when a scathing review of Seinfeld's stand-up show in Irvine, California, ran in the *Los Angeles Times*. In January 1989, Lawrence Christon wrote: "He's expressive. He's clear. And he's completely empty. . . . There isn't a single portion of his act that isn't funny — amusing might be a better word — but ten minutes or so into it, you begin wondering what this is all about, when is he going to say something or at least come up with something piquant."

As Seinfeld fretted over the review, Shapiro asked a staffer to photocopy a bunch of Seinfeld's positive reviews and deliver them to Littlefield and Ludwin at NBC. In the end, though, it seemed that Seinfeld and

Shapiro were far more concerned about Christon than NBC was. They didn't bat an eye. Seinfeld and Shapiro desperately wanted this show to happen — and NBC didn't care much either way.

By the early months of 1989, David and Seinfeld were assembling a sitcom pilot called *The Seinfeld Chronicles*.

2
THE PLAYERS

Larry David popped into the apartment across the hall that belonged to his neighbor, Kenny Kramer, unannounced as usual. But this time he had an unusual request: He wanted to write a character based on Kramer into his pilot script with Seinfeld, to make Kramer the Dean Moriarty of his new work. Kramer gave David his okay, thinking the chances of it coming to anything were slim, as Kramer later told me. *Larry David is going to write a sitcom for prime time,* he thought, *and nobody's going to put it on the air.* Even David didn't seem to think it would amount to much.

David lived in the Manhattan Plaza apartment complex in Midtown Manhattan, a subsidized development for struggling artists. Across the hall lived Kramer, another comic, a handsome, laid-back guy with a head full of thick, dark curls. David and Kramer would leave their doors open so that they could wander in and out of each other's places at their leisure. Kramer wore a bathrobe as he grazed in David's refrigerator while David watched Knicks and Yankees games. Kramer would ask the score, then leave again. In their more conversational times, Kramer shared tales of his previous and current efforts to make a living — making disco jewelry, managing a rock-reggae band.

Kramer dragged David along on errands, somehow turning David into his unwilling sidekick, to David's perpetual irritation. "Come take a ride for ten minutes," Kramer begged. "I've just gotta run into this building and pick up a package." Of course, it was never ten minutes; it was always more like forty minutes, with David stuck in a car by himself. Then Kramer would say he had just one more thing to do, and another one more thing, and before David knew it, it would be 5:00 P.M.

David would cook dinner for comedian friends, promise them dessert — meaning ice cream bars — then scream at Kramer when he found the bars were missing from his freezer. "It's embarrassing!" he would yell. "I have company!"

Of course, this arrangement worked the other way, too. Because David hated to shop or do dishes, he once decided to reduce all of his food-related accoutrements to one plate, one knife, one fork, and one spoon. With nothing to eat in his apartment, David wanted to be able to "borrow" Kenny's food without feeling guilty. So he decided that he'd pay his friend for everything he ate. If he ate one Mallomar, he'd figure out how many were in a box and compute how much he owed based on percentage. He wrote it all down on a legal pad and paid Kramer every few weeks.

Kramer witnessed David and Seinfeld at work on early versions of their script, writing them out in longhand with their Bic clear-barrel pens on their yellow legal pads — a practice they would continue throughout the show's run. At the time, much of their discussion centered on whether to include a Kramer-ish character. Seinfeld worried the wacky neighbor was too cliché, but David was convinced he could make the character fresh. David prevailed. Seinfeld emphasized one thing: He wanted to use Kramer's real name for the character. It was funnier-sounding than any alternative they came up with.

Despite David and Kramer's friendly living situation, complications ensued when Castle Rock presented Kramer with a release to clear use of his name. Before David could shoot the script with Kramer's name in it, he had to have explicit permission from Kenny, it seemed. And the release stipulated that Kramer wouldn't get a cent for its use.

Kramer would have none of that. Once there was fancy studio paperwork at hand, it seemed to him that there should be some compensation in the offing.

David tried to call his bluff. "We'll just use the name Bender then."

Script drafts went through several phases, marked by which name they used for the neighbor character. Bender. Hoffman. Kessler. (A vestigial reference to "Kessler" remained even in the final taped pilot.) But Kramer still felt like the best name. (The character would never go by his first name, they decided, so the "Kenny" part was moot.) David's and Seinfeld's musical ears for comedy couldn't settle for anything else. That plosive consonant K sound is known to be among the English language's funniest phonemes. (H. L. Mencken argued this in *The New Yorker;* Neil Simon made this point in his play *The Sunshine Boys.*) They couldn't resist.

Finally, Castle Rock ponied up some cash to Kenny Kramer, though he had one more demand: He wanted to play this Kramer fellow.

Absolutely not, David and Seinfeld said.

He signed the contract this time anyway. Hey, a guy had to try, but he had to take what he could get, too. He would, in time, become a symbol of that new dimension, the first person who could pass freely from real life into Seinfeldia and back again.

When the NBC executives read the pilot script, they okayed it with yet another shrug. It had a sensibility about it. It seemed fun. That's what pilots are for: to see how the script works out in the flesh.

David would write the show but didn't even consider starring as the character based on himself. (*How can I write and act at the same time?* he asked himself, even though Jerry planned to do exactly that.) So he needed a stand-in character to engage in the comedic dialogues that he and Seinfeld had conceived as the show's centerpiece. For this purpose, Larry David created George Costanza. David and Seinfeld got his last name from Seinfeld's real-life New York friend Mike Costanza, another name they found funny. David and Seinfeld had a rough idea of who George would be: at least a little bit of David himself, but more than anything, they were looking for someone who could serve as a counterpoint to Seinfeld's character. Castle Rock executives had complained during early drafts of the pilot that George and Jerry were too similar. David wondered why the two guys would be friends if they weren't similar, but also saw the sense in having two main characters who were distinguishable from each other.

The producers and casting director Marc Hirschfeld saw dozens of actors who fit the basic age parameters. Stage actor Nathan Lane, sitcom vet Danny DeVito, indie film actor Steve Buscemi, bit-part actor David Alan Grier, comedy writer Brad Hall, *Top Gun* costar Anthony Edwards, and Seinfeld's actor friend Larry Miller read for the role. Stand-up Robert Schimmel auditioned as well, but spent the whole time picking apart the script — never a great move. Particularly unwise when auditioning for Larry David.

But Castle Rock executive Rob Reiner had seen Jason Alexander in the play *Jerome Robbins' Broadway,* and Seinfeld had noticed Alexander's work in a Neil Simon play called *Broadway Bound.* And Hirschfeld had cast Alexander in a short-lived 1984 hospital sitcom called *E/R.* All agreed that Alexander could serve as a perfect physical counterpoint to Seinfeld — short, stocky, and balding to Seinfeld's beanpole build and thick hair.

Alexander had toiled in the trenches of TV commercials throughout the '80s, singing and dancing in praise of McDonald's McDLT and pushing nearly fifty other products, as he said later, "from chicken to carpet fibers." He had struggled to find a niche as an actor. In his early twenties, casting directors wanted to peg him as "a young Belushi." He had a baby face but started losing his hair as soon as he hit adulthood. Sometimes he was cast as a Belushi-like wild man; other times he was cast as a suburban dad. On *E/R*, he played a villainous hospital administrator, even though he was only twenty-four and unlikely to be running an entire institution at that age.

A New Yorker who loved the theater, Alexander hated being in Los Angeles. Eventually, when *E/R* ended in 1985, he and his wife couldn't afford to stay because she'd taken a leave of absence from her New York job to come west with him. While his wife went back to work in New York, Alexander stayed at the urging of his agent, who felt like Alexander was just gaining momentum in TV. For four months, he continued to audition. He knew he definitely hadn't gotten the job whenever the casting directors said, "That's great!" The more enthusiastically they responded, the less likely you were to get the part. In New York theater, directors would simply say, "Thank you," no matter how good or bad the audition. In L.A., a veneer of fake niceness covered everything, and it drove him crazy.

Finally, he returned to his wife and New York, vowing never to go back to Los Angeles unless he had a solid job lined up. He was happy to revisit the stage in Neil Simon's *Broadway Bound,* then star in a short-lived 1987 sitcom shot in New York called *Everything's Relative.* It was the first time he served as one of the leads of a TV show. Reviews were decent — the *Christian Science Monitor* compared Alexander to a young George Burns, "wearing a squint that seems to be viewing life from far off and almost laughing." But the show lasted only ten episodes.

In 1989, Alexander starred in *Jerome Robbins' Broadway,* playing an aspiring comedy writer. For that, he won a Tony. Having achieved one of his major dreams at age twenty-nine, he quoted *Pippin* to his wife after the ceremony: "I thought there'd be more plumes." He wasn't sure he had anything left to aspire to.

Amid the hype for *Jerome Robbins' Broadway,* Alexander was invited to read for the *Seinfeld* part from New York via video. He figured actors rarely got jobs by reading on tape for them, so he tried to determine what he could do to stand out. He knew little about the show — just that it would be about how a comedian goes about getting his material. He had only a few pages of the script, which was common practice for New York–based auditions; there, actors often got "sides," or small packets of just the pages they needed for their part. Alexander knew nothing about the character besides his name and his lines of dialogue for the audition. He interpreted the character as a Woody Allen prototype because the dialogue about misreading women's signals sounded a little Allen-esque. After working hard at Boston University to lose his native New York accent, Alexander now went right back to it, reading lines in Allen's nasal, stuttering cadence while he wore wire-framed glasses. (The actor himself could see just fine.)

David and Seinfeld watched Alexander on tape in a Los Angeles screening room with Shapiro and his partner, Howard West. After two lines out of Alexander's mouth, they knew: *That's the guy.* They could see his talent and comedic prowess, as well as his strong acting ability, in just those few lines. They wanted a particularly polished actor to anchor the show against Seinfeld, who had less-developed acting skills.

About a week after Alexander first made the tape, he got a call asking him to come to Los Angeles to audition before Castle Rock and NBC executives. Alexander later said that when he got to the tryout and saw comedian Larry Miller there as well, he thought the audition was "a complete waste of time" because he figured Miller, as Seinfeld's friend, was a shoo-in; he assumed he was there as a formality, possibly to keep Miller from asking for too much money.

But David gave him a little direction — "Not so obviously Woody, but the glasses, great, the accent, great." When Alexander read, David could see the chemistry between Alexander and Seinfeld right away. Everyone in the room laughed. Whereas Miller had been good, they could see Seinfeld rise to Alexander's performance.

Alexander got right into a car afterward and headed to the airport. By the time he landed at New York's John F. Kennedy International Airport, he had an offer to play George Costanza.

■ ■ ■ ■

David's former *Fridays* costar Michael Richards seemed to Seinfeld like the perfect person to play the Kenny Kramer–like neighbor. Richards had appeared in bit parts on *Cheers, Night Court, Miami Vice,* and other shows, always stealing scenes thanks to his manic energy and wiry hair. He used his long limbs, rubbery muscles, and expressive face to such a degree that he didn't need lines to get laughs. He practiced yoga, and the resulting suppleness clearly helped his comedy.

On *Fridays,* he was known for his one strange contract demand: Give him a thousand pounds of dirt on the set, he said, and he'd do the show. The producers delivered; he used it for a memorable bit he improvised with army toys that lasted an extraordinary seven minutes and involved truly disturbing battle scenes, real fire, and "amputating" a plastic soldier's destroyed limbs with wire cutters.

Seinfeld knew Richards's work from *Fridays* and elsewhere, so he was excited by the possibility that Richards might be available for *Seinfeld.* David remained doubtful about Richards, who didn't match up with

David's vision of his neighbor.

Richards, in touch with his intuition, was sure he'd get the part the first time he met Seinfeld at his audition. The magic felt so palpable to him that he didn't worry about the other guys waiting to read, which included TV regular Tony Shalhoub and character actor Larry Hankin. How could the producers pass up this chemistry? Seinfeld felt it, too: as he later described it, it was "the mysterious hand of the universe going, 'You two are going to be together.'"

Richards worked perfectly as Kramer, the mysterious ne'er-do-well across the hall, who existed apart from the normal demands of humanity. Richards got the character from the beginning: Kramer was a guy who could fit into any situation, make it his own, and make it a little funnier.

Seinfeld had made up his mind. But to get final network approval, Richards had to read for the producers and NBC's head of entertainment, Brandon Tartikoff. Tartikoff would cram him in between meetings in a suite at the Century Plaza Hotel, a nineteen-story crescent of a luxury hotel in the middle of a Los Angeles business park.

Outside the room, Richards paced the hotel lobby, guests hustling by as he mumbled his lines to himself. Richards exploded into the room from the start, his hyperki-netic energy in full force. David excused himself and listened through the door to avoid throwing his old *Fridays* friend off. Richards read his lines opposite Seinfeld, confident in their connection. Everything he did elicited screams of laughter, not the least of which included finishing the scene standing on his head.

When Richards left the room, Tartikoff said to the producers, "Well, if you want *funny . . .*" Richards got the job.

For the final potentially regular role, David and Seinfeld had to cast a woman to play the waitress at Pete's, George and Jerry's regular diner where they'd have many of their obsessive discussions. At the top of their list was Lee Garlington, a redhead who had mastered a tough-chick, Stockard Channing vibe. When she walked into the audition room, she was surprised to find Jerry and another actor seated at a makeshift dining table, ready for her to deliver her audition lines to them. She was used to reading lines to a camera, with a casting director filling in for the other characters.

When she finished, Seinfeld said to the others, "See, see, what'd I tell you?" Gar-lington got the feeling she'd get the job, and she was right. Soon, she was rehearsing with Seinfeld, Richards, Alexander, and David at Desilu-Cahuenga Studios in Hollywood. She lunched most days with Richards, Alexander, and Seinfeld, laughing the whole way through.

She enjoyed being the only woman among the main cast. While she hung out with her three costars, she whipped out her new video camera and shot some footage of them goofing around together. A security guard approached. "You can't videotape," he warned them, oblivious to who they might be.

Of course, she didn't get too attached to the new job, either. She'd starred in enough TV pilots to know she couldn't tell which would work and which wouldn't.

Alexander had also done his share of pilots and short-lived shows, and he felt the same. Seinfeld asked him, "So, Mr. Experience, what do you think?"

"No way," Alexander said of the show's chances. "I think the No. 1 show right now is *Alf*. Who's going to watch this? The audience for this show is me, a white guy, Jewish-Italian, who lives in a big city, between eighteen and thirty-two. And I don't watch TV."

As soon as Alexander got the full pilot

script, he noticed a major difference between *The Seinfeld Chronicles* and other shows he'd done. The pages contained few to no behavioral cues or stage directions; they had nothing but dialogue. He had no idea what he was supposed to do during all this talking. He and his costars would have to come up with that themselves, lest they end up standing in the middle of the stage, simply reciting line after line. As they rehearsed on the set, he and Richards and Seinfeld started helping one another move around: Maybe go get something out of the refrigerator. Maybe doodle on a notepad.

This process grew in time and eventually helped to build a strong team mentality.

The resulting pilot episode turned out to be a lightweight affair, with only glimmers of potential. Looking back on it, its quiet calm would be shocking to anyone familiar with what the show eventually became. The plot focuses on misinterpreted social cues between Jerry and a female acquaintance he'd met on the road. She comes to town and asks to stay with him. George and Jerry discuss it in the diner and in the Laundromat. Does this mean she wants to sleep with him, or not? (George: "All right, if she puts the bags down before she greets you, that's a good sign.") Jerry and George, with a bit of input from Kramer, debate this for the entire twenty-two minutes until the ironic conclusion: She takes a call from her fiancé while at Jerry's place, just as Jerry's about to make his move.

The inconsistencies with later episodes jump out in the pilot: George comes off as both supportive and *better* at reading women than Jerry; Kramer knocks before entering Jerry's apartment. Seinfeld himself is, as he later recalled, uncomfortable as an actor, even when playing a version of himself. The show we'd come to know as *Seinfeld* only peeks through in this episode's obsession with social details, its attempt at being an Oscar Wilde for television.

Its first test came at a screening for a few dozen NBC suits — from programming, advertising sales, marketing, management — in the network's Burbank offices, a regular occurrence for pilots. When the lights came up, anyone could see that *The Seinfeld Chronicles* was no *Cosby Show* or *Golden Girls* — the same room had erupted with wild applause at the end of those pilots. But the executives had laughed throughout *The Seinfeld Chronicles,* despite its lack of high-stakes story, and noted that the show was fresh, different. Tartikoff wasn't sure:

"Who will want to see Jews wandering around New York acting neurotic?"

He felt he could say this because he was a Jew from New York.

Seinfeld's biggest network supporter, Rick Ludwin, countered, "I'm not from New York, I'm not Jewish, and I thought it was funny." As the head of late-night, he had no preconceived notions about what a sitcom should look like. He just responded to anything he thought was funny, and he'd had his eye on Seinfeld's late-night performances for a while.

About a week later, though, came the pilot testing phase, which garnered a much stronger reaction. This round of testing involved about four hundred households, recruited by NBC via phone, who watched new pilots on unused local cable channels. In the first week of May, Littlefield got the test results on all his pilot contenders — the results phase always came around his birthday, and usually ruined it. This proved no exception: Viewers were unimpressed with *The Seinfeld Chronicles*. "You can't get too excited about going to the Laundromat," one viewer told researchers.

"No segment of the audience was eager to watch the show again," the report concluded. "Jerry Seinfeld, who was familiar to about a quarter of the viewers, created, on balance, lukewarm reactions among adults and teens, and very low reactions among kids. . . . None of the supports were liked, and viewers felt that Jerry needed a better backup ensemble." Then, the final blow: "Pilot performance: weak."

Littlefield had hoped for the best for the show, but the research report concerned him. *The Seinfeld Chronicles* did not make the cut for the fall schedule, which would instead feature shows starring Cloris Leachman as "the oversexed head of housekeeping at a family-owned New York City hotel," as the press release announced, in *The Nutt House;* Stephanie Beacham as "a hard-edged, adventurous nun placed in charge of an unruly group of orphans who are surprised to discover that she is no pushover" in *Sister Kate;* and David Hasselhoff in the sexy lifeguard drama *Baywatch.* The network's Thursday lineup remained its powerhouse, with *The Cosby Show, A Different World, Cheers,* and *L.A. Law.*

The Seinfeld Chronicles would air as a onetime "special" during the TV dead zone of summer. In the bit of press it got, Seinfeld described it to the Associated Press as a show full of "aimless wandering."

■ ■ ■ ■

No one at NBC knew what to do about *The Seinfeld Chronicles* after it ran to tepid reviews and okay ratings. And for months afterward, they chose not to do a thing. Ludwin got nervous as the network's rights to *The Seinfeld Chronicles* neared expiration at the end of 1989. He and several of his colleagues liked the show and were disappointed when the testing went so poorly. He and Littlefield hatched a plan: Since Ludwin had commissioned the series, and Ludwin was in charge of late-night and specials, why not use that department's more fluid budget to its advantage? One axed two-hour Bob Hope special could mean four new episodes of Seinfeld's show.

And, in fact, the equation would play out just that way, the world never knowing of the Bob Hope special it had missed. Littlefield asked Ludwin to call Hope with the bad news while he called Seinfeld with the good news. Seinfeld, however, knew this wasn't the *greatest* news. He greeted Littlefield's "four episodes" offer with a few seconds of silence, followed by: "Has any show, in the history of television, ever succeeded with a four-episode order?"

He took the deal anyway, and the minuscule episode order suited Larry David just fine. "That's all I got in me anyway," Shapiro recalled him saying.

However, the executives had some caveats in picking up the show: First and foremost, David and Seinfeld would need to add a major female character to the core cast. Garlington's wisecracking waitress in the first episode wasn't enough to counteract the fact that, as Seinfeld later said, the show "lacked estrogen." Littlefield worried the waitress character would have a hard time getting out of the coffee shop to involve herself in the guys' adventures. The music, too, could use some help. And though only four episodes were on deck for now, David and Seinfeld would have to launch a real show operation, with directors, staffers, producers, and a set. They would air again in the summer, returning to NBC on May 30, 1990. But their battles with the network that gave them life were far from over.

3
THE NETWORK

Jeremiah Bosgang reported to his new job at NBC in 1990. He was assigned to work for Rick Ludwin, who oversaw late-night and specials, which sounded cool enough to Bosgang. But soon after Bosgang got there, he got the feeling that he was in the wrong place. Comedy and drama development were the places to be, while the late-night and specials department was nothing more than paper-pushing purgatory.

Ludwin's division handled the least glamorous series — *Unsolved Mysteries, TV's Bloopers and Practical Jokes* — and those running on autopilot, such as *The Tonight Show* and *Saturday Night Live,* both of which had been on for decades. It didn't make new hits. Still, Bosgang knew he was lucky to get a corporate job, as he later told me. A struggling actor, he'd moved from New York to Los Angeles, telling himself if he hung out in Hollywood enough, he'd get some real work.

Instead, he got this glorified internship at NBC at age twenty-eight. As a "program associate," he'd help Ludwin in whatever way he could while he tried to prove over the next two years that he had what it took to become a development executive.

But just when Bosgang thought he understood how uncool his assignment was, he heard about this sitcom pilot that was also under Ludwin's purview. *The Seinfeld Chronicles* had run the previous year as a onetime special buried in the summer, but Ludwin explained to Bosgang that he'd done some fancy accounting to make room in the budget for four more episodes to give it another chance.

Somehow, despite being stuck in specials and late-night, Bosgang found himself tasked with serving as the office's main liaison to a cool new sitcom, one that wasn't like any other on TV, one that he actually thought was funny. A cool new sitcom no one watched, but a cool new sitcom nonetheless. Bosgang considered himself a comedy writer and performer, or at least an aspiring one, so he couldn't have been more thrilled.

As the point person, he'd give Larry David and Jerry Seinfeld the network's notes at table reads each week. He thought that was funny. What the hell did he know? It didn't matter; he was on his way to becoming a network executive. Years later, he'd remember sitting in Ludwin's office when entertainment president Brandon Tartikoff stopped by to tell them the show's name was changing — at Seinfeld's request, and to avoid confusion with ABC's *Ferris Bueller's Day Off* rip-off *The Marshall Chronicles*. Now, it would be called simply *Seinfeld.*

Ludwin, known for protecting the creative talent behind the shows he supervised, impressed upon Bosgang the importance of empowering David and Seinfeld to make the kind of show they wanted to make, even when the network didn't understand what the producers were doing. Ludwin said their department's job was to fight for *Seinfeld* at the network. While the comedy division and the higher-ups were focused on making a new sitcom called *Wings* a hit — because it shared producers with the huge hit *Cheers* — Bosgang and Ludwin should make sure *Seinfeld* didn't fall through the cracks.

The day of the first table read that Bosgang would attend on NBC's behalf, he hopped onto the motorcycle he'd driven across the country from New York and roared over to the show's Hollywood lot.

He parked, dismounted, and took off his helmet, carrying it to the office with him. His scraggly brown hair brushed his collar. As he approached the building, the suited men standing outside eyed him suspiciously. They turned out to be some Castle Rock executives, along with Seinfeld's managers, George Shapiro and Howard West. And here, *he* was supposed to be the "suit."

"This is what NBC thinks of us," Bosgang remembers one of the Castle Rock executives scoffing.

But at that moment West embraced Bosgang and rubbed his forearm. "This is for good luck," West said.

"That's right," Shapiro said. "You're going to be our good luck charm." Shapiro was right: Bosgang was one of several people who would become a key part of Seinfeldia's earliest history.

Tom Cherones was key as well. Cherones was among the few people who'd already heard good things about this *Seinfeld*. A fifty-year-old manly presence with a thatch of graying hair and a thick beard, and with a pipe often in his hand, he had his share of television experience, a long career that had recently turned to sitcoms. He had worked on *Annie McGuire,* a short-lived comedy that starred Mary Tyler Moore, and before that the grown-sibling comedy *My Sister Sam* and the hit family show *Growing Pains.* Castle Rock offered Cherones a directing job for the first two episodes of *Seinfeld,* then upped the offer to a producing credit when one staffer left. Soon he was developing and producing all four episodes in this mini-season.

That didn't mean he *got* it, though. He read the scripts, like the one where Jerry's character frets about his girlfriend seeing him with dental floss stuck to his hand, and wondered: What the fuck was this?

He was pretty sure only Larry and Jerry knew what this thing was about. But he didn't care much about that. He took the job for one reason: For the first time, he had creative freedom. The network had demanded the show be shot before a live audience, but he liked the idea of making it look as un-sitcom-like as possible, and no one seemed to be watching him too closely. He had worked for productions as diverse as *Mister Rogers' Neighborhood* and *National Geographic* films. He wasn't locked into the sitcom mind-set when it came to visuals, and now he had some room to play.

He could tell that the network guys, because they were from the late-night and specials department, were unusually hands-off; they wouldn't fuck this up like the comedy people always did. It seemed to him that Bosgang, Ludwin, and their colleagues were saying, "We don't know what you're doing, but go ahead and do it."

Seinfeld paid Cherones more than any other show he'd worked on thus far, because he got checks as both a producer and a director this time. He worked long hours, of course, with production, budgeting, staffing, and postproduction to handle. But his wife was writing novels and TV scripts, so she was busy, too, and they had sent their kids off to college already. He had the time.

His first idea: Keep the lighting lower and more natural than the normal glare of sitcoms. Hire lighting experts who would set it up like a single-camera show. Meanwhile, let the writers write what they wanted, and shoot it the way they envisioned, whether he understood it or not.

Jonathan Wolff got a call from his old friend George Wallace, a comedian who'd lived with Seinfeld in New York City, asking for a huge favor: Wolff was now a big shot in the TV theme song world, having written and arranged music for *Who's the Boss?, Married with Children,* and others. Would Wolff write a song for Seinfeld's new sitcom?

Wolff and Wallace had met on the road

when Wallace was touring and Wolff was a musician, and they had become close enough that Wolff couldn't help but say yes. Wolff still looked like a lost member of Def Leppard with his long golden curls, but he ran a serious business operation now. He handled thirteen shows at the time and didn't need the work or the hassle for some sitcom he hadn't heard of. Still, he loved Wallace.

Seinfeld called Wolff to chat about the project. Music, he told Wolff, would be important to the show's aesthetic. Wolff wasn't impressed; stars and producers always told him such things while they courted his services. But Wolff grew a bit more intrigued when Seinfeld dug into the specifics. *Seinfeld* had a unique sound design problem: The opening credit sequence would revolve around Jerry's comedy monologues. And while Seinfeld wanted distinctive music, the audience had to hear him talk. For that reason, the pilot music hadn't cut it.

This piqued Wolff's interest. Sometimes musical choices were obvious, and sometimes he had to find clues in everything from the show to the time slot and target audience, which made for interesting work. He watched *The Seinfeld Chronicles* pilot, listened to Seinfeld's delivery. The language had a rhythm, a musical quality of its own. This inspired him. A strong bass line could work, since its pitch wouldn't compete with Seinfeld's voice. Wolff could build bass lines around Seinfeld's routine, holding for punch lines or accenting gestures. He thought about New York City energy, people buzzing around all the time.

He had a kind of crazy idea.

Nobody thought of '80s TV theme songs as art. Wolff himself felt that he'd written a lot of stupid stuff. (Lyrics from the woodwinds-heavy *Who's the Boss?* theme: "There's a path you take and a path untaken / The choice is up to you, my friend." Never has a truism been so catchy.) He'd started out trying to be a musician because he wasn't much good at anything else. He tried to fix cars, but it didn't take. So in 1976, at seventeen, he moved to Los Angeles from Louisville, Kentucky, and got work as a session musician. As it happened, a lot of his gigs were playing for film and TV scores.

Soon, the composers handed him their extra work — arranging a rhythm section, for instance. Then it occurred to him: Why didn't he just do the whole job himself, for the whole pay? He sent a letter to a bunch of studio music departments declaring himself a composer for hire. It worked, like a switch. The same studios who'd been calling him to do their cleanup work started giving him composing assignments. Soon he ran his own company, which focused solely on half-hour television comedies. Half-hour shows meant twice as much money in an hour — with two of his theme songs playing in an hour of programming, rather than just one for an hour-long — so the choice was a no-brainer.

Wolff would get to write something interesting only if he could find some producers — and a network — willing to break from convention. As it turned out, he'd found those people in *Seinfeld:* producers who wanted something unique, and a network that was barely paying attention.

Seinfeld came to Wolff's studio for the official music pitch. Wolff proposed the slap bass hc had imagined — plus a scatting, beatboxing riff he'd produce with his very own lips, tongue, and teeth. That was it.

Seinfeld loved it, no questions asked. He called Larry David from Wolff's office. "This is kind of cool," he told his partner.

David said a quick "okay" — he was busy writing the next episodes — and that was that. *Seinfeld* had official music. Wolff

71

retrofitted the music to the pilot episode so that it could rerun with the new episodes. The slap bass would become *Seinfeld*'s sonic brand, making Wolff, over time, the most famous slap-bass player since Bootsy Collins.

As the growing team churned out new footage, a tape of each episode appeared in Wolff's office, a commercial building he'd purchased when his scoring business took off in 1986. There, a copy of every half hour on three-quarter-inch video piled up, a stipulation in his contract. Unlike some of the other shows he worked on, he enjoyed watching his complimentary copies of *Seinfeld*.

When the network suits heard the new music in a meeting, however, they balked. It sounded like they couldn't afford real music or something. Was that popping noise an instrument? Some weird electronic effect? It all seemed annoying.

Annoying? David loved that! Even when Wolff pulled David and Cherones aside and suggested they change the music so they could fight with the network on other issues, David would hear none of it. "No, no, the music stays," Wolff remembers David saying. "Next."

Larry David was already garnering a bit of a reputation for resisting outside interference and unwelcome suggestions when it came to his sitcom. Some of the cast even got the idea that his sensitivity contributed to the show's next big change: dropping Lee Garlington, who appeared as a waitress in the pilot, in favor of a major female character not hampered by serving duties. According to Alexander's recollections in later interviews, although Garlington has no memory of this, she had a conversation with Larry David that infuriated him. David told the other cast members that Garlington said she could write something better than he had, according to this version of the story. Even though she understands that's what he heard, it was certainly not what she thought she was saying.

Garlington could get a little bit excited over a new role and sometimes offered suggestions: What if Claire did this? I have an idea for that! David, however, sometimes took "suggestions" personally, as a direct criticism of his writing.

She had worked a lot, even though she wasn't a household name; she had done stints on *Roseanne, Coach, Quantum Leap, Who's the Boss?,* and many others. She'd done nine pilots in ten years. So she didn't even realize that she'd been "fired" from *Seinfeld;* her contract simply wasn't renewed.

The network did, however, also emphatically suggest a stronger female presence when it ordered more episodes. The network executives wanted a woman on par with George and Kramer. The producers considered TV regulars Patricia Heaton and Megan Mullally, as well as stand-up turned actress Rosie O'Donnell, for the job. None of them quite did it for the *Seinfeld* producers.

But Julia Louis-Dreyfus had a contract at Warner Brothers that was about to expire, and David had a personal connection to her from their working together on *Saturday Night Live* in 1982. The day after she got out of the deal, David threw her name into contention. She got the four *Seinfeld* scripts via her agent. She would have preferred a bigger part, but she loved the scripts' writing.

Louis-Dreyfus had comedy chops and a sexiness that wasn't overbearing — tons of dark curls, huge brown eyes. Like David, she had barely survived her *SNL* time, though she endured three seasons to his one. And she'd had a good excuse for being eaten alive: She joined at twenty-one, the youngest female cast member in the show's history at the time. She had struggled to hold her own against a powerhouse cast that included Eddie Murphy, Martin Short, Christopher Guest, Billy Crystal, and Joe Piscopo. She was shocked to find a cut-throat atmosphere instead of the ensemble energy she'd experienced doing improv in college, but she endured, if only just.

She and David had bonded in their misery at *SNL*. When David asked her to audition for his new *Seinfeld* character, she agreed partly because of her connection to him. Once she walked in, David and Seinfeld knew, for the first time, who Elaine Benes was. Louis-Dreyfus understood the New York sensibility, having been born in the city. She spent some of her childhood there, but she brought a worldly perspective as well. She'd lived in Washington, DC; Sri Lanka; Colombia; and Tunisia because of her stepfather's medical charity work.

Louis-Dreyfus had grown up, in fact, quite comfortably: Her father, William Louis-Dreyfus, ran a billion-dollar commodities firm called the Louis Dreyfus Group. As she traveled the world with her mother and stepfather, and her father made major financial deals, she dreamed of being Lucille Ball, Mary Tyler Moore, Madeline Kahn, Teri Garr, or Diane Keaton. She loved film-maker Preston Sturges's funny, sexy hero-ines.

Her parents wouldn't allow her to pursue acting as a child, so she waited until she went to Northwestern University in Chi-cago, where she met her husband, fellow actor Brad Hall (an early candidate to play George Costanza), and got spotted in a comedy revue by *Saturday Night Live* pro-ducers. She left Northwestern before gradu-ating; she and Hall both appeared on *SNL* for three seasons, from 1982 to 1985, then moved to Los Angeles.

When Louis-Dreyfus arrived for her *Sein-feld* audition, she found Jerry eating cereal and waiting to trade lines with her. She saw Larry at the audition and felt at ease, a Pavlovian response to the presence of the one bright spot from her most miserable years. She sat on a sofa with Seinfeld and read lines. When Seinfeld heard her read, he thought she'd mesh well with George and Kramer. "That," he told his colleagues afterward, "is Elaine." She would, David later said, give the show "luster."

After her audition ended, Louis-Dreyfus

left, and David ran out onto the sidewalk after her. "What do you think?" he asked.

"I don't know," she said honestly. The even more honest version would have been: *I'm not sure if this is the right move for me.*

But in the end, she accepted David and Seinfeld's offer to join the four-episode "special" series, as an NBC press release categorized it. Her hard time at *Saturday Night Live* had paid off, though she didn't know yet how much. She figured this thing would get canceled in a week, but it beat her recent film projects, such as the self-explanatory *Troll.*

When she showed up on the set in cowboy boots, Richards knew: Oh, yes, this is our girl.

She became one of the guys on *Seinfeld,* getting lines as funny as the other cast members' without (too often) having to play just "the girl." An early rant, for example, questioned people's affection for cats: "What evidence is there that cats are so smart, anyway? Huh? What do they do? Because they're clean? I am sorry. My uncle Pete showers four times a day and he can't count to ten. So don't give me hygiene." As Jerry's ex-girlfriend, Elaine could play up her feminine energy when she wanted to or rib Jerry like only a former girlfriend could.

As an ex instead of a current girlfriend — a compromise with the network, which would have preferred the female addition be a potential love interest, and would continue to push for romantic involvement — she and Jerry could both maintain healthy dating lives, and thus dating story lines.

David modeled Elaine partly on an ex of his own named Monica Yates. The two had transitioned seamlessly from dating to being friends, a feat he thought was extraordinary. David and Yates dated for three months in the summer of 1983, when Yates, twenty-five at the time, had just been fired from her job as an assistant at *Vanity Fair.*

The real woman Elaine was based on was tall and athletic; she couldn't be bothered to dress up much or fuss with makeup except for eyeliner. She had dark, shoulder-length hair and liked to frown a lot. She was mourning the loss of her glamorous gig and living low on unemployment when she accompanied a friend to a recreational softball game involving a bunch of New York comics. The pitcher, David, had just finished a year at *Saturday Night Live.* She and her magazine assistant friends were impressed. When the group went out for beers after the game, David and Yates bonded over what she later called "the same aesthetic distaste for lots of things." After the breakup, the two remained such good friends that as David wrote his new scripts for *Seinfeld,* he often called Yates in New York to read scenes to her.

Louis-Dreyfus helped to shape the character of Elaine from the beginning, even though she'd never seen herself as a comedian or written her own material before. She knew part of her lack of comedic confidence came from her upbringing. Boys were always encouraged to be funny, whereas humor wasn't something cultivated in girls. Even after being part of the Second City comedy troupe in Chicago and on *SNL,* she didn't identify herself as particularly hilarious.

She ended up being good enough to worry Alexander, though. *He* was supposed to be Jerry's confidant. If she was another friend, and a network-mandated one at that, where might this leave him? Still, Alexander and Louis-Dreyfus bonded in her earliest days on the set, mainly over their mystified reactions to the scripts. Why were there heated conflicts that were never resolved? Why didn't the characters ever learn anything? What had they gotten themselves into?

As David and Seinfeld wrote Garlington out and Louis-Dreyfus in, they made one other little change. They had George and Jerry switch to a new diner, so as to sidestep the entire issue of the waitress we'd met in the pilot. Because there was a Thelonious Monk poster in the office where David and Seinfeld worked together, they named the new fictional place Monk's.

In their new studio home, behind the distinctive white Ren-Mar Studios entryway arch, David and Seinfeld refined their routine together, careful not to settle into their office too much just yet. They were making only four episodes, after all. Jerry crunched on cereal while the two bandied about premises for shows. What if Kramer starts a make-your-own-pizza restaurant? What if Elaine plots a hit on her boyfriend's cat?

David chomped on his after-lunch cigar, which gave him an air of absurd authority. He looked and felt contemplative, reminding Seinfeld of what he'd thought about David since first talking with him at the club years earlier: "This guy's got some head on him."

And now, no one seemed to be stopping them from doing what they wanted on TV. NBC would probably cancel the show soon enough, but that would come as a relief for

David. He wasn't sure he wanted to do any more of these things anyway.

As these four new episodes started to air, *Seinfeld* began to feel more and more like a real television show. It had exceeded David's and Seinfeld's own expectations twice now: first, by getting on the air at all, and second, by getting all four follow-up episodes on. Even better, the episodes aired after reruns of NBC's biggest current sitcom, *Cheers*. *Seinfeld* surprised everyone in the business by holding on to most of *Cheers*' audience and suddenly showing up in the TV ratings' top five every week.

Once again, NBC executives faced a decision about committing to *Seinfeld* or moving on for good.

As NBC dithered over whether to pick up *Seinfeld* yet again, David got a call from Joe Davola, the guy who'd once asked him to write for MTV's *Remote Control*. Davola now ran the alternative-programming department at the three-year-old Fox network. He'd kept track of David since then because David's manager turned girlfriend, Laurie Lennard, had been a friend of Davola's since his MTV days. He'd also seen *Seinfeld* and liked it.

David and Lennard went to meet with Davola at Fox. Davola tended to ramble a bit in his thick Brooklyn accent, but he eventually got to the point: He thought *Seinfeld* was great. He'd told his boss, Peter Chernin, that Fox ought to pick it up if NBC didn't, Davola later told me.

They thanked him and awaited a verdict from NBC. Others, like Castle Rock's Glenn Padnick, later recalled Fox rejecting the idea of picking *Seinfeld* up from NBC at some point. But surely any interest from another network helped spur NBC to a decision.

With the deadline approaching to renew *Seinfeld* after the first four episodes, Bosgang, Ludwin, Littlefield, and their colleagues locked themselves in a conference room and watched all five episodes again. Once again they said, "It's too Jewish. Too New York." Yet an overriding sentiment emerged: "They don't tell stories, but the fucking thing is funny."

Preston Beckman, the network's executive vice president of program planning and scheduling — in other words, the top ratings guy — wrote a memo debunking the New York and Jewish myth: The show played as well in Chicago and Seattle as it did in New York. People across the country (and presumably not just Jews) responded to it equally, many not even thinking about its "Jewishness" or lack thereof. (Personal note: My family was among the many in the Midwest who thought nothing of Seinfeld's ethnic background.)

Buzz was building, too. *Philadelphia Inquirer* critic Ken Tucker was an early supporter, noting the show's "brisk funniness" and writing that NBC was making a mistake if it didn't pick the show up. *Washington Post* critic Tom Shales wrote, "This Jerry Seinfeld is a very funny fellow. . . . [*Seinfeld*] is sweet and breezy and, as cowritten by Seinfeld, full of witty, pithy asides about modern social behavior."

NBC was finishing up its fifth season in first place among the four networks. It could afford a gamble, and comedies were still hot — four of the top five shows of the 1989–90 season were sitcoms: ABC's *Roseanne* and NBC's *The Cosby Show, Cheers,* and *A Different World.* In fact, the network needed to take some fresh chances: None of its five new shows from fall 1989 would live to see the 1990 schedule. And *Cosby* was fading in its later years, while Fox's new hit animated show *The Simpsons* was siphoning off the young viewers advertisers most coveted. *Seinfeld,* though a long shot, showed promise among the young audiences the network was losing.

And though NBC executives didn't know it at the time, they may have prevented a true nightmare scenario for them: With Davola's interest in *Seinfeld,* NBC could have found itself competing with a *Seinfeld/ Simpsons* superpowered comedy block.

The decision was made: NBC would take its chances on Jerry Seinfeld again. *Seinfeld* would get a respectable order, thirteen whole episodes (only twelve would be made after the start of the season was unexpectedly delayed by a week). Of course, the show wouldn't return until midseason, starting in January 1991. But the order was hope. Hell, it was a miracle.

Of course, there was one person who didn't quite see it that way. When David and Seinfeld got the news at their office, David told Seinfeld not to accept the offer. Already, this was becoming a tradition: David, afraid he'd run out of creative juice, didn't want to come up with an entire thirteen episodes' worth of stories. It reminded him of when he used to drive taxis for a living. When he dropped off a passenger, he always thought it was his last fare. There were so many cabs in the city — why should anyone else choose him?

Seinfeld accepted the offer anyway, and promised to give David $15,000 toward buying a car.

David told his comedian friend John De-Bellis, who was visiting that day, "I'm going to get a Lexus. I'll never be able to afford one again." David figured this was as good as his career would ever get. Which was just fine with him. In fact, he sort of wished the show would be done with so he could return to New York. Instead, he realized he'd be settling in Los Angeles for at least a little while.

As *Seinfeld* took to the air in January 1991 for its first regular-season spot, Littlefield took over as NBC's entertainment president when Tartikoff left to run Paramount's movie studio. With NBC's lead slipping, Littlefield felt the pressure.

The first episode was scheduled to premiere on January 16, 1991 — the day the United States bombed Baghdad at the start of the Gulf War. The *Seinfeld* premiere was preempted for news coverage. When the show finally debuted the following week, it began to build an audience, though a select one. It lost out most weeks to CBS's crime drama *Jake and the Fatman*.

Cherones was happy to hear the good news about the full season order, even though he was still a little mystified by this show he'd signed on to direct and produce. He'd worked in network television since 1975 and had never seen anything quite like it; it was a little like directing something in a language he didn't speak, though he got the feeling there was something special about it. As he read scripts for the upcoming thirteen-episode "second" season, he was still flummoxed. This story line all about Jerry buying a suede jacket and everyone flipping out about the lining being pink-and-white striped . . . Why was the lining of a jacket such a big deal? Who fucking cared? Why were they doing this?

Eh, at least it was no ordinary show. He kept his questions to himself and went with it, figuring it had to end soon enough. But as he and David planned for *Seinfeld*'s certain demise, TV viewers were just starting to catch on to this new show.

4
THE CULT HIT

Peter Mehlman believed that *Seinfeld* could not fail. He believed it was too good to fail.

Peter Mehlman was not in the television business.

And yet, in what was becoming true Seinfeldian form — outsiders only, please — he became one of the first writers whom Larry David trusted with a script.

David, who was now clearly in charge of all of *Seinfeld*'s backstage operations while Seinfeld concentrated on being the star of the show, assigned Mehlman the fifth installment of the thirteen-episode season in 1991. When Mehlman turned it in, David told him, "If by some off chance we get picked up again, you've got a staff job." Mehlman figured this was a sure thing, he later told me. He had no idea that quality was not a reliable predictor of longevity in television. In fact, it usually doomed a show to "cult" status and a short life at that time.

Mehlman looked a bit like a younger David, with blue eyes, scraggly eyebrows, and wild, graying hair. At thirty-four, he'd written one other TV script, a sample episode of *The Wonder Years* that never got shot. He was a freelance magazine writer, and when he moved to Los Angeles from New York in 1989 for a change of scenery, he figured he should take a shot at scriptwriting, since everyone around him was doing it. He believed his spec script would magically get sold and cover his moving expenses. His script never even made it near *The Wonder Years* office, but it did land him a TV agent.

Still, the agent didn't lead to any jobs; an old acquaintance, Larry David, did. When Mehlman bumped into David at a Los Angeles party, about a year after moving west, David mentioned some show he was doing with Jerry Seinfeld. Maybe Mehlman could write a script?

David had no idea that Mehlman had never written dialogue. Mehlman, unsure what this little show even was, offered David a writing sample: not his *Wonder Years* script, but a piece he'd written for the *New York Times*'s About Men column, a bittersweet, funny essay called "Star Trekking" about wandering the city while getting over a recent breakup. David liked it and passed it on to Jerry Seinfeld, who felt the same. Soon Mehlman had his first TV assignment — which, when word got out, would make him an inspiration to freelance magazine writers everywhere.

Later, Mehlman heard that David had made similar offers to many of their mutual friends — give him a writing sample, and he and Seinfeld would consider it. Many of them had real scripts to offer, and had known David much longer than Mehlman had. For whatever reason, though, Mehlman was the first to get through.

The *Seinfeld* cast and crew switched stages once again, taking up permanent residence on the CBS-MTM Studios lot in the San Fernando Valley, where *Get Smart, The Bob Newhart Show,* and *The Mary Tyler Moore Show* were shot. They reached back into sitcom history to come up with a more ironclad production schedule. A typical show started its weekly cycle on Monday, leading up to a Friday shoot; but *The Dick Van Dyke Show*'s producer, Carl Reiner, figured out that if he started on Wednesday and shot on Tuesday, he'd have weekends to rewrite. David and Seinfeld had no personal lives at the time, so that sounded like the perfect approach to them.

Even the Reiner-style schedule began to slide away from them, though. Time had little meaning in Seinfeldia. The Wednesday table read would slip from 10:00 A.M. to 3:00 P.M. Then cast members would get another call: "It'll be at ten on Thursday." Then: "Take Thursday off." They could end up coming in on Saturday or Sunday afternoon. The three weeks off meant to be built into the regular schedule would disappear. Between David's and Seinfeld's inexperience at running sitcoms and Rick Ludwin's inexperience with overseeing them, nothing went quite as expected.

Of course, this led to the show's unusual take on comedy as well as its disorganization. David and Seinfeld had written jokes and sketches in their past, so they considered stories that typical producers wouldn't; Ludwin, too, approved stories that average network executives wouldn't. As Seinfeld said at the time, "Some of the writers who want to work on the show, they have a hard time getting a grip on what funny is. They give us all these sitcom ideas. I tell them we don't want sitcom ideas. I tell them what we don't want to do, but it's hard to explain what we do want."

■ ■ ■ ■

Seinfeld thought he had Mehlman pegged. When they met, Mehlman remembers the comedian saying to him, "God, you seem like such a total New Yorker. I can't believe you moved out here." Mehlman didn't feel that way at all. He grew up in Queens, but when he came to L.A. to cover the 1984 Olympics for ABC Sports, he fell in love with the place. It seemed fun. New York exhausted him, which could be good — it was nice to, as he said, "put out some effort once in a while." But he was ready for some sunshine and laid-back attitudes.

In fact, he used just that feeling as inspiration for his first *Seinfeld* pitch. He suggested a story in which Elaine was exhausted by New York and wanted to leave, which would make Jerry confront any feelings he had for her. Producer Larry Charles, however, suggested that instead Jerry could accidentally get her an apartment in his building. Mehlman agreed that was better — more opportunity for humor, less worrying about Jerry and Elaine's relationship. This resulted in "The Apartment," which first aired in April 1991.

With almost no rules or outlines to write

by, Mehlman could throw whatever he felt like into the script for "The Apartment." George could wear a wedding ring to a party to see if it helped pick up girls! Mehlman put it in, and it sailed through without a change. Most other shows planned out every episode beforehand, scene by scene, and then handed it to the writer to flesh out. *Seinfeld*'s free-for-all approach was unusual, although Mehlman didn't realize it at the time.

After he turned in his script, he started hanging out at the *Seinfeld* offices even though he wasn't an official staffer. That's when he got nervous about this TV writing thing. It seemed like such a great place to work; now he *wanted* this possible staff job for this possible next season.

He got a glimpse of how smart his new bosses could be when he saw them discuss Elaine and Jerry's relationship. One of the season's episodes, "The Deal," had the characters committing to a romantic relationship after first trying to sleep together with no strings attached. But David made a quick, critical decision for the show's direction and longevity: They'd back out of this thing while they still could, and never go back to that easy plot-generator, romantic tension between major characters. They were not to become another *Cheers,* with its antics between barkeep Sam and waitress Diane.

NBC executive Warren Littlefield loved the Elaine-Jerry dynamic and pushed for them to have a real relationship that the audience could invest in. David and Seinfeld agreed to the "happy" ending to "The Deal" because they thought it might be their series' final season. When they returned for another unexpected season, they dropped the romantic relationship, never acknowledging it on-screen.

Mehlman had a knack for dating stories, so he was relieved that all four main characters would remain available for such plotlines. He believed in the show more than ever, even though he wasn't so sure about himself. He had never written even a word of fiction, aside from this one episode he had somehow faked his way through. He had no idea what he was doing.

David faced the pressure to produce a season three times as long as the last, four-episode run, by mining his own life for plotlines — it seemed easier than making stuff up. This turned the show, at times, into an almost documentary-style reenactment of incidents from his past. Some of the most memorable episodes during this season came from his experiences, all of them noted in his piles of yellow, lined notepads, waiting to be excavated for scripts.

"The Jacket," which ran in February, was the pinnacle of this phenomenon, almost pure autobiography for David. It featured the imposing Lawrence Tierney as Elaine's father, novelist Alton Benes, modeled on *Revolutionary Road* author Richard Yates — that is, the father of Monica Yates, David's ex. When Monica and Larry first met, she told him her father was "one of the greatest American writers." Larry read the book, then reported back, astonished: "Oh my God, you're actually right." David's comedian friends, including Richard Lewis, all took up reading Yates at David's urging.

David once suffered a harrowing meeting with Richard Yates in 1985 when he agreed to a dinner with father and daughter at the Algonquin Hotel, just like Jerry and George do in the episode. And Monica had arrived late, leaving David alone with her gruff, alcoholic father, just like Elaine had left Jerry and George hanging. Even the jacket story line — about a new suede coat with a flamboyantly patterned lining, its pristine condition threatened with falling snow — was straight from David's life.

Monica was living in L.A. at the time the episode was shot, so she attended the taping. ("I think you can hear my laugh on the laugh track," she told me.) Her father was living and teaching in Alabama, nearly broke, without a television. Monica thought he would enjoy the cheeky send-up, so she encouraged him to find a grad student whose TV he could watch. He did, and several students planned a little get-together to view Richard Yates's television "debut" with him. But Monica had gotten the airdate wrong, so after quite a bit of fanfare, the group turned the TV on only to find an episode all about Jerry offending an old woman by saying he hated people who grew up owning ponies; not a hint of anyone Yatesean. Suddenly it looked like Richard had possibly imagined the whole thing: *Sure, your daughter's friend wrote this television show all about you.*

But a slightly smaller group gathered with slightly less fanfare the following week, and there it was: "The Jacket," airing on February 6, 1991, three days after Richard Yates's sixty-fifth birthday. In it, Tierney — known for playing gangsters — grimaces when Jerry and George order nonalcoholic drinks while waiting in his hotel bar with him for Elaine to arrive. He tells "funny guy" Jerry,

95

"We had a funny guy with us in Korea. Tail gunner. They blew his brains out all over the Pacific."

Richard Yates watched the scenes play out, stone-faced, as his students tried not to laugh. It went on.

When George and Jerry escape Alton's withering stare for the restroom, George wonders: "How could she leave us alone with this lunatic?" Elaine finally appears, and as the four head outside to dinner, Jerry panics. It's snowing, which will ruin his pricey new suede jacket. He turns it inside out to reveal the candy cane–striped lining. "You're not walking down the street with me and my daughter dressed like that. That's for damn sure," Tierney snarls. Jerry ruins his jacket to placate the terrifying tyrant.

As the grad students later recalled the evening to Yates's biographer, Blake Bailey, the credits rolled and Yates watched, silence descending. Finally, one of Yates's friends said, "Well, it was *kind of* funny, Dick."

Yates's response: "I'd like to kill that son of a bitch!" With that, he left the room.

Monica believed the story was apocryphal, embellished, or at least a demonstration of her father performing for an audience more than an honest reaction to the episode.

("These kids clearly didn't get him," she said of the students.) Richard did later enumerate to his daughter all the particulars David had gotten "wrong" in his script. Yates would never wear a fedora like Alton Benes did. He served in World War II, not Korea. And, he insisted, "I'm not *that* scary." But Monica suspected it pleased him more than he let on. She loved the episode for what David had left out of the character — her father, at the time of the original incident, was frail and shriveled, prone to runny noses, a constant cough, and heavy drinking. But Alton Benes embodied only Yates's powerful, old-fashioned masculinity, coming across as an intimidating intellectual presence.

Tierney, for his part, really turned out to be scary, at least to the cast and crew of *Seinfeld*. David had conceived Alton Benes as a possibly recurring character and loved Tierney's performance, but noticed something odd during the filming: a butcher knife from Jerry's apartment set was missing. Seinfeld tried to lightheartedly confront Tierney about it: "Hey, Lawrence, what do you got there in your jacket?"

Tierney "joked" that he thought it would be funny and mimed the *Psycho* stabbing scene with the knife pointed in Seinfeld's direction. Tierney was not invited back, but David liked to threaten director Tom Cherones in the years to come with writing another Tierney script if Cherones's work wasn't up to par.

Monica Yates was disappointed; she had hoped to see "her father" show up again on *Seinfeld.*

Right around this time, Jason Alexander finally unlocked his character. After one table read, he questioned George Costanza's motivation in the script. He went to David with his concerns. "Larry, please help me. No one would react like this."

"What are you talking about? This happened to me, and this is exactly what I did."

Ah, so George wasn't Woody Allen. He was Larry David. Alexander began to study the executive producer more closely. Larry, he determined, was constantly trying to decide whether others' actions were an attack on him and, if so, whether to respond in kind. Whenever David did this, he put his tongue against his bottom teeth, opened his mouth and tilted his head as he figured out whether to say something or let the moment pass. It was, as Alexander described it, David's way of saying, "I see what you did. You just took a shot at me."

David was, Alexander noted, also constantly balancing his sense of utter worthlessness with an inflated ego. David attacked one minute, then apologized for being an idiot the next. Over time, Alexander started to tip George's balance toward the worthlessness, though he maintained plenty of simmering rage as well. Monica Yates saw shades of David in both the George and Jerry characters. "Larry is cooler than George," she said, "and he always was."

George did take on his own unique characteristics: a bumbling Inspector Clouseau, but with no cases to solve; an entitled Gordon Gekko, but without the money, power, or sex appeal. He slipped ever farther away from any semblance of integrity. He always chose to lie to protect himself. But he possessed a self-awareness that made him charming, and an underlying humanity courtesy of the much more functional human playing him. George knew he was a mess, so we could forgive many of his foibles.

Jeremiah Bosgang and his boss, Rick Ludwin, found themselves in a real bind after the table read for an episode late in *Seinfeld*'s midseason run in 1991. The script they'd just heard — for the eleventh episode of the season's twelve, called "The Chinese Restaurant" — had Elaine, George, and Jerry doing nothing in the script except waiting for a table at a Chinese restaurant. (It was the only episode that didn't include Kramer, because David, at the time, was still sticking with the idea that Kramer was a shut-in.) The waiting would happen in real time. No scene changes, no progress, no action beyond a pay phone call and an attempt to bribe the maître d'. Bosgang and Ludwin had championed many of the show's stranger moments, but now they were considering shutting down production.

They'd been worried about the script from the first time they'd read it. A half hour after receiving it, Bosgang came into Ludwin's office and exchanged worried looks with him. Was this thing missing pages or something? There was no story! What would the other NBC executives say if Ludwin and Bosgang allowed this to move forward?

To Bosgang, it confirmed the network's worst fears about David and Seinfeld — that they couldn't hack it making a sitcom long-term. Ludwin and Bosgang liked the show and wanted it to succeed, for their own sakes as well as David's and Seinfeld's. But they didn't think they could sell their

NBC colleagues on a show concept this flimsy.

They'd decided to go to the table read in hopes of seeing some progress. But there'd been no substantial change. Now Ludwin and Bosgang sat together in Bosgang's car, a used, white Mercedes-Benz 190E he'd recently bought from *Seinfeld* director Tom Cherones to replace his motorcycle. Both executives agreed that telling producers to kill a script was a provocative action. Larry David, in particular, would not receive this sort of directive lightly.

But the two also knew how precarious *Seinfeld*'s future was at the network, what a critical time it was for the series. They had a responsibility to say *something*. "This is really their show," Bosgang recalls Ludwin telling him. "We should explain to them that we, personally, Rick and Jeremiah, feel we should not go forward with this show, but we will ultimately support them."

Indeed, David balked even when Ludwin said — gingerly, but still getting his trepidation across — "If you feel passionate about this, which you obviously do, go do it, and we'll hope for the best."

Ludwin took David for a walk around the lot and allowed him to vent his frustrations. David wanted Ludwin to understand that this episode was in the spirit of the show. It was a funny half hour of television about life's little frustrations. It was *Seinfeld*. If the network executives didn't like this, they didn't like the show.

In fact, the script baffled even the man who played the Chinese restaurant host. Actor James Hong expressed his confusion. Cherones understood it as similar to his own feelings in his early days with the show. "That doesn't matter," he told Hong. "Just go with it."

The episode did not go over well with Ludwin and Bosgang's colleagues, but no one stopped it from airing.

And when it ran on May 23, critics understood what NBC did not. "Like real life, but with better dialogue," wrote Kit Boss in the *Seattle Times*. "*Seinfeld* doesn't feel like sitcom television," *New York* magazine's Chris Smith said. "It feels more like a conversation with your funniest friends." Over time, the episode would stand as a turning point for the series and a groundbreaking bit of television; NBC executives would gain a reputation for supporting creativity instead of foisting their own opinions on their talent.

In summary, everyone won: The producers made the show they wanted, and the network looked good for airing it. In fact, the episode showed that a sitcom could take on more highfalutin qualities than the form had previously attempted: In this case, modernism, a TV take on Samuel Beckett's *Waiting for Godot*.

"The Chinese Restaurant" hinted at where *Seinfeld* was headed after two uneven seasons. The question remained, however, whether that was a direction NBC wanted to bet on again.

And *Seinfeld* still had one last little stylistic flourish to invent for the final episode of this season — possibly its final episode ever, yet again. In "The Busboy," George accidentally gets a busboy fired, then makes matters worse by allowing the busboy's cat to run away when he tracks him down at home to apologize. Eventually, the busboy thanks George for saving his life: A few days after he'd been fired, there had been an explosion at the restaurant that could have killed him; plus, he found a new job while out looking for his cat. Meanwhile, in an unrelated plot, Elaine desperately tries to dump her boyfriend.

As David struggled to end the script, he saw an opportunity in the coincidence that the busboy and the boyfriend show up at Jerry's apartment around the same time.

Wouldn't it be funny if they got into a fight in the hallway on the way to the apartment? And wouldn't it be even funnier if it had catastrophic results for both plotlines? In the end, because of the hallway altercation, the busboy loses his new job and Elaine's boyfriend is bedridden in her apartment for several weeks.

From then on, David decreed: All plotlines on *Seinfeld,* should the show continue, would dovetail into one explosive ending. Writing it would be even harder that way, but that's the way David preferred things.

The network was now monitoring *Seinfeld*'s every move, every success and failure, like a parent trying to get a kid into a good college. Bosgang filed reports to Ludwin that assessed every script's quality. "The Ex-Girlfriend" (in which Jerry wants to date George's ex), "The Jacket," and "The Revenge" were among those deemed "above average." "The Busboy" was "average, . . . although it tested poorly."

David and Seinfeld took the scrutiny the same way they took every hardship: with pride and humor. They knew they were regularly losing to *Jake and the Fatman* and *Doogie Howser, M.D.* They simply didn't plan to do much about it. They displayed their own monitoring system, tacking the weekly ratings charts on a wall near their office with an additional column labeled EXCUSE: BASEBALL PLAY-OFFS. COUNTRY MUSIC. DOOGIE GETS LAID. Even though they knew their status as outliers in TV comedy made big ratings less likely, they stuck to their vision. David told the writers they must adhere to one rule in their scripts: "No hugging, no learning." They even had jackets made up with this credo imprinted upon them.

The NBC executives once again pored over the reports and the ratings numbers, as well as audience and critical reaction, and decided: *Seinfeld* would get a spot, at last, on the network's fall schedule.

Perhaps the first indicator that they'd chosen correctly — that *Seinfeld*'s hip factor was growing — came when Bosgang was hired away to be a full-fledged executive at Fox, where he'd report to the head of comedy development: the job he'd wanted at NBC from the beginning.

As a memento of his time with the show, *Seinfeld*'s prop department gave Bosgang one of the several copies of the tiny, plaster woman they'd made for the title art in the episode "The Statue." He took it with him to his new office at Fox, a nod to *Seinfeld*'s unexpected halo effect on his career. The industry was starting to take serious notice of this weird little show. As CBS Entertainment president Jeff Sagansky said that year, "All hits are flukes." *Seinfeld* was becoming one of those flukes.

Seinfeld and David pushed their matching, facing desks together in their shared office and went to work on their third season — their first full-length, twenty-two-episode, regular-season run. They had run up a deficit of possibly $10 million at Castle Rock — the difference between what NBC had paid for the show and what it cost to make — that they had yet to make back, but this was their chance to try. They spent their days debating with Cherones about, say, where to put a Pez dispenser for maximum comic effect, and their evenings and weekends rewriting scripts. Occasionally, Seinfeld would speed off in his Porsche down Melrose Avenue to the Improv, do a little stand-up, then come back. Seinfeld got anxious if he went too long without doing a live stand-up set.

Now the question became whether this fluke — impressive for its mere survival up until this point — could really become a hit. Getting onto the fall schedule signified that it had arrived, but the show now faced a much tougher road, competing with the onslaught of new series on both network television and the growing cable channels. Standards for hits loomed much higher in the fall. Anything without sufficient numbers could die an unceremonious death. Experimental shows, such as the previous fall's musical disaster *Cop Rock,* could become instant industry punch lines. And NBC was losing its grip on the top spot; while it finished the 1990–91 season still in first place, less than half a ratings point separated the Big Three networks overall. *Seinfeld* was entering treacherous territory.

At least Larry David now had a backup team to help him feed the idea-eating monster that would be this third, twenty-two-episode season.

Peter Mehlman had officially joined the writing staff for *Seinfeld,* along with a handful of other staffers, most of them sometime stand-ups. As Mehlman sat at lunch with them, along with David and Seinfeld, he noticed that they were all fighting to talk, fighting to tell the joke that would get a laugh from the table — from David and Seinfeld, especially. He had no idea how to compete with them. He wrote a note to himself: "Just shut up and learn." The next year would not prove easy.

The workload had doubled yet again. The writers worked at the office with David and Seinfeld constantly, every day, weekends, too. Scriptwriting on *Seinfeld* remained an exercise in both freedom and terror — the writers worked as individuals, not in a room full of staffers pitching jokes, the way other sitcoms worked.

It became clearer that the writers were to function mainly as an idea farm, and they were to harvest these ideas from their own lives. David had already plucked his own past nearly bare by writing most of the episodes so far himself. Mehlman carried a notebook everywhere to write down any little thing that happened that might make a story. As a journalist, he had spent years observing professionally, but he usually noticed things that went on around him, not *inside* him. For *Seinfeld,* he trained himself to notice his own smallest thoughts, the things he worried about and obsessed over. For instance, he met a woman he liked, and as they made out, all he could think about was the fact that every woman had her own "kissing system." Like, lip here, hand here, open mouth, close mouth. Then he realized: He wasn't in the moment, even when kissing a beautiful woman. He was merely observing his own life. *Seinfeld* had consumed him.

Jason Alexander's sense of indignation was raised to George Costanza levels once again. He would have no more of *this*.

He had never confronted Larry David with a problem, but now, in the fall of 1991 as *Seinfeld*'s third season began, he had to. Alexander had felt a little territorial ever since Julia Louis-Dreyfus had been cast in the second episode. In the third episode of the third season, his worst fears came true: The new script, called "The Pen," contained neither Michael Richards nor Alexander. Just Jerry Seinfeld and Louis-Dreyfus's Elaine, going to visit Jerry's parents in Florida. Alone.

Alexander didn't need this TV career. He had won a Tony on Broadway! He still had a New York apartment. He could go back. He didn't want to waste a minute in Los Angeles that he didn't need to.

After the table read for the episode, Alexander pulled David aside. "If you write me out again," he said, "do it permanently." David stammered, tried to explain the difficulties of servicing every character equally every week. "Don't tell me your problems,"

Alexander snapped. "If you don't need me here, I don't want to be here."

At the same time, Louis-Dreyfus was routinely voicing her own similar complaints to David: She felt that *she* wasn't getting enough quality screen time. In this case, the producers saw her point, though they were still struggling to find exactly the right comedy groove for Elaine.

Louis-Dreyfus even came into the writers' office crying one day to talk to producer Larry Charles, David, and Seinfeld about her concerns that she wasn't being used to her fullest abilities. Though she clocked plenty of face time in front of the camera, she felt she wasn't getting material as funny as the boys'. They promised to do better.

But George was also a breeze to write for; the basis for him was walking around the set all the time. Jerry's character, too, often came naturally — he was, after all, among the first sitcom characters to acknowledge his similarity to the actor who played him by sharing the same first *and* last name. Kramer's dual poles — real-life inspiration Kenny Kramer (though Richards never studied him the way Alexander studied David) and Richards's genius with physical comedy — made him a rubbery character who could stretch to almost every extreme.

Then there was Elaine.

Of course she was distinctive, and played by the gifted Louis-Dreyfus, whose giant smile and dark hair made her the object of many a secret crush in the writers' room (and among many of those watching at home). But her story lines came the hardest for a lot of the writers. Most of them were men, for starters, though that didn't stop them from throwing her story lines inspired by their own lives — that was part of what gave her such a liberated persona. In fact, David and Seinfeld told writers to feel free to write her "as if she were a guy." While she was no doubt a heterosexual woman, her femininity did not stop her from doing whatever she pleased.

What vexed many writers about her more than her gender was her functionality. She was the most well-adjusted of the *Seinfeld* characters: She was the only one who almost always had a steady day job, a robust dating life, plenty of confidence, and even friends outside the core four. She was smart; she'd graduated from Tufts (and that was, as she often noted, her safety school). Perhaps Elaine's functionality was what made Louis-Dreyfus's portrayal of her seem so effortless; Richards reported that he "never saw a process with Julia when she worked."

Peter Mehlman felt like he was the only one on staff who liked to write for Elaine and Jerry — the more "normal" characters — than for George and Kramer. He loved to see what new shades Louis-Dreyfus would bring to his lines. He developed a theory that Elaine was the linchpin in the entire series, that if she didn't have a strong story line in an episode, it would fall flat no matter what else went on. He had the most trouble with Kramer stories, in fact. It took him a few years to figure out that if he had what he thought of as an "extra" Jerry story lying around, he should give it to Kramer. A normal story for Kramer would become big and cartoony through Richards's acting. Thus an idea originally intended for Jerry — switching to boxer shorts due to low sperm count, for example — became a Kramer idea, and seemed wackier for it.

One of the *Seinfeld* cast's most remarkable feats, in the end, was that almost none of these cracks showed in the final product. The actors nailed their characters so completely that no one watching could imagine any of them feeling shortchanged in the funny-line department, or experiencing an identity crisis via the writers. Viewers could hardly guess that a story line meant for one

112

character had been transferred to another. The *Seinfeld* cast and writers were on their way to becoming legendary, and for good reason.

5
THE PRODUCTION

A beautiful brunette looks into George Costanza's eyes and pleads, "Save the whale, George. For me." A hopeful crowd surrounds them on the beach where a whale emergency has occurred. Only a marine biologist can rescue this magnificent creature. Unfortunately, George has told this woman that he is a marine biologist. But he is not a marine biologist. George has, once again, lied for personal gain. And once again, he will not cop to the truth, even when caught in the most incriminating circumstances.

He heads, with grand purpose, straight into the ocean.

The audience titters, expecting more. But the script is supposed to end there. On *Seinfeld,* however, the script should end with a huge laugh. A wow moment.

It would be another long night on the set of *Seinfeld.*

Seinfeldia was not built on lukewarm audience reaction. It needed a wow moment. A ho-hum ending meant pitching ideas on the shoot; any and all good ideas were welcome. The producers huddled, then Larry David asked Jason Alexander: "How long would it take you to learn a monologue?"

Soon, Alexander was presented with new pages. He focused his nearly photographic memorization skills on those pages, then settled into the gang's favorite coffee-shop booth opposite Seinfeld and Michael Richards. The cameras rolled.

George speaks. "I don't know if it was divine intervention or the kinship of all living things, but I tell you, Jerry, at that moment, I *was* a marine biologist." A solid laugh. "The sea was angry that day, my friends. Like an old man trying to send back soup in a deli." An even bigger laugh. "I got about fifty feet out, and suddenly, the great beast appeared before me. I tell you, he was ten stories high if he was a foot. As if sensing my presence, he let out a great bellow. I said, 'Easy, fella!' . . . And then, from out of nowhere, a huge tidal wave lifted me, tossed me like a cork, and I found myself right on top of him, face-to-face with the blowhole. I could barely see from the waves crashing down upon me, but I knew something was there. So I reached my hand in, felt around, and pulled out the obstruction."

He produces one of Kramer's golf balls from his pocket to bring back the episode's other story line. "Is that a Titleist?" Kramer asks. One of the show's longest sustained laughs, and applause, follows.

The moment would become Seinfeld's favorite of the entire series.

Another episode nailed, another long night. The cast and crew of Seinfeld could pull off such Olympic-level feats of television now — George's speech not only saved an episode, it made that episode into an oft-quoted classic — because of the tonnage of talent at work on each side of the camera.

Alexander's George Costanza was growing into an autonomous being — separate from his creator, Larry David. By the show's fourth season, Alexander thought of the character as George, not as Larry David in disguise. This George had his very own tendency to snort-laugh — or at least more of a tendency than David had — and to double-take in disbelief.

George couldn't have been more different from the guy who played him. George was an avid baseball fan who went to work for the Yankees, while Alexander knew nothing about sports. He'd never followed a team in his life. But when Alexander played George, the baseball references flowed like they were straight from a kid who grew up at Yankee Stadium.

George found his own path to some level of personal success over the seasons, too. He'd started the series as a real-estate broker, then fallen into unemployment and lived with his parents, but then he got a great apartment, produced Jerry's TV pilot, worked in the head office at the New York Yankees, and dated his share of beautiful women. Even Alexander's own wife asked him at one point, "How are you getting all these girls?"

Maybe it was his charm — or at least his portrayer's charm, which few of his costars were immune to. Director Andy Ackerman referred to "this little twinkle in his eye that you can't help but love." Even Alexander acknowledged that his own sensitivity "became an underpinning of George's sensitivity." In the sixth-season episode "The Kiss Hello," writer Carol Leifer played a bit part as a physical therapist's assistant. When George, a patient, writes a check to the therapist and hands it to the assistant, Alexander wrote profane messages to Leifer on the small slip of paper, a new one every take, just to get her to crack up. He did not fail.

Like Seinfeld, Michael Richards began his career as a stand-up, though he didn't get started until after serving two years as an army draftee in the Vietnam War. He graduated with a bachelor's in drama from Evergreen State College in 1975 after serving, and got his first major break as a stand-up with a spot on Billy Crystal's first cable TV special in 1979. On *Fridays,* Richards gained a measure of fame as the cast member on-screen with guest host Andy Kaufman when Kaufman refused to deliver his lines on live TV. Richards brought the cue cards to Kaufman on camera, Kaufman threw a drink in Richards's face, and a small melee erupted. Richards and other *Fridays* cast and crew later revealed he was in on the joke.

But Richards made his pre-*Seinfeld* name, at least around the industry, in his many, many guest spots on TV sitcoms and dramas — *Cheers, Night Court, Miami Vice, St. Elsewhere* — always stealing the spotlight with his physical performances. His wild, wiry dark hair, expressively lined face, and easy way with a cigar made Kramer into the kind of character who could become an icon.

Richards was sometimes compared to Jacques Tati, a French acrobatic satirist from the 1930s known for his music hall act in which he took mime to a new level. Novelist and performer Colette (known for her book *Gigi*) wrote of Tati's *Impressions Sportives* at the ABC Théâtre in Paris: "His act is partly ballet and partly sport, partly satire and partly charade. He has devised a way of being the player, the ball and the tennis racquet, of being simultaneously the football and the goalkeeper, the boxer and the opponent, the bicycle and the cyclist. Without any props, he conjures up his accessories and his partners. . . . How gratifying it was to see the audience's warm reaction! Tati's success says a lot about the sophistication of the allegedly 'uncouth' public, about its taste for novelty and its appreciation of style."

Kramer was idiosyncratic to the extreme. He refused to wear an AIDS ribbon at an AIDS walk. He often talked of a close friend named Bob Sacamano who never materialized. He prepared dinner for guests while in the shower. He authored a coffee-table book — a book that folded out into a coffee table. He watched surgery from the viewers' gallery. He impersonated the Moviefone voice when his number was mixed up with the service. He told a woman she needed a nose job. He drank beer with a cigarette in his mouth.

For Richards, who was forty when *Seinfeld* started, Kramer was the role of a lifetime. Richards got audience applause every time he slid, stumbled, or fumbled through Jerry's apartment door. David eventually requested a preshow announcement to get the audience to stop cheering Richards's every appearance. The applause breaks were distracting.

When Richards didn't nail his part, he took on a pained expression that his costars began to recognize. While Alexander, Louis-Dreyfus, and Seinfeld networked with industry types after a taping, Richards escaped to his dressing room, emerging only to do reshoots, which were often requested by him. Richards always thought he could do better, and berated himself if he couldn't. He always found a way to give lines an extra hit with a gesture or sound effect, a technique he swiped from watching Gale Storm, the star of the 1950s sitcom *My Little Margie,* in which she played a twentysomething woman living with her widowed father in New York City.

Over the first sporadic months and seasons of working together, Alexander began to understand that Richards was executing a "subtle, powerful reinvention," as Alexander later put it. "Michael, instead of playing the dumbest guy in the room, decided he's the smartest guy in the room." This way — changing a word or two in his lines as he went — Richards showed David and Seinfeld who Kramer could really be and created an evolution for the character, from a shut-in weirdo to a guy who was too cool for normalcy. Other times, these changes came from the comedy gods above. In one of the earliest episodes, Richards accidentally rammed into the doorjamb of Jerry's apartment as he exited, which caused the studio audience to erupt in laughter. Thus his entrances and exits became one of his signature moves.

Even Richards's own instincts and his forethought could contradict each other. In the episode in which Kramer had seizures every time he heard *Entertainment Tonight* anchor Mary Hart's voice, Richards told Alexander — who was directing the episode — that he didn't want "to be grotesque about it." He'd *tastefully* shake and then fall behind the sofa. As soon as Richards got in front of the audience, however, he nearly destroyed the set with the intensity of his antics. As the audience reacted, he instinctively amped up his performance.

"Dude, now we're screwed," Jason Alexander said to Richards. "We've just lost the set. Why didn't you tell me?" But he also understood: That was all part of working with Richards. Preparation and spontaneity in equal, heaping measures.

Richards went to a place of deep concentration where he rarely broke character or laughed while taping, but he was so good his costars couldn't help cracking up. This caused a vicious cycle; he hated when costars' laughter broke his momentum. When Alexander laughed during a scene when the three guys go to see an overly serious shaman, Richards begged, "You can't, please, you don't know how hard it is for me." (Because the laughter meant they had to reshoot the scene.) Another time, during a hospital-room scene in "The Junior Mint" with a giggly Louis-Dreyfus and Seinfeld, Richards griped without cracking a smile, "I had a line, if I could just get to it." Even an uncooperative rooster costar caused him to lash out. The rooster wandered all over the set instead of walking in a straight line down the sidewalk as intended. "Why don't I just be carrying him?" Richards asked.

"This is the dumbest bird I've seen."

Richards's costars didn't feel like they knew him, even later, after years on the set together. He often sat in a back corner with his eyes closed, muttering lines, between takes. When he wasn't doing that, he was walking around backstage, mumbling lines as he poked at the air. But others on the set knew him in strangely intimate ways: Charmaine Nash Simmons, the show's costume designer, found him to be extraordinarily appreciative of her contributions. Richards worked on Kramer's look with her, developing the idea that Kramer was wearing the clothing he still owned from the 1960s and '70s. They chose fabric together for shirts she'd make for him; he needed a few "copies" of each in case one got ruined in a particularly physical take. This paralleled the several sets of door hardware the crew kept on hand in case Richards took out a hinge during an entrance. Richards also came and got Kramer's shoes to rehearse in every day on the set as a way of stepping, physically, into his character.

Alexander saw an "insanity" in Richards that allowed him to play Kramer but went beyond the boundaries even of the crazy character. Louis-Dreyfus did more than see this phenomenon; she felt it. Whenever

Richards was about to perform one of his great physical comedy bits anywhere near her, she tensed, and for good reason. In one scene, he nailed her in the head with a golf club, leaving a welt just above her eye. Just before the scene, when she expressed her concerns about her own safety, he had told her, "Don't worry, I've never hurt anybody."

But others relished his methods. Estelle Harris, who played George's mother, loved to work with Richards because he'd never do a scene the same way twice. Danny Woodburn, who played Kramer's friend Mickey, enjoyed going off with Richards alone to rehearse the physical gags they often played together, contrasting Richards's height with Woodburn's short stature.

Richards faced some strange contradictions as his career took off. He found himself ambushed by paparazzi, but the shots they took were never published in the celebrity tabloids. He felt hurt that the photos didn't seem to interest anyone, and yet he wore a disguise when he ventured outside his home. He was the least known of the *Seinfeld* stars as a personality, but he was the one whose classic comedy skills could translate to any audience, any language, time, or place. He also won the most accolades for his showy role: He got *Sein-*

feld's first acting Emmy, in 1993, and would go on to win two more, enjoying the rare company of Don Knotts, John Larroquette, Art Carney, and Ed Asner as a multiple-Emmy winner in comedy.

In the 1890s, artist Charles Dana Gibson made a series of black-and-white, pen-and-ink illustrations of women he thought represented the ideal of feminine beauty, his composite view of "thousands of American girls." Gibson girls had thick, wavy, dark hair that they piled into gigantic, messy bouffants atop their heads. They were thin and youthful, with delicate features.

They were also stylish and modern, imagined to have jobs and some sense of independence. They were single, and often dominant in relationships with men. One drawing, called *The Weaker Sex,* shows four Gibson girls examining a tiny man under a magnifying glass as if he's an insect. In *The Crush,* a Gibson girl looks bored by a young man trying to woo her. In *Love in a Garden,* two men faithfully follow a Gibson girl's instructions to plant a tree root-side up.

The model and inspiration for the Gibson girls, Gibson's wife, Irene Langhorne, was a society girl who'd gotten more than sixty marriage proposals before she accepted his. Langhorne met and married Gibson in New York, where they settled into a home designed for them on East Seventy-Third Street. Langhorne was "a proper lady who also could hail a taxi with a sharp whistle, play a rousing piano tune, and hike up a mountainside in long skirts," according to the magazine at Hollins University, which proudly advertised even her brief ten-day stay at the school in 1889 before she decided to drop out.

Entertainment Weekly critic Lisa Schwarzbaum once referred to Elaine's "sexy modified Gibson girl coif," but the similarity went beyond hair. (Though hair was certainly important: The style George once described as "a wall of hair," that pouf atop cascading curls, was becoming a signature '90s trend that would be eclipsed only by the *Friends*-inspired Rachel haircut a few years later.) With her wit, obvious intelligence, and liberated sensibilities — not to mention a combination of physical comedy skill and sex appeal — Louis-Dreyfus became the sitcom's biggest step forward for womankind since Mary Tyler Moore and Lucille Ball.

Elaine wasn't perfect, which was why she could hang not only with boys but also with these particular dysfunctional boys. She rejected dates almost as often as Jerry did, and for equally superficial reasons — when her hunky boyfriend Tony, for instance, is mangled in a rock-climbing accident, she wonders how long she must wait before she can break up with him. Her inspiration, Monica Yates, saw her as a rare "male-minded" female character.

Over time, Monica found Elaine "too feministy" for her own taste, or at least for Elaine to be truly "based on" herself. Whenever *Seinfeld* writers heard about a liberal cause they thought could spark a good story line, it went to Elaine: David wrote the sixth-season episode "The Couch" after he heard that the Domino's pizza chain was owned by a supporter of the extreme pro-life group Operation Rescue. Thus was born Elaine's avoidance of pro-life foodstuffs — she refuses to order from a similar chain — and her reluctant breakup with a hot boyfriend who doesn't share her principles. "I'm sure he's pro-choice," she says before she confirms the truth. "He's just so good-looking."

Her liberal politics, in particular, came from one of the women who helped shape her behind the scenes, comedian Carol Leifer. Used to the male-dominated world of comedy, Leifer knew what it was like to be surrounded by men. She had written a well-received Showtime special called *Gaudy, Bawdy, and Blue* in 1992, in which she played a foul-mouthed comedian looking back on her '60s career, featuring a cameo by Seinfeld. When Leifer joined the *Seinfeld* writing staff in season five, she pitched many of Elaine's most memorable story lines, giving the character her own neurotic-girl twist and giving rise to the commonly cited idea that Elaine was "based on" Leifer.

Leifer used her status as an inspiration for Elaine — that is, her gender — as an advantage over her male colleagues. Leifer trafficked so well in "girly" *Seinfeld* stories, in fact, that she was often asked if she'd written "The Sponge," the episode (actually written by Peter Mehlman) in which Elaine hoards her favorite form of birth control when she hears it's being discontinued. Luckily, being accidentally credited with a Mehlman episode wasn't a bad thing.

Leifer also learned that she should look to her own life for material. She was, after all, one of the few women on the writing staff, the Mary Richards of this newsroom, and Elaine needed stories every week. Leifer struck gold, for example, with: "Elaine thinks the manicurists at her nail salon are talking about her in Korean behind her back." As a bonus, Leifer got free mani-pedis at her own salon from then on, after the show used the establishment's real name in the episode.

She had more where that came from: "Elaine thinks that the mirrors at Barneys are skinny mirrors." Leifer had to explain the concept of skinny mirrors to the guys, a good sign — this would be a plot. Similarly, she went as a fake date with a gay banker friend on an outing with his boss to the Hollywood Bowl and came up with the plotline for the episode "The Beard."

Of course, Louis-Dreyfus injected plenty of her own personality into Elaine — like Jason Alexander, she had a real-life warmth that offset some of her character's brutality.

When I met her for an interview once, she arrived at the designated restaurant first, and called my cell to thoughtfully ask if she could order me something; I insisted I wasn't hungry, but when she heard I'd been driving for several hours when I arrived, she begged me to share her turkey sandwich with her. It was delicious, and I was starving.

This was her good-mom instinct coming out: Though Elaine was a new model of single-womanhood who hated the idea of having children, Louis-Dreyfus gave birth to both of her sons during the show's run (Henry in 1992, Charles in 1997), spending months hiding her growing belly behind cushions, pillows, boxes, furniture, and oversize clothes while on camera. Because of Elaine's aggressive singlehood, Louis-Dreyfus reported that fans were flummoxed when they saw her out and about with her young son. "Oh my God," they'd gasp. "I had no idea."

Costars often cited Louis-Dreyfus's gutsy approach to comedy, her willingness to do anything or look ridiculous to get a laugh. But her pregnancies pushed her limits. When she was about four months pregnant with Charles, Seinfeld told her, "I have an idea for how to play this out. What if Elaine gets fat?" Louis-Dreyfus burst into tears.

Years later, she acknowledged that it could've been a great plotline, but it would have "taken a few lunches" to talk her into it.

As the show took off, Louis-Dreyfus also found herself balancing moments of stardom — taking interviews with the *New York Times* as she visited her wealthy father at his estate — with feeding her ten-month-old son, Henry, mashed peas.

■ ■ ■ ■

As the third season progressed, the production grew. While *Seinfeld* still tended to focus on the inner annoyances of life, its budget allowed for larger expressions of those feelings. "The Parking Garage," in which Jerry and the gang visit a mall and forget where they left the car for an entire episode, required the construction of a fake garage building. It marked the first time of many that they'd shoot off set, away from a studio audience. Seinfeld, David, and the rest of the crew were amazed by how good it looked when it came time to edit the tape.

A more typical taping night would begin with about two hundred people — recruited by the studio in the early days, lucky ticket-holders as the show got more popular — filing into the audience bleachers on the soundstage. No matter how in-demand the tickets were, they were always free. There, the studio audience would sit and wait an hour or so for the production to begin, though they were entertained with thematically resonant treats — Snickers bars, for instance, after Elaine caught her boss Mr. Pitt eating one with a knife and fork. There was always a "warm-up" comedian who performed, to get the audience in a laughing mood; Seinfeld often came out and chatted the audience up a bit, too.

This made the warm-up comedians' jobs extra-hard, since the audiences had come to see Jerry's stand-up, not some guy they'd never heard of. Comedian Pat Hazell said that "sometimes it's like being on a cruise ship all alone with a bunch of people who don't like you." He did try to tailor his jokes to the audience, using a Seinfeldian conversational approach and taking audience questions. An older woman once, hilariously, asked if the episode being taped was a rerun. For the rest of the evening Hazell kept asking her, "So what's coming next?"

Watching *Seinfeld,* or any other show, being filmed was very different from watching the zippy, twenty-two-minute final product. Scenes might be repeated two, three times or more. Breaks might ensue as writers and producers made adjustments to the script or wrote entirely new lines and scenes. A taping could last up to three hours, making the audience restless.

For off-site episodes like "The Parking Garage," Cherones and the producers devised an innovative system wherein they showed tapes of the location footage to the next week's studio audience to record "live" laughs. They were pioneering a middle ground between live taping and the more filmic "single-camera" approach. So they'd act out some sequences and show others on tape, in the sequence in which they would appear in the final cut. Other times — if there was a car scene, for instance — the actors would shoot it away from the audience for the final cut, but then reenact it onstage for the crowd, sitting in chairs and pretending to be in a car, like a little play for the live viewers. The on-location, off-set shooting would become one of the show's most distinctive hallmarks, and would help to usher in an age of "single-camera" comedies, shot cinematically and without an audience or laugh track, the way David had intended *Seinfeld* to be.

The snippets were shot in front of different live audiences but they were cobbled together. But *Seinfeld* often shot far more than required for a twenty-two-minute episode. *Seinfeld* tended to shoot at least eight minutes more material than it could use in the final cut. Even the episodes shot in front of one, consistent audience required editing together various takes. All of this made *Seinfeld* a particular challenge for the postproduction sound mixer — that is, the "laugh track guy." Even though the writers and producers proudly emphasize that they didn't have to *add* laugh tracks, they did need technical smoothing of the laughs recorded at the taping.

One of their favorite laugh track guys, writer Jeff Schaffer told me, was "a very sour man." All day, this guy sat at his custom-built laugh-editing machine, complete with foot pedals, like a court stenographer's contraption. When Schaffer and his partner, Alec Berg, arrived for editing, he'd say, "Oh, it's you two. I thought it'd be Fucko and What's-His-Name." They would ask him to bring the laughs down a little in one part, and he'd say, "I thought this was a comedy!" If they asked to bring the laughs up a bit in another part, he'd crack, "They can't all be winners!"

At this point, *Seinfeld* had survived the part of a normal show's life cycle during which the network seemingly tries to kill it. Even the network notes were now less intrusive than before. After a table read, Ludwin would say, "Great script, guys!" and then be off. David and Seinfeld could execute their own vision, without even the cursory network notes they'd experienced in the beginning. Because they hadn't worked in television before, they had no idea how rare this was.

The actors had settled into their roles to the point where they embodied their characters and nearly directed their own performances. Richards worked out his own, distinctive physical comedy bits to add to what was written in the script — sliding through Jerry's door to make an entrance or falling down and bumping into things. Alexander stopped worrying so much about Louis-Dreyfus stealing the show from him. Seinfeld, David, and Cherones started to see themselves less as producers and director and more as facilitators of the actors' talents.

By halfway through the third season, in February 1992, *New York* magazine called *Seinfeld* "TV's funniest, smartest sitcom" and "the purest New York show in years." Seinfeld's managers were receiving movie offers for their client, envisioning him in Billy Crystal–type roles, even though Seinfeld insisted he'd return to stand-up when the show ended. David and Seinfeld had either perfected their marriage-of-opposites shtick or had very different visions for their shared show. Seinfeld told *New York* that it was "about two idiots trying to figure out the world." David cautioned, "A lot of people don't understand that *Seinfeld* is a dark show. If you examine the premises, terrible things happen to people. They lose jobs; somebody breaks up with a stroke victim; somebody's told they need a nose job. That's my sensibility."

The *Atlantic,* meanwhile, opined that "*Seinfeld* shows why television is today's best medium for comedy."

As buzz built for *Seinfeld,* NBC announced that *The Cosby Show* would end that spring, at the end of the 1991–92 season. Hollywood started to take even more notice of NBC's stealth comedy weapon. Agents showed up on the set, and, still oblivious to how these things should work, David and Seinfeld just let them hang out. The floor of the *Seinfeld* set became a showbiz scene as big-name agents waited around to poach writers from the smaller agents who'd originally represented them.

Many agents were after Mehlman, because, as he said, "I was with a boutique agency, almost more like a bodega agency." He later found out that the Creative Artists Agency and ICM Partners — two of the biggest in the business — had agents assigned to him, to tail him and persuade him to leave his agency for them.

He resisted. The little bit of New Yorker left in him preferred the bodega.

Jerry and Larry's creation had ranked forty-sixth for its third season but was gaining viewers. For the first time in *Seinfeld*'s history, the question was not whether the show would get picked up for another season but how NBC would use it to its advantage.

In the first week of June 1992, loyal TV viewers pored over the grids in newspapers across the country that laid out the networks' new fall schedules. And many of them faced a dilemma come September: ABC had moved its hit family sitcom *Home Improvement* — the nation's fourth-most-popular show and the highest-rated new series of the year — from 8:30 P.M. on Tuesdays to 9:00 P.M. on Wednesdays. That is, opposite the rising favorite on NBC, *Seinfeld*. *Home Improvement* had done well, but it had succeeded with the help of a cushy slot on the schedule between hits *Full House* and *Roseanne*. The face-off would pit two former stand-ups, Tim Allen and Jerry Seinfeld, against each other. *Sun Sentinel* TV writer Tom Jicha called it "the most intriguing showdown since Fox sicked *The Simpsons* on *Cosby*."

The Wednesday-night battle meant a lot

137

to the networks because so many other nights were locked down. CBS ruled Sunday and Monday, ABC Tuesday and Friday, NBC Thursday. Whoever took Wednesday could win the season, and NBC needed a win to prove it could survive the loss of *The Cosby Show* and the impending ending of *Cheers* the following year.

Tim Allen expressed his disapproval of making his show cannon fodder. "They tell us it will work out fine," he told reporters through gritted teeth. Then he added a sarcastic, "Yeah, we're just thrilled."

Seinfeld shrugged it off, more used to fighting for his show's life. "I mean, what are you supposed to do?" he said. "Do anti-tool jokes? There's really nothing we can do but do our best work, which is what we would have done anyway."

NBC recognized *Seinfeld*'s growing potential and had given it a promotion, but this came with a huge responsibility: winning the battle for Wednesday night.

The cast now found themselves treated as stars — photographed in punk drag for the cover of *Rolling Stone* and in an homage to the Beatles on the cover of *Entertainment Weekly* — but the adjustment wasn't easy. Alexander and Richards still drove practical cars: Alexander a 1988 Toyota, Richards a slightly nicer Lexus, but certainly nothing near Seinfeld's two Porsches. (Alexander and Richards were known to freak Seinfeld out by sprinkling a few fall leaves on the roof of Seinfeld's midnight-blue Carrera in the studio parking lot.) Richards was often surrounded by men yelling "Kramer!" at him, and women wanting to touch his hair.

Alexander realized he couldn't tell fans to "blow off" when they wanted an autograph, but as an introvert, he also craved a sense of boundaries. Even as he grocery shopped, he faced constant cries of, "George Costanza! Can't stand ya!" — in reference to a flashback to Jerry and George's high school days in the third-season episode "The Library." He felt himself creating a kind of public persona: actor Jason Alexander, who could deal with this sort of thing affably, not Jay Scott Greenspan (his given name), who could not.

He really knew the show was taking off, though, when he did an interview for *Entertainment Tonight,* during which a van drove by with an African American family inside. A nine-year-old girl shot her head out the window and yelled, "I love you, George!" The show had reached far beyond the audience he'd anticipated for this little show about white, Jewish, thirtysomethings men in New York.

That said, there was no better crowd to keep the *Seinfeld* cast humble than uninterested New Yorkers themselves. After shooting their *Rolling Stone* cover in 1993 in New York, the four core cast members decided to go out for dinner. They wanted to sit outside, and they figured people were going to freak out when they saw the four of them together, outside, in New York, right on Columbus Avenue. But no one stopped except for a homeless man asking for money.

Finally, fall came, the time for the ratings showdown. Within weeks, it was clear: *Home Improvement* had destroyed *Seinfeld.*

And it mattered not one bit.

NBC, happy with *Seinfeld*'s upward trajectory and the demographics of its young, wealthy audience, moved the show to the big leagues by the middle of the 1992–93 season: Thursday nights, just after *Cheers,* which was entering its final days after lead Ted Danson had decided to quit. At first, network executives viewed the move as an emergency extraction of *Seinfeld,* its critically admired cult hit. With *Cheers* still doing great numbers, it wasn't like *Seinfeld* could ruin NBC's Thursday. NBC's programming vice president, Preston Beckman, said of the show's ratings, "*Seinfeld* wasn't showing signs of improving. It was literally wallowing. We had to get it out of there. It wasn't a time to be proud."

Jerry's manager, George Shapiro, ran into Danson shortly thereafter at a party and hugged him tightly in greeting, like a father greeting his long-lost son. "Thanks for quitting *Cheers,*" he told the baffled star.

Larry David, however, hated the idea of moving to Thursdays. "I don't want to be *Cheers'* little brother," he complained to Alexander.

David complained more to the writers. "We're on Wednesdays," writer Alec Berg remembers him saying. "That's when we're on. If they're not watching us on Wednesday, I don't want them watching us on Thursday."

Fortunately, no one cared what Larry David wanted.

Then, in *Seinfeld*'s first four weeks in the new Thursday spot, its ratings rose by 57 percent, taking it from TV's fortieth-most-popular program to its fifth. NBC had thought it was rescuing *Seinfeld,* when, in fact, *Seinfeld* was now rescuing NBC. *Seinfeld* was being groomed to replace NBC's biggest show on its biggest night.

6
THE WRITERS

Bill Masters — a tall, handsome former stand-up with thinning brown hair and a thick mustache — stood before Larry David and Jerry Seinfeld in their office, ready to make a pitch.

He knew Seinfeld from the days when they both did comedy and lived near each other on Eighty-First Street in New York. Like Seinfeld, Masters had worked the club circuit back then, but he also collected a paycheck for doing the audience warm-ups at *The Cosby Show* tapings in Brooklyn. Now, in the fall of 1991, Masters was in Los Angeles after he had sold a feature script and gotten a three-movie deal with Disney's Hollywood Pictures. As he waited for his film scripts to be made — and waited, and waited — he hoped to get a writing assignment from David and Seinfeld.

Masters had no idea how to pitch for

sitcoms, he later told me, but he went in that day in 1991 with five ideas and winged it. The first didn't fly. The second, he'd gotten from a script he'd written on spec for *The Cosby Show* that never went anywhere, about a guy whose job is to move cars from one side of the street to the other to comply with New York City's constantly shifting parking rules. That pitch was obviously more *Seinfeld* than *Cosby,* and it got him the holy grail of sitcom pitching: hard laughs in the room.

Satisfied, Masters went on to his next idea, but producer Larry Charles, who sat right next to him, stopped him and whispered, "Go back. They liked that one."

Masters reversed gears to the parking story and fleshed it out some more. David and Seinfeld bought it. He had his first sitcom assignment, reworking his idea from a traditional sitcom of the old guard — with limited, indoor sets and a limited concept of what makes a story line — to the new approach for which *Seinfeld* was now known — on-location shoots, quick cuts, and a boundless sense of where plots could go.

Masters was amazed by writing for television, even though so far he'd gotten only this one freelance script deal. He'd written several movie scripts, none of which had escaped the stacks of paper on which they had been written. Even though the scripts had been purchased, Masters hadn't seen anyone say a word of his dialogue. With this TV thing, he wrote something, and then David rewrote a lot of it, granted. But within a few weeks, he saw his words performed at a table read, and a few weeks later acted out on a stage, and a few weeks later shown on television.

After selling that *Seinfeld* script, however, Masters hit a run of bad luck. By the following year, his movie deal had collapsed, and his wife, Gail Berman, who worked in a production office on the Fox lot, was consigned to bed rest after she became pregnant with twins. At forty-one, Masters had no idea what he wanted to do with his life, but he knew he needed to do something soon, something more permanent than a one-off *Seinfeld* script.

After visiting his wife at her office before her maternity leave, he called to check his messages, and one was from Larry David, who left a callback number that was in New York. Masters was annoyed. Before moving to Los Angeles, his wife had made her name as a wunderkind Broadway producer, so Masters figured David was calling to ask them to get him theater tickets.

Masters said to his wife, "I'm not calling him. Fuck him."

However, Masters did eventually return David's call, and it turned out David wanted to tell him that *Seinfeld* was hiring writers for its next season. Masters had a full-time job on the fourth season. His luck had instantly turned back around.

Peter Mehlman got a call from David at that time as well: He was the only writer who'd been on staff hired back for the fourth season. Everyone else on the third-season staff had been let go, which became a common pattern on *Seinfeld:* David would bring in a batch of former stand-ups, use all the best material from their lives for plots — the only way to keep that Seinfeldia dimension between fiction and reality alive — then start fresh with a new batch of lives to harvest the following year. Larry and Jerry didn't go in for traditional sitcom procedure and rarely hired writers with much, or any, sitcom experience. The pile of spec scripts they'd gotten from writers who attempted a *Murphy Brown* or a *Cheers* sat ignored.

It was a particular honor to be asked back, so the rehiring boosted Mehlman's confidence. He'd been nervous throughout that year, his first in the *Seinfeld* office full-time, given his total lack of experience with television writing. Now he felt better. He was embarking on what would become a great season for him, possibly his best.

Masters went to work at the *Seinfeld* office along with Mehlman and four other new writers. He particularly loved working alongside Mehlman, whom he knew from the mid-'80s back in New York, where Mehlman's then girlfriend had worked with Masters's wife. They had become friends back then, and Mehlman even wrote a *Washington Post* piece in which he followed Masters through his life as a comedian for a week.

Masters soon learned that being on staff at *Seinfeld* meant being an idea factory — specifically, turning your own life experiences into pitches, and using your life as a laboratory for possible pitches, and listening to other people's life stories so that you could turn them into pitches. If David and Seinfeld liked one of your pitches, you'd get to write a script. Masters ran across a typo on a Trivial Pursuit card: The answer to a question was "the Moors," but the card read, THE MOOPS. That went into an episode called "The Bubble Boy," featuring a climactic Trivial Pursuit match between a sick boy forced to live in a plastic quarantine "bubble" and George. Masters sat in on a freelance writer's pitch to David for a story line that would turn into "The Pick," featuring Elaine's accidentally X-rated Christmas card. The guy brought a visual aid: a photo of a man smiling for a camera on Christmas morning in a robe as he unknowingly exposed himself.

If a pitch didn't sound real, David didn't want it.

Besides mining real life for stories, the writers also, once in a while, helped David with a script problem. He'd come into the writers' offices and present the issue; then they'd pitch solutions. If he liked a writer's solution, he'd walk out without another word. If he hated a writer's solution, he'd walk out without another word. The writers never knew which had happened until later, when they saw the script. Once, for instance, David came into a room full of writers and said he was writing a script about a contest in which the three guys would see who could abstain from masturbation for the longest. But he needed a story for Elaine.

One of the writers suggested that Elaine participate, too. David had, of course, already considered that, but he needed the right way to challenge her. "Who would be the guy that Elaine would be hot for?" Hot enough, in other words, to take her out of the running.

One of the writers knew: "John F. Kennedy Jr."

In this case, David walked out and went right back to work, writing that into the script that would become "The Contest."

As each new season began, the writers knew their goal: Get time with Larry and Jerry to pitch some stories. Get into that office where the two worked with their desks pushed together, and get enough material approved to write a script. Assignments didn't happen here like they did on other sitcoms.

Pitching them was difficult, especially when it came to pleasing Larry. When he was bored, which was most of the time, he'd stretch one of his shoulders in circles, one direction and then the other. To reject an idea, he'd say, "No, I don't love that one." If he hated something, he'd say, "I could see that on another show."

Both Larry and Jerry loved a quick pitch that came through in one or two sentences. Anything longer and they drifted off because they knew an idea too convoluted couldn't be that funny.

■ ■ ■ ■

After each raucous table read, David held court in the office he shared with Seinfeld. The two would sit at their facing desks, surrounded by writers sitting on chairs and sofas. The network reps would find themselves with no place to sit — perhaps by design. A rep might offer a small suggestion: "Jerry's too harsh in this scene." David would fidget with the golf club he kept in his office, then answer: "Nah, I don't think he's that harsh." Occasionally he might promise to work on it. No demands, no arguments. David and Seinfeld were in charge now that they were on their way to their vaunted Thursday-night time slot and No. 1 ratings ranking.

The writers braced themselves, however, for a confrontation with the network over "The Contest," that masturbation episode David had been working on.

The trick, in a broadcast situation comedy, was to launch this as a plotline without offending standards and practices. Thus George explains it to his friends this way: "My mother caught me." Doing what, Jerry asks. "You know. I was alone. I stopped by the house to drop the car off. . . . My mother had a *Glamour* magazine. . . . So one thing led to another. . . ." George explains that his shocked mother screamed, fell, threw her back out, and ended up in traction at the hospital.

But the real action begins when George says to his friends, "I'll tell you one thing. I am never doing *that* again."

"What, in your mother's house?" Elaine asks. "Or altogether?"

"Altogether." George's certainty elicits groans all around. "What, you don't think I could do it?"

"Well," Jerry says, "I know I could hold out longer than you."

George smirks. "Care to make it interesting?"

George, Jerry, and Kramer wager $100 each on who can hold out the longest. Elaine wants in, too, but the guys balk. "It's easier for a woman not to do it than a man," Jerry protests. "We have to do it. It's part of our lifestyle." But they relent, as long as she gives them odds; she'll put up $150.

To keep this up as the main plotline in a prime-time network television show, the *Seinfeld* writers had to come up with a euphemism for masturbation. In fact, they went one better: They came up with a new term that meant something new. To abstain from masturbation was to be "master of your domain." This allows the characters free and easy discussion of their sexual thoughts and exploits throughout the episode without one dirty word. Part of the humor came from the script's abstinence from even the word "masturbation," much less anything more graphic. An early draft had George using the word "tugging," but even that was cut. Kramer caves because of the woman walking around her apartment naked with her shades open, and later sleeps with her. Elaine caves when she stands behind John F. Kennedy Jr. in a workout class. Sly scenes depicting each character in bed at night clarify the status of everyone in the contest: Those who are still "masters" toss and turn, while those who have been satisfied sleep well.

As with most *Seinfeld* plotlines, it came from a real-life bet David was involved in. (He claims to have won.)

The table read for "The Contest" had gone well, with even more laughs than usual the first time through. Still, the subject matter left the writers with little doubt that the network would protest. Louis-Dreyfus, meanwhile, kept waiting for the executives to object specifically to her character's participation in it. A woman talking about

151

masturbation on prime-time television seemed like an obvious place to draw the line.

Instead, a shock. "It's perfect," the network reps said. "Don't touch it." They had come a long way since the showdown over "The Chinese Restaurant."

The episode helped *Seinfeld* win its first Emmy, and was often cited as the show's breakthrough episode. "Master of my domain" became *Seinfeld*'s first catchphrase.

Andy Robin got his first *Seinfeld* script assignment in the fourth season, after he was already a fan of the show. Robin felt a kinship with David and Seinfeld. Even though he was in his twenties — with a boyish handsomeness and dimples that made him look even younger — he loved stuff from the '50s and '60s, smooth crooners like Johnny Mathis and Petula Clark, the '69 Mets. He knew *Seinfeld* was the kind of operation where he could throw some Burl Ives into a script, and Larry and Jerry would get it.

Robin had come to Los Angeles to work for Tom Gammill and Max Pross, who'd eventually also write for *Seinfeld,* but at the time ran a sitcom called *Great Scott!,* starring a young Tobey Maguire. While Robin worked on his script for Gammill and Pross, he got a call from the *Seinfeld* office saying they were ready for him to submit some stories. Soon, *Great Scott!* was canceled, and all three guys headed over to the *Seinfeld* staff.

Robin had been editor of the *Harvard Lampoon* and worked at *Saturday Night Live* as a writer. He knew he'd stumbled onto something big with *Seinfeld,* his favorite show. He felt a huge responsibility to help keep the show so great. How would he maintain that level of quality? Or would he be the one to ruin it?

Now he couldn't write a thing without ripping it apart. He grew hypercritical of others' work on the show as well — that whole thing where you don't want to be a member of any club that will have you.

He found that desperation led to some bizarre pitches, none more so than the one that became his first episode, "The Junior Mint."

He had some reasonable plots lined up: Jerry dates a woman whose name he can't remember; Elaine visits an old artist boyfriend in the hospital to rekindle their romance when she sees he's lost a lot of weight; George buys a piece of art by Elaine's paramour in case he dies in surgery and the value increases. Tying them all together was the tough part, and out of that difficulty came one of the series's first memorably absurd moments, when Jerry and Kramer observe the artist's surgery from the gallery above while they snack on Junior Mints, eventually dropping one into the open body cavity below.

Robin was happier at *Seinfeld* than he had been back in New York at *Saturday Night Live.* At *SNL,* he found himself in a surprisingly corporate environment, nothing like the creative haven he'd expected. Instead, all anyone talked about were ratings. Everything felt overly cautious and bureaucratic, full of fiefdoms. People who had been there for decades were protective of their power.

After he landed at *Seinfeld,* he was happy he had escaped for sitcoms. But now, with his very first *Seinfeld* script, he was sure he had wrecked his career, and possibly an entire sitcom, with this dumb Junior Mint plotline. Robin couldn't believe David had approved it. As he went to his office to write his script, Robin thought, *This is crazy.* People would say, "They let some amateur in and he came up with this stupid, unsterile-hospital-environment story."

He called David while mid-draft and said, "I just realized, this can't happen."

David's response: "Just write it."

When Robin had finished with it, he was proud of one part: the story line in which Jerry couldn't remember the name of the woman he was dating. Robin always forgot people's names, so that idea came naturally to him.

In the episode, Jerry tries to find out his girlfriend's name through acts of subterfuge, like digging in her purse. She mentions that her name rhymes with a female body part. Exasperated, he guesses: Is it Mulva? Maybe Bovary? No, but she realizes: "You don't know my name, do you?"

Jerry finally figures it out when she leaves in a huff, and he shouts his final guess out the window after her: It's Dolores. (We don't know for sure, but we assume he's right.) Could this have been the first network-television acknowledgment of the clitoris? It seems likely. Cloris had been the scripted choice for her real name, but when the warm-up comedian asked the studio audience, just before the taping, to guess the woman in question's name, someone guessed Dolores. David and Seinfeld decided that was a better choice and subbed it in at the last minute.

Director Tom Cherones liked Robin's "Junior Mint" script more than its author did. He always enjoyed *Seinfeld*'s weirder little directorial challenges, none more so than the climactic fall of a piece of candy into a body mid-surgery. The quarter-size chocolate disk wouldn't show up on camera while in flight, so he shot a York Peppermint Pattie — about four times the size — instead. Viewers wouldn't be able to tell the difference without other objects in the shot to allow for comparison.

As the episode proceeded through the production process, Robin was shocked that no one raised an objection. The audience at the taping laughed, but he figured that was just because they were excited to be on the *Seinfeld* set. He saw the edited version and still hated it. Finally, it aired. And though the public revolt he expected did not happen — many fans and critics loved the episode — he was still certain he had ruined the show. Regardless of what people thought, *he* still hated the episode. It wasn't up to his own expectations of himself or of *Seinfeld.*

In fact, Junior Mints became almost synonymous with *Seinfeld,* and Seinfeld himself cited the episode's success as one of the signs that the show had reached another milestone: If it could pull this off, it could do no wrong. Anything was game. Even

Jerry's own character reached a new level of darkness in this particular script. Once the show's anchor for normality, TV Jerry was getting closer to the edgier real Jerry. As Kramer begs Jerry to join him in the surgical gallery to observe, Jerry sighs, "All right, all right. Just let me finish my coffee, then we'll go watch them slice this fat bastard up." You can see the barely contained glee on Seinfeld's face at getting away with this line.

After the episode, however, Robin could barely function, so cowed was he by the pressure of working on *Seinfeld.* The acclaim for "The Junior Mint" made matters worse, pressuring him to top what he'd done on his first try. He often started a script, then gave up on it about two-thirds of the way through when it didn't click. He didn't feel much support from fellow *Seinfeld* writers, given the solitary way the *Seinfeld* staff worked. David and Seinfeld were too busy to take much time for mentoring, and Robin's fellow writers were all working on their own pitches and scripts.

Gammill and Pross — who were both in their mid-thirties and looked like an older Clark Kent and a fair-haired suburban dad, respectively — were thrilled to land at *Sein-*

feld after *Great Scott!* ended. They had met while at Harvard, working on the *Lampoon,* and had been writing partners ever since. They were New Yorkers who'd moved to Los Angeles in 1987 to work on *It's Garry Shandling's Show* — a Showtime sitcom with some proto-*Seinfeld* qualities: a neurotic comedian who plays "himself" and a tendency to go meta. When *Seinfeld* first started, they hadn't watched, because they had just finished working on *Shandling* and needed a break from anything close to it.

But by the fall of 1992, when they were struggling to keep *Great Scott!* afloat, they would watch *Seinfeld* every week and wish they were working there instead of on their own show. Everything they saw on *Seinfeld* was what they wished they could do, and it looked so effortless. Among the few people who were watching *Great Scott!* was Jerry Seinfeld, who liked it enough to do a cameo appearance. When he shot the scene, he told Gammill and Pross, "When your show is canceled, and it will be, you should come over and work on our show."

Their résumés contained the usual stepping-stones to *Seinfeld: Saturday Night Live, Letterman* (where they first met Seinfeld, who was doing some of his late-night stand-up appearances). Their experience with showbiz in early-'80s New York made them a great match with David and Seinfeld. "*Seinfeld* was a show written in the '90s about people remembering their New York lives in the '80s," Pross later told me. "So we had that in common with those guys." In fact, they loved working at *Seinfeld* because it made them miss New York a little less: They could stroll "New York Street" (the set built to look like a Manhattan block), read the *Village Voice* and the *New York Times* in the office, and make obscure references to local New York television from the '60s.

When they finally reached refuge at the *Seinfeld* offices, they were at home, in a place where a lunchtime anecdote they told about a friend who'd worked on Wall Street and ate his Snickers bars with a knife and fork could become a script. That time Gammill bought a cigar store Indian, and his Native American next-door neighbor told him it was "like having a lawn jockey"? (Historically, lawn jockey statues were black and commonly used in the South — not considered in great taste for a modern liberal.) Another script.

Even though that fourth season demonstrated that *Seinfeld* was on an upward trajectory — in terms of both ratings and creativity — Mehlman, now an old veteran among the writers, saw signs of a direction he didn't like — "The Bubble Boy" episode, for instance. It parodied the simpering news coverage of immune deficiency patients who had to live in quarantine bubbles, who were always featured in heart-tugging portraits. *Seinfeld*'s Bubble Boy, however, was obnoxious. To Mehlman, the story exemplified a move away from the show's original intent to examine the smallest conflicts of everyday life and toward high-concept zaniness.

Of course, he still liked working on *Seinfeld,* and he didn't mind the social benefits, either. He didn't always know if the beautiful women dated him for his connections or because they liked him. But he got to date a lot of them. Even one of his friends, a lawyer unconnected with show business, got dates by saying he was friends with a *Seinfeld* writer.

Mehlman tried to preempt any awkward conversations about whether a date might end up inspiring an episode by saying, "Well, if you say some really funny things, that would be great."

Despite his disagreements with the show's direction, Mehlman churned out winning scripts as fast as he could. "The Virgin" had

160

Jerry in the unlikely position of dating a sexually inexperienced woman, played by the beautiful up-and-coming British actress Jane Leeves. "The Implant" had Jerry dating a woman whom he suspected of having fake breasts, played by the beautiful up-and-coming American actress Teri Hatcher. The idea for that one struck Mehlman while he talked to a female friend at a health club; when she caught him staring at a woman walking by, the friend said, "They're fake." At first, he considered using it as a throwaway interaction between Elaine and Jerry, but then he realized he could make it into an entire story line.

Both of his episodes generated next-day discussions, particularly the parting shot from the "Implant" girlfriend: "They're real, and they're spectacular." Mehlman was sure he'd now cracked the code of *Seinfeld* scriptwriting. He had four or five funny scenes that he'd come up with himself and gotten into that one script for "The Implant." (The same episode also included an oft-quoted rant against "double-dipping" chips at a party.) He knew how to do this.

But when he headed back to the drawing board for his next episode, he realized he knew nothing. Every episode was just as hard as the last. Still, he soldiered on.

Mehlman's script for "The Smelly Car" had Jerry battling the lingering body odor of a valet attendant — a story line swiped from the life of his lawyer friend. The friend constantly pitched Mehlman ideas for *Seinfeld* scripts, but they were never good. Then one day he told a story about a valet with B.O., never mentioning *Seinfeld.* Mehlman knew his friend had finally, unknowingly, provided him with a winner.

Mehlman's knack for conversation-starting episodes became one of *Seinfeld*'s defining trademarks.

As he drove to work in his dark blue 1992 Saab 900 convertible one day in 1995, he heard an NPR report on his radio: The Today Sponge had been discontinued. He thought, *Oh my God, what if Elaine is a sponge user?* She would, of course, have to buy out the entire West Side's supply. But she'd have a limited number, which would change her whole screening process.

This was the kind of story inspiration that came straight from the heavens.

In fact, Elaine's trendsetting carried over into real life on this issue, causing many of the Today Sponge's 6.4 million fans to agitate for its return to shelves. At the time, the manufacturer had said the stoppage was a temporary one, to fix a "water filtration"

problem with the design, but Elaine had been right to hoard them; six years later women were still lamenting the sponge's demise to *Ms.* magazine. "I should have stocked up early like Elaine," one woman told the publication in 2000.

Life was also about as good as it could get for Bill Masters, the former *Cosby Show* warm-up turned *Seinfeld* writer for the fourth season.

He had, along with fellow writers Steve Skrovan and Jon Hayman, written a memorable episode that season called "The Movie," with the four main characters continuously missing one another while they try to meet up at a theater. His wife gave birth. A comic friend of his, upon hearing that Masters now wrote for *Seinfeld,* marveled, "You know, you're writing for *The Mary Tyler Moore Show* of our time. It's that good."

Masters had gotten to appear in another episode, "The Airport," playing the shuttle-van driver who picks up Elaine and Jerry. Even though Masters had plenty of stand-up experience, he knew he always froze when he had to do something on camera. Still, he didn't want to say no to Larry David. His instructions were complicated, too, for a bit

163

part: After Elaine and Jerry load their stuff into the van, he was supposed to say, "Okay!" and then hit the gas. He was terrified he would screw it up somehow and ruin his writing career forever. As it came time to shoot, crew members were standing within inches of where Masters had to drive. Cherones told him, "Just floor it and go!" He worried he'd kill them all.

Finally, the cameras rolled. He said his line. He floored it. He didn't hit anyone. One take. Cherones called it — on to the next scene. He was a success.

His year at *Seinfeld* had turned out okay.

Then, in the summer of 1993, after the fourth season had ended, Masters got a call from Jerry and Larry telling him he wouldn't be invited back to the staff the following year. David said they'd wanted to keep him, but felt funny choosing some of that season's writers and not others. So they'd clear the deck of everyone except Mehlman, who'd been around longer. Masters wondered if David just said that to be nice, but a yearly staff purge was, in fact, standard practice at *Seinfeld.*

In any case, Masters felt okay about leaving *Seinfeld.* It had saved him when he needed it most, and now he was on his way to a career in television. Even though he'd been too busy at *Seinfeld* the previous year to see what was going on with other shows, he felt confident he could get another job. In fact, he soon had a job writing for the sitcom *Grace Under Fire,* starring another comedian, Brett Butler.

Robin left of his own accord. Despite his success with "The Junior Mint," he remained disenchanted with show business and his own writing.

An NBC executive called Larry David and Jerry Seinfeld with an idea leading up to sweeps month in fall 1994, the beginning of the sixth season: The network wanted to have a blackout-themed night that would span all of the Thursday lineup. Now known as "Must See TV," the night was a powerhouse on the rise. It included *Friends,* a new show about six comely twentysomething friends in New York City; the two-year-old *Mad About You,* starring Paul Reiser and Helen Hunt as a young couple; and *Madman of the People,* a destined-to-disappear sitcom in which Dabney Coleman played an irascible newspaper columnist. All the shows took place in New York City. So, you see, they could all experience the same blackout. Characters from one could even appear in another! And somehow, the suits figured, viewers would just *love* this.

When the appointed Thursday came, there it was: On *Mad About You,* Jamie causes the blackout while trying to steal cable; on *Friends,* Chandler gets stuck in an ATM vestibule with Victoria's Secret model Jill Goodacre; on *Madmen of the People,* the blackout ruins Coleman's character's birthday. On *Seinfeld,* Jerry dated an Olympian, with no blackout.

NBC was no longer in a position to push *Seinfeld* too much. When Mehlman heard about the idea, he told David, "You know, we could have, like, the David Schwimmer character from *Friends* on our show, and we could kill him! Like, he dies! Maybe we should consider this."

Perhaps it sounded brutal. Perhaps it seemed as if the *Seinfeld* writers had grown snotty from their success, with no interest in being team players anymore. But network suits with so-called ideas just rubbed them the wrong way. They were banging their heads against the wall to come up with ideas, rejecting forty-nine out of fifty of their own thoughts every day. Then these NBC guys come up with one idea in a year, and they're making calls.

The fact was, the *Seinfeld* writers were right, and NBC was wrong, in ways that went beyond Blackout Thursday. (Though at least NBC was right enough to let *Seinfeld* do its own thing.) As *Seinfeld*'s growing ratings would prove, its detached, sardonic outlook was gathering steam across pop culture. With Johnny Carson stepping down from his longtime late-night throne, a new generation of hosts invaded the airwaves wielding an ironic edge: David Letterman, Conan O'Brien, a young Jon Stewart in his first major hosting gig on MTV. Other fringey shows were getting more mainstream, too, like *The X-Files* and *Twin Peaks*. TV was changing, with *Seinfeld* leading the way.

Fred Stoller wandered into the thickening cloud of hubris at the *Seinfeld* offices that season.

When the stand-up comedian and character actor — who looked like a cross between Seinfeld and fellow comic Ray Romano — showed up at *Seinfeld* to join the writing staff in its sixth year, he was amazed by the way the writers worked, each completely isolated from the other. It reminded him of homicide cops working their own cases. Even to a socially phobic guy like him, it seemed extreme.

Soon, he learned that he had to get four

story lines approved before he could start even one script: a Jerry, a Kramer, a George, and an Elaine. The real problem was that this required getting David and Seinfeld's attention for a pitch. In the first few weeks of the season, before shooting started, this wasn't so hard.

After that, it felt impossible. ("If a woman doesn't return one phone call, I'm not like John Cusack holding the boom box outside," Stoller later told me, turning his overtly whiny delivery onto his favorite comedy subject: his own shortcomings. "You know what I mean?") One time, he sat outside David and Seinfeld's office for an hour, waiting for the door to open. It didn't until two other writers showed up, went right in, and shut the door again. Stoller went back to his office and napped. Another time, he thought he'd take some initiative by mapping out an episode with a story line that had yet to be approved. When David saw it, he barked, "Hey, why'd you write up that outline?"

David didn't mean to upset Stoller. Once, after he yelled at Stoller, he apologized, and offered some advice. "You've got to be more aggressive," he said. "These other guys are aggressive. You've just got to track me down, give me any idea, throw it out."

"All right, now that I've got your attention . . . ," Stoller said, then proceeded to pitch an idea.

"That's stupid!" David responded. Stoller hung his head. "I'm sorry," David added. "I did tell you to throw anything. But that's stupid, Freddy."

David had been the reason Stoller got the job. The two met back on the New York comedy club scene, waiting in many smoky, sticky-floored rooms together to hear when they would go onstage. But David was a decade older than Stoller, and Stoller had always been intimidated by him. David perhaps took some advantage of that when he routinely greeted Stoller back then with "How are you doing? When's the last time you got laid?"

But then Stoller ran into David at a surprise birthday party for *Seinfeld* writer Steve Skrovan. The two started chatting about what they were up to now. At that time, in 1994, everyone in Hollywood wanted David to read a *Seinfeld* spec script; another partygoer interrupted David and Stoller's talk to ask about submitting one. David then asked Stoller, "How come you never wrote a spec script?" When Stoller said he was focusing more on guest-starring roles than on writing, David insisted: "Write one. Nothing will happen, but I will read it."

At first, Stoller wasn't going to bother. But then he realized how lucky he was to have Larry David *ask* him for a writing sample. He also thought it might be good to have a sample on hand in case any other similar opportunities came up.

What he wrote then did, in fact, get him a job on *Seinfeld*. It also meant one assignment for the following season, based on his sample script, revised by David into what would be titled "The Soup." Like most writers, Stoller mined his own life for the stories: He once bought an open-ended ticket to the United States for a woman he'd met while doing stand-up in London. But when she arrived in America, he felt like she was a different, terrible person.

In his spec script, Stoller gave that story to Jerry. But David felt ladies' man Jerry couldn't stoop so low, so he gave the plot to Elaine instead. Jerry got another story from Stoller's life: A comedian friend named Bruce had given him an Armani suit and wanted Fred to buy him a meal to pay him back. Fred took him to Jerry's Famous Deli in Los Angeles, and Bruce got soup and a soda, saying, "I'm going to save the meal for another time."

Stoller hoped that he'd get a box of free Armani suits when the episode ran. Other writers had gotten swag from companies whose products they'd mentioned. No such luck this time, though.

Stoller found pages of the original banter he'd written struck from the final version. (Among the deleted lines were George's, on Elaine giving her frequent flier miles to a guy she met in London so he could visit her: "When attractive people do things like that, it's passionate and spontaneous. Any move I make with a woman is desperate.") Stoller started another episode that never got made, stymied by David's meticulous attention to the tiniest story questions. A major plotline hinged on Kramer calling a cruise ship Jerry was on to give him his messages, but David dispatched this with one scrawled note on Stoller's outline: "Why can't Jerry call for his messages?"

Stoller didn't want to get back on the stand-up circuit, traveling all over and vying for stage time. But he had been a little nervous about taking nine months out of his acting career to lock himself in a tiny, blank room in the *Seinfeld* office and do this writing thing. It never occurred to him that he could leverage his *Seinfeld* experience into other writing jobs, or maybe even into a deal to make his own shows. He saw the *Seinfeld* job as a way to pocket a regular paycheck for a while and save up.

As it became clearer that he'd have little to do at this job, he gave up on writing and spent his days wandering around the studio lot, playing pinball at a pub across the street, where he could also get a beer or a taco. He bumped into other comics he knew who wrote for *The Larry Sanders Show, Third Rock from the Sun, Just Shoot Me!,* and *Roseanne.* Stoller had no friends at *Seinfeld* and made none at *Seinfeld.* One fellow writer (whom he won't name) pretended to be his mentor, he said, then spent all their time together trying to undermine Stoller. When Stoller approached David's office, his "mentor" would intercept him and say, "This is not a good time, bro. I'll read the room. I'm good at reading Larry. I'll tell you when to go." Looking back, Stoller is sure he was sabotaged.

The "mentor" did give him one good tip, though: He told Stoller that Writers Guild members could see movies for free at the Galleria mall in Glendale. Stoller ditched work once to go see *The Professional,* a thriller about a hit man directed by Luc

Besson. So at least his time on *Seinfeld* wasn't a total wash.

When he stayed on the *Seinfeld* stage, he spent his time bonding with security guards and stand-ins. He became friends with Ruthie Cohen, who played the cashier at Monk's and, in fact, became the answer to a trivia question: Who appeared on *Seinfeld* the most besides the four regulars? A widow with no income, she had started doing extra work and ended up with a regular job for nearly a decade, manning the register at the fictional restaurant. Later, when Stoller guest-starred on *The Nanny,* he got Cohen some extra work on that show as well.

Being a guest star had made Stoller sensitive to the outsiders on the set; he was so often an outsider himself. Once, his heart sank when he heard David say of a guest actor, "This guy has one fucking line and he can't get it." Stoller knew how hard it was to do, saying one thing out of context, possibly among actors you'd long admired but didn't personally know.

Even as the months dragged on without another script for Stoller, he began to see the time as a learning experience. He realized, for instance, the importance of taking your ideas to the actual person in charge, the person who gets to say yes or no

— in this case, Larry David. When Stoller bounced ideas off of his "mentor," his confidence would fall when the guy said, "I'm very concerned about that, bro, very concerned." Later, he realized he should have gone straight to David without worrying what anyone else thought.

After months of striking out with ideas and trying to find David and Seinfeld in the maze of backstage rooms and hallways for pitch meetings, Stoller got at least one more story line in before the season ended. David took it for a subplot on a script he was writing for the episode "The Face Painter." When Stoller was a kid, his family went to a wildlife park in Miami called Monkey Jungle, and he saw men throwing rocks at the animals. "What are you throwing rocks at monkeys for?" a woman asked. One of the guys responded, "They started it."

That became a Kramer story line, and Stoller was thrilled that he got to meet the monkey who appeared on the show. He even had his picture taken with the animal. Because of his social phobias, he had always loved animals. At parties, you could find him with the pets. His time on *Seinfeld* had, if nothing else, allowed him to get himself a cat because he was off the stand-up circuit and home every night.

As the sixth season wound down, things did not look good for Stoller to get another season at *Seinfeld*. He heard Mehlman talking about buying a house and mentioned it to David. "Yeah, that's not for you," David responded.

Indeed, Stoller was not invited back onto the staff for another season. Years later, he'd still have nightmares that he was back in the *Seinfeld* offices, waiting again to be chosen, having flashbacks to clubs like New York's Catch a Rising Star, where comics had to wait around and hope for a prime spot. "There was no dream where I'm on staff and it's working out," he later cracked.

But he returned to the set just a year after he'd left — this time, with something specific to contribute.

In the episode "The Secret Code," he was cast as a guy Elaine was interested in only because he never remembered her. It was David's idea to bring Stoller in for the role. After the table read, Michael Richards complimented his acting: "That was good. I do that, too, sometimes, where you hold back." As if Stoller were Robin Williams or something! To return as a guest star felt like redemption. Everyone seemed happy to see him. Julia Louis-Dreyfus was particularly warm, a blessing since most of his scenes

175

were with her.

Thanks to that part, Stoller got more guest-part offers than ever: *Mad About You, Wings, Murphy Brown, Suddenly Susan, Friends,* and many others. People remembered him from the *Seinfeld* role, and often thought he'd appeared on more than one episode.

He was one of many whose appearances on *Seinfeld* — as actors, as characters, or as characters named for them — would change the course of their lives in (there's no other way to say it) really weird ways.

Jason Alexander, music director Jonathan Wolff, and Jerry Seinfeld pose together at Wolff's studio after recording some early radio commercials for *Seinfeld*. COURTESY OF JONATHAN WOLFF

Jerry Seinfeld on the set with writer Andy Robin's grandmother-in-law, Helen Farr, and sister-in-law, Polly Macgregor Ford. COURTESY OF ANDY ROBIN

Writer Andy Robin's sister-in-law, Polly Macgregor Ford, snaps a shot with Seinfeld's 40th birthday cake. COURTESY OF ANDY ROBIN

Larry David and Seinfeld prepare to shoot the show's final episode, captured by photographer David Hume Kennerly. GETTY IMAGES

THE CRUISE

A) COMEDY CLUB

CRUISE MANAGER OFFERS JERRY WORK ON A SHIP. GEORGE TALKS TO
WOMAN WHO WORKS TICKET BOOTH BUT THEN STOPS TALKING TO HER
AND TELLS JERRY HE DOESN'T THINK HE'S INTERESTED IN HER.

B) JERRY'S APARTMENT.

JERRY PACKS FOR CRUISE. ELAINE'S COMING AS HIS GUEST. JERRY
ASKS GEORGE WHY HE'S CALLING THE WOMAN WHO WORKS IN THE
TICKET BOOTH (MARLA) SO MUCH IF HE'S NOT INTERESTED IN HER.
MARLA TOLD JERRY TO TELL GEORGE TO STOP CALLING HER. THEY
ARE CONFUSED BECAUSE GEORGE SWEARS HE NEVER CALLED HER.
JERRY THEN FIGURES OUT SHE MUST BE CONFUSING GEORGE WITH
THIS OTHER GEORGE THAT WAS HANGING OUT AT THE CLUB. GEORGE
IS LIVID THAT HE WAS REJECTED BY SOMEONE HE NEVER ASKED OUT.
KRAMER COMES IN AND TALKS ABOUT HOW HE'S DYING TO GO TO
MONKEY JUNGLE. JERRY TELLS KRAMER AND GEORGE TO CHECK HIS
MESSAGES AND CALL THE SHIP IF THERE ARE ANY URGENT ONES.

C) TICKET BOOTH

GEORGE GOES BECAUSE HE RESENTS HE WAS REJECTED BY SOMEONE HE
DIDN'T ASK OUT. HE THEN SEES HOW SHE LOOKS GOOD. SHE LAUGHS
WHEN SHE SEES HIM AND SAYS SHE CAN'T BELIEVE AFTER SHE SAID
TO NOT CALL HER, HE ACTUALLY CAME DOWN THERE. SHE STILL
THINKS HE'S THE OTHER GEORGE. GEORGE TRIES TO EXPLAIN AND
SHE LAUGHS AND THEN ADMITS SHE'S FLATTERED HE CAME DOWN AND
NOW SHE IS GOING TO TAKE HIM UP ON THESE WILD WEEKEND PLANS
HE OFFERED HER. GEORGE LEAVES AFRAID TO SAY THAT WASN'T HIM
THAT OFFERED THOSE PLANS BECAUSE NOW HE LIKES HER.

D) ELAINE'S CABIN.

ELAINE IS UNPACKING. SHE'S HEARS POUNDING ON THE WALLS. A
NOTE COMES UNDER THE DOOR. WHEN SHE READS IT OUTLOUD IN
DISBELIEF, THE WOMAN NEXT DOOR POUNDS AND SCREAMS SOME MORE
FOR HER TO SHUT THE HELL UP.

E) SHIP DECK. AN ANNOUNCMENT IS MADE FOR JERRY TO REPORT TO
DECK. HE HAS A PHONE CALL. IT'S KRAMER CALLING FROM JERRY'S
APARTMENT WITH HIS MESSAGES THAT REALLY COULD HAVE WAITED.
GEORGE TAKES THE PHONE FROM KRAMER AND DWELLS ABOUT HIS
SITUATION.

Larry David's notes on an outline for an unproduced episode that Stoller pitched.
COURTESY OF FRED STOLLER

An excerpt from a draft of the episode "The Soup," with lines that were cut from the final version. COURTESY OF FRED STOLLER

SEINFELD   Jul 26 1994   2.
"The Soup"

                    GEORGE
Make fun. You don't know what it's
like! Everytime I see an attractive
woman in the street I want to go
right up to her and scream, "You've
never been lonely! You have no
idea!"

                    ELAINE
Come on, lots of....

                    GEORGE
Don't give me the beautiful women
sit alone on Saturday nights
number! That's just something made
up by people who work at the sucide
hotline.

                    JERRY
George, she's resorting to flying a
guy in from London.

                    GEORGE
It's different. When attractive
people do things like that it's
passionate and spontaneous. Any
move I make with a woman is
desperate.

                    ELAINE
Flying him in? It's not like I'm
paying for his flight.

Stoller and Kenny Kramer, the real-life model for the character of Kramer. PHOTO BY ADAM ANSELL

Writers Andy Robin, Larry Charles, and Peter Mehlman backstage. COURTESY OF ANDY ROBIN

TV producer Joe Davola—who willingly lent his name to the character of "Crazy Joe Davola" on *Seinfeld*—at a TV industry event in 2012. GETTY IMAGES

Writer Alec Berg in the *Seinfeld* offices. COURTESY OF ANDY ROBIN

Writer Jeff Schaffer hamming it up for the camera next to Carol Leifer. COURTESY OF ANDY ROBIN

Kenny Kramer hosts "Soup Nazi" actor Larry Thomas at Kramer's "Seinfeld Reality Tour" of New York City in 2006. GETTY IMAGES

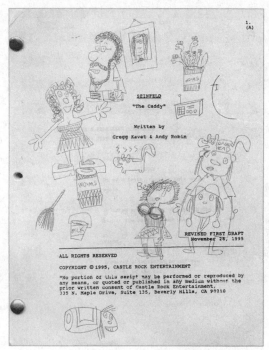

Writer Max Pross's expert illustrations adorn a *Seinfeld* script. COURTESY OF ANDY ROBIN

Andy Robin's grandmother-in-law, Helen Farr, in his *Seinfeld* office, next to the all-important white board full of story ideas for each of the four characters. COURTESY OF ANDY ROBIN

Writer Max Pross at his *Seinfeld* desk. COURTESY OF ANDY ROBIN

Writer Andy Robin, right, and his wife, Anna Macgregor Robin, backstage at a *Seinfeld* taping. COURTESY OF ANDY ROBIN

7
THE BIZARROS

Larry David walked up to Joe Davola at a Robin Hood Foundation fund-raising party in Los Angeles in 1992 and greeted him thusly: "Joe Davola, Joe Davola, Joe Davola, Joe Davola."

Davola replied, in his deep Brooklyn accent: "What the fuck are you doing, Larry?"

"I like your name. Can I use it?"

Davola shrugged. Sure, why the fuck not?

Six months later, Davola, now an executive at Fox, got a visit at his office from Castle Rock cofounder Glenn Padnick. Padnick had two fourth-season *Seinfeld* scripts in his hands, one with a blue cover, one with a yellow cover. Padnick seemed nervous, Davola told me, though he often did. "Joe, you need to read these," Davola remembers Padnick saying.

Davola took them home with him that night and tossed them to his wife. "I'm in these *Seinfeld* scripts," he said. "Can you read these?"

She did, and reported back. In them, the character "Crazy" Joe Davola develops a pathological hatred for Jerry out of professional envy; as Jerry is trying to sell a script to NBC at the time, so, too, is Joe. After that, he continues to stalk Jerry and George. "The guy's a lunatic," Davola's wife told him. "He's nothing like you. But you should do it."

Later, people often asked Davola what he'd done to David to deserve such a character named after him. They didn't realize that he'd not only read the scripts beforehand but also went through quite a process to sign off on them. Davola even had to go to his own boss, Fox chairman Peter Chernin, for his approval. Under Davola's Fox contract, the network owned his name and likeness, so Chernin had a say. He gave it his okay.

David's penchant for using real names and real-life stories in *Seinfeld* scripts, week after week, without any effort to conceal it, had a magical effect. It constructed a third dimension: There was reality; there was television; and there was Seinfeldia, where elements of both commingled, passed through, and, as the show's audience grew, enticed fans into feeling like this was more than just another sitcom. This was a feeling, a place, another world, and one they could visit whenever they wished.

And the longer this went on, the stranger things got.

At the same time that Joe Davola was meeting his script doppelgänger, another onetime Fox executive had his own through-the-looking-glass moment with *Seinfeld*.

Seinfeld's first NBC liaison, Jeremiah Bosgang, had left to work for Fox, cutting some of his hair and losing some of his hair along the way. Now resembling a square-jawed Jason Alexander, he had since quit the executive ranks to follow his comedy-writing dreams. He did a two-week tryout in New York as a writer at *Saturday Night Live* but didn't get a job offer. He returned to Los Angeles and instead got a full-time gig writing for Fox's upstart sketch show *In Living Color*. At his office one day, he got a call from an actor friend, a guy he knew from back in the days when he himself had been trying to act. "I just got out of the strangest audition," his friend said. "I was auditioning for a role where the character's name is Jeremiah Bosgang, over at *Seinfeld*. A young network executive."

When Bosgang hung up with his friend,

he tried to figure out what to do next. He hadn't spoken to David or Seinfeld in the two years since he left NBC. He called George Shapiro. "I just heard that there's some character on the show called Jeremiah Bosgang," he said when he reached Seinfeld's manager.

"Oh, yeah. This season they're planning to arc out over the course of the season that Jerry and George are approached by NBC to do a sitcom. It's going to culminate at the end of the season with them actually casting the cast."

"George, wait a minute. How about this? Jeremiah Bosgang as himself! I can do this."

"Well, I don't know. You're an actor?"

"George, I toured with Second City when I was in college. I'm trained. I studied acting in New York for years."

Shapiro promised to talk to David and Seinfeld and get right back to Bosgang. An hour later, Bosgang's phone rang. "Listen," Shapiro said, "I talked to the guys, and they said if you'd like to come in and audition, they'd be happy to see you."

"Wait a minute. I've got to audition? For Jeremiah Bosgang?"

Shapiro explained to the former network executive that the network had to approve all casting choices. He needed to go through the same process as everyone else. He had an hour before they finished auditions for the day. "I'm on my way," Bosgang said.

He hopped into his car — still the used Mercedes he'd bought from Cherones, still with his credentials on the windshield for the Radford lot, where *Seinfeld* shot. He drove from the KTTV lot where he worked, up and over the hills to where he'd visited *Seinfeld* two long years before. He felt like he was going back in time. Unlike when he'd been there, though, the *Seinfeld* offices now displayed an expensive logo sign and had receptionists.

The front-desk secretary directed Bosgang down the hall, to the third door on the left. The last time he'd been there, doors weren't even an option — they didn't have enough rooms to worry about such luxuries. There, another receptionist greeted him, surrounded by four guys looking over scripts. When he explained that he was there to audition, she asked his name. "Jeremiah Bosgang," he said, still out of breath from the rush.

"No, not the character's name," she said.

He smiled. "Actually, I am Jeremiah Bosgang."

She looked at him with impatience. She'd dealt with her share of method actors: I am

181

Jeremiah Bosgang! I am Julius Caesar! "Okay, *Jeremiah,*" she humored him.

He felt his fellow actors scoot as far away from him as possible when he sat down to wait his turn.

The door to the casting room opened, and out walked an actor. David and Seinfeld spotted him. "Jeremiah!" one of them called. At least he had been vindicated with this waiting-room crew.

Bosgang went in and chatted with David and Seinfeld for a bit, explaining that he now wrote for *In Living Color* and that he would very much like to play himself on *Seinfeld.* They asked him to read. His official line: "That's right." He performed it several times, several ways. Angry. Happy. Confused. *"That's* right." "That's *right."* He nailed it.

He floated out of the room, thrilled. At last, he had won a role in a major production; he was sure of it. He returned to his office. He didn't hear anything that day. He didn't hear anything the next morning. Around 2:00 P.M., with still no word, he called Shapiro.

"I just don't know where I'm supposed to go," he said to Shapiro, "or what I'm supposed to wear."

"Well, Jeremiah, I'm sorry, Jerry said he

was going to call you." Oh no. "They decided to go in a different direction with the Jeremiah Bosgang character." As a comedy writer, Bosgang couldn't deny the greatness of that line.

But Shapiro went on to explain: David and Seinfeld didn't want to imply that any of the characters at the network were real. They wanted the network characters to be free to engage in their share of Seinfeldian weirdness, like, say, the network president wrecking his career after falling for Elaine, or the female executive dating George. So they couldn't have any obvious crossovers between reality and fiction — like Jeremiah Bosgang playing himself. They had, in fact, decided to change all of the characters' names to avoid confusion.

As the episode's airing grew closer, Bosgang heard through industry contacts that David and Seinfeld had, however, tried to cast actors who looked like their real-life inspirations. He was terrified in anticipation of seeing who played "him." He felt at least a little bit better when at last a hunky young guy appeared on-screen playing "Jay Crespi," the character Jeremiah Bosgang had become.

Strange things started to happen to Davola

early that fall, even before Joe Davola episodes aired. When he went to the set of *The Edge,* a sketch comedy show Fox was producing, he ran into Wayne Knight, who'd guest-starred in several recent episodes of *Seinfeld* as Jerry's nemesis neighbor, Newman. When Knight heard Davola's name, he looked terrified and tried to avoid Davola in meetings.

Davola pulled him aside. "Wayne," he said, "I know about it. It's not a bad thing."

When Davola ran into David at the Emmys at the end of August, David told him, "You're not in two episodes. You're in five."

When the episodes started to run in September, Davola figured the weirdness was behind him. Granted, the character had gotten worse as the fourth season of *Seinfeld* progressed: Davola dates Elaine and becomes obsessed with her, cornering her in his lair until she escapes by spraying him in the face with Binaca. There's also a bit where he dresses like the scariest clown ever. But the real Davola figured he and *Seinfeld* would now go their separate ways.

Then he suggested to his wife that they go to Hollywood hot spot the Ivy for dinner one night. "You can't just call the Ivy an hour before and get in," she insisted.

But Joe Davola did.

From then on, he noticed everyone treating him differently anyplace he dropped his own name. Better restaurant tables, better Clippers tickets, upgrades wherever upgrades were possible. He'd been a well-regarded producer and executive before. Now people thought he was famous. And they were, just possibly, a little frightened of him.

Once in a while, someone would have the guts to ask, "Are you that guy?" The bold ones would whisper, "What did you do to him?"

Davola was now constantly explaining: "I didn't do anything! I did him a favor." (This was a *favah* in Davola's accent.) "He liked me. It's fine."

Every meeting he had: "Can I ask you a question?"

Davola decided to use his *Seinfeld* predicament to his advantage. He'd long harbored a crush on Julia Louis-Dreyfus. Now that he was part of the *Seinfeld* family, he sent her a dozen roses, signed, "From the real Joe Davola." He figured she knew the origins of the character's name.

After a few weeks went by, Davola heard no response. He mentioned it to George Shapiro. "I didn't even get a note or a call! I was trying to make this funny gesture."

The following week, he got a signed photo from Louis-Dreyfus: "To the real Joe Davola: Leave me alone!" Until Shapiro mentioned it to her, she'd thought the flowers were from a real stalker.

For the most part, viewers didn't yet get the joke that *Seinfeld* was in the habit of taking reality, chomping it up, and spitting it out funnier than before. Then they saw the episode that fourth season when Jerry is supposed to pitch executives at NBC an idea for a show in which he could star. He asks George to help him brainstorm.

George has an idea as they chat: "See, this should be the show. This is the show."

"What?" Jerry doesn't get it.

"This. Just talking."

"Yeah. Right . . . Just talking? What's the show about?"

"It's about nothing." This is the best that George can come up with.

"No story?"

"No, forget the story."

"You've got to have a story."

"Who says you gotta have a story? Remember when we were waiting for that table in that Chinese restaurant that time? That could be a TV show."

With that scene, *Seinfeld* would forevermore be known as the show "about nothing" — to the annoyance of most who worked on it — and a new level of meta infiltrated the series. Despite his initial misgivings, fictional Jerry gives in to his desire to have *something* to pitch, even if it's *nothing.* Or maybe he's giving in to his penchant for wordplay: "Nothing?" George says.

Jerry replies, "I think you may have something here."

George takes command when the two go in for their meeting with the NBC executives. "I think I can sum up the show for you with one word: nothing." He continues, explaining, "Nothing happens on the show. You see, it's just like life. You know, you eat, you go shopping, you read. You eat, you read, you go shopping."

Russell Dalrymple, the NBC president based on Warren Littlefield and played by character actor Bob Balaban, is skeptical. "No stories? So, what is it?"

George, invigorated by the challenge, responds with a question: "What did you do today?"

"I got up and came to work."

George is not deterred. "There's a show. That's a show."

"Well, why am I watching it?" Dalrymple asks.

"Because it's on TV," George replies.

"Not yet."

This progressed over several episodes until the 1992–93 season culminated in a spectacular in-joke of a finale in which *Jerry,* the fictional sitcom, becomes a "reality," filmed with other actors playing the characters within the show. Jeremy Piven, doing double duty at the same time on the acclaimed *Larry Sanders Show,* plays fictional George as a balding ranter in sweatpants and thick glasses. (George is not amused by the portrayal.) Kramer, mimicking his real-life inspiration, demands to play himself and is denied. Larry Hankin, who also read for the role but lost out to Richards, plays the actor who plays Kramer.

The layers of the plotline folded into and out of one another, into real life and then fiction and back again. *Seinfeld* writers Bill Masters and Steve Skrovan had planned to pitch Larry David a story idea at work, but David had to stay home sick that day, one of the rare times he didn't make it to the office. David asked Masters and Skrovan to come to his house for the meeting instead. They did, and just as they started to pitch,

David ran to the bathroom. The writers could hear him vomiting.

"So, how do you think it's going?" Masters said to Skrovan. Both were laughing as David returned.

When they explained their laughter to David, he said, "This is good."

"Did you like the pitch?" Masters said.

"No, it's terrible," David said. "But this, what just happened, is good."

That scene ended up in the episode "The Shoes," in which George and Jerry go to Russell Dalrymple's apartment for a pitch meeting because the network president is ill after eating some bad pasta primavera. The episode was the first *Seinfeld* to air in its Thursday-night spot following *Cheers.*

In the end, TV Jerry's deal falls apart — because of Elaine. Dalrymple falls in love with her and joins Greenpeace to impress her, then dies at sea. (Balaban later said his character was initially supposed to sleep with Elaine and give her her first orgasm. But as an actor, he enjoyed having a good death scene, complete with pretending to be on a boat in front of a green screen on the soundstage, while the crew sprayed him with water.) The new network president pulls *Jerry* off the air.

In a double loop from reality to fiction to

reality again, Balaban landed a role as NBC president Warren Littlefield in a separate production, an HBO adaptation of Bill Carter's book about the late-night television wars, *The Late Shift.* Then, in a denouement of the meta joke, the actor made an appearance at the NBC up-front presentations to advertisers during the heights of the Must See TV era. Littlefield hired Balaban himself, over the objections of his fellow executives, who thought the gag would be too insidery.

When announcer Don Pardo proclaimed the arrival of Littlefield, Balaban took the stage in a new Armani suit Littlefield had bought for him. The crowd roared as Balaban talked through NBC's corporate achievements. Eventually, Littlefield joined him onstage. "Bob, what are you doing? You're a wonderful actor, but I'm Warren."

John Peterman took a red-eye flight from California back home to Lexington, Kentucky, after a business trip. Operating on no sleep, he stumbled into the office from which he operated his clothing catalog company. All anyone would say to him was, "You were on *Seinfeld.*" It felt like the strangest of dreams. He kept replying, "I was on an airplane. I wasn't on *Seinfeld.*"

But one of his employees had taped the TV show that aired the previous night. He popped the videocassette into the VCR and watched. Sure enough, a character named Peterman appeared, and he said he operated a clothing catalog company. He met Elaine on a rainy night in New York City and offered her a job writing for his catalog, famous for its literary descriptions of clothes. It wasn't Peterman himself, though. The real John Peterman was a good-old-boy Kentuckian with thinning gray hair, wire-framed glasses, and a mustache. This TV version was a chiseled, silver-haired actor who was playing "him," or at least some character with his name and profession, with the booming voice of a television announcer and a dramatic flair for storytelling.

Peterman's employees fretted. The character was a buffoon, bombastic, nothing like the real Peterman. But Peterman, despite his lack of sleep, had pulled out ahead of his employees. "It's a good thing he's nothing like me," Peterman said, "because then he wouldn't be on *Seinfeld.*" He looked up the ratings: Thirty million viewers now watched the show every week. Tens of millions of people were suddenly aware of the J. Peterman Company.

Soon, Peterman was getting *Seinfeld* scripts to vet before they aired. This character would continue to appear, and NBC's lawyers didn't want to take any more chances. David and Seinfeld had gotten a particular kick out of Peterman's catalog, of which they were sometimes customers, and they loved the idea of having this obscure, unusual little company involved with their show. The catalog was known for its stylized writing about such items as chambray shirts and moleskin trousers. To wit, from the real J. Peterman catalog: "When a man puts on this authentic French farmer's shirt he may very well find that his hands look bigger. . . . Is that woman over there giving him the eye and nodding toward the haystack? Yes, and he knows what to do."

Whatever anyone else thought of his catalog's prose, Peterman knew from experience with his own staff writers that he shouldn't try to interfere too much in the *Seinfeld* writers' process. He'd sign off on the scripts and send them back without question. Only once did a script preview cause him to take any action at all. When he read the one in which Peterman's mother dies, he called his sister to prevent any panic from his own mom, who was in her eighties. "Does Mother watch *Seinfeld*?" he asked. Yes, and she was adequately fore-warned of "her" coming death.

As the Peterman character caught on with viewers, Peterman and John O'Hurley, the actor who played him, did a flurry of publicity together. When the two did their very first news show together, a talk show called *Fox After Breakfast* — meeting for the first time on camera — all Peterman could think was, *What the fuck am I doing here?* The two looked at each other for several moments in silence. Peterman saw the host starting to sweat the moment. Would this be okay?

Soon the two started talking, though. They became friends. Peterman sent O'Hurley clothes and wine. Sometimes they traveled together to do promotional appearances, and often fans would approach and say, "Hey, J. Peterman, how are you doing?" Peterman himself soon learned to ignore such greetings; they were for O'Hurley, not for him.

Further blurring the lines between reality and fiction, O'Hurley often hung out between scenes on the set of Peterman's fictional office simply because he liked the décor. He leaned back in Peterman's comfy black leather desk chair and put his feet up on the glossy, knotted-pine desk, feeling at home among the African masks and mounted butterflies adorning the walls as he watched scenes being filmed on other parts of the set. He even took a few of the masks from the set, once the show was over, to hang in his home in Vermont. He also kept several of the real J. Peterman Company's jackets in his closet there.

Surprisingly, however, the show had little positive effect on J. Peterman's real-life business. Betting on the increased name recognition, Peterman opened several stores across the country, with plans for up to fifty locations. Peterman sat outside his first West Coast retail store in Newport Beach, California, and watched customers coming and going on its opening night in 1998. Over and over, he heard passersby saying, "I didn't know that was a real company!" Most *Seinfeld* viewers didn't realize it, either. (Some still don't.) Most of those who did know were already customers, and they enjoyed the joke, but they didn't buy more clothing because of it.

A year later, that discrepancy between name recognition and real business became apparent. J. Peterman filed for bankruptcy after expanding too much, too quickly, listing debts of more than $14 million.

Dan O'Keefe had grown up in Mount

Pleasant, a Westchester County suburb of New York City, celebrating a holiday that his father invented in 1966. His father — Daniel O'Keefe Sr. — was an editor at *Reader's Digest,* a scholarly writer (he published *Stolen Lightning: The Social Theory of Magic* in 1982), and a man of many odd ideas. Festivus was meant to be an alternative to other holidays that were over-commercialized or just "some dead guy's birthday," as Dan O'Keefe explained to me. It began as nothing more than a celebration of the first anniversary of O'Keefe's parents' first date. After their kids were born, it became an annual tradition that involved looking at old photos and taping everyone in the family talking about the previous year, usually centered on a theme. (Theme in 1976: "Are We Scared? Yes!" Theme in 1977: "Are We Depressed? Yes!") Inspired by Samuel Beckett's play *Krapp's Last Tape* — a copy of which Mr. O'Keefe had lent Mrs. O'Keefe on that first date — the holiday was built around an annual "airing of grievances."

The name for the holiday came from a derivation of "feast" in Latin (*festum*). Strange hats and dress-up clothes served as the traditional garments. The decorations included a FUCK FASCISM! sign, handwritten on cardboard and displayed on the mantel. Bowing to Mrs. O'Keefe's objections, Mr. O'Keefe changed it one year to SCREW FASCISM! The American flag went out on its front-porch perch. Poems were read. ("To which we sing, each Festivus, which we hold for the Rest of Us.") There were songs, like the "Bird and Duck Chorus," quacks sung to the tune of "The Mirlitons" from *The Nutcracker Suite;* a German song about pigs; and an Irish song about the hanging of a terrorist. Plate licking and talking with one's mouth full were encouraged.

Though O'Keefe and his two brothers agreed not to talk about "that strange piece of psychodrama," as he called Festivus, to outsiders, one of the brothers eventually described it to O'Keefe's colleague, Jeff Schaffer.

Unfortunately for O'Keefe, he and Schaffer worked together as writers for *Seinfeld.* Next thing he knew, Schaffer and Schaffer's writing partner, Alec Berg, cornered him over dinner at a diner and said, "We want to do this on the show." O'Keefe stood his ground, even though Berg and Schaffer had seniority over him as executive producers at the time: No way. Well, they'd already told Seinfeld about it, and he wanted it. So that was settled.

Writing this script, O'Keefe felt like he was writing a tell-all about growing up in a cult.

The *Seinfeld* version of the holiday evolved during the drafting of the episode to include a ceremonial pole, something never involved in the O'Keefes' Festivus. The main harbingers of Festivus in the O'Keefe household were a clock and a bag, the significance of which the children never knew. The fictionalized version of the holiday also evolved to include father-son wrestling. On *Seinfeld,* it took December 23 as an official date, though in the O'Keefe household, Festivus could come at any time, and was most likely to occur in March, October, or November. Mr. O'Keefe felt the uncertainty made it more exciting.

Shooting the three-minute Festivus scene itself, in the December 1997 episode "The Strike," became a six-hour ordeal. Jerry Stiller, as George's father, Frank, had almost all the lines, and he was having a hard time, as usual, remembering the longer soliloquies. He had to do all of them in small chunks, over and over again. The more this happened, the more the others messed up their lines and erupted into laughter. O'Keefe described it as "like rapture of the deep" by the final hours, with the actors losing oxygen to their brains.

Dan O'Keefe waited as long as possible — until the week before the episode aired — to tell his dad that Festivus would soon make its prime-time debut. He wasn't sure his dad grasped what he was saying at first.

O'Keefe was astonished when the episode ran and fans embraced the holiday. He was stunned that anyone reacted with anything but scorn. At first, his father was uncomfortable with his secret reaching the masses. Then he began to embrace it: Maybe this was vindication for every odd idea he'd ever had! Perhaps he *should* revive his idea for a book called *The Accursed Corporation,* about how the rights of big business must be curtailed to save us all from certain doom. Perhaps Dan *should* spend his summer hiatus learning Vietnamese, American Sign Language, and Romanian from his father in a ramshackle Vermont cabin.

Strangers began celebrating it across the country. Wagner Collaborative Metal Works in Milwaukee, Wisconsin, launched a Festivus-pole division. For some reason, Pennsylvania's Full Pint Brewing Company made a caramel-flavored beer called Festivus. Ben & Jerry's ice cream launched a Festivus flavor — brown sugar cinnamon with gingerbread cookies and ginger-caramel swirl — that Dan O'Keefe hated, even though he loved the brand's other ice creams. One guesses there was, perhaps, a psychological element to his hatred.

A slight, redheaded twenty-two-year-old girl sat one morning in a standard New York diner on Manhattan's Upper West Side, waiting for her coffee at the counter. The waiter had filled her cup halfway when he noticed someone coming in. "It is always nice to see you," he said, not to the girl, but to the woman coming in, who was shaking her umbrella. He rushed to kiss the woman hello while the girl poured milk into her cup.

This was the scene that emerged from a morning in the early 1980s that singer-songwriter Suzanne Vega spent in Tom's Restaurant at the corner of Broadway and 112th Street. The diner had sat in that location for more than thirty years, operated by the Greek-American family of Minas Zoulis dating back to the 1950s. The building was owned by Columbia University and housed some of the school's programs, along with NASA's Goddard Institute for Space Studies. It fed affordable eggs, pancakes, coffee, tea, and the dozens of other standard Greek diner offerings to hungry students, professors, administrators, scientists, and Upper West Siders. But on this morning, Tom's Restaurant — its name spelled out in all-capital, red neon lights across its front, seen only as RESTAURANT on its north-facing side, the TOM'S hidden — got its first big break when Vega visited.

Vega's smoky alto would narrate her disconnection that day, a cappella, in a song called (misnamed, slightly) "Tom's Diner," a track that first appeared on a January 1984 compilation album from *Fast Folk Musical Magazine.* It popped up again three years later on Vega's own *Solitude Standing* album, though her record company released two different songs, "Luka" and "Solitude Standing," as singles in the United States.

In 1990, "Tom's Diner" became a surprise radio hit, this time as a dance remix by British producers DNA. The producers combined Vega's a cappella vocals with a Soul II Soul beat and repeated Vega's original outro — "doo doo doo doo, doo doo doo doo, doo doo doo doo doo doo doo doo" — throughout as a hook.

The song and Vega had secured their place in music history. Tom's wasn't quite as famous — there was that confusing switch from "restaurant" to "diner," and the song didn't make the location clear. Soon it would have another, even bigger, shot at fame.

Tom's was an unlikely candidate for any kind of notoriety beyond its Upper West Side neighborhood. Its cramped space, even by New York City diner standards, contained only two rows of dark brown wooden booths with red and tan upholstered seats. Its continuous rows of windows on both sides of the restaurant did make it feel more spacious, though. And it had its special qualities: Among the clanking dishes, friendly Greek chatter was a constant among its staff and even some of its customers, giving it a warm, family-run atmosphere. It smelled of its exceptionally good French fries.

A location scout from some Los Angeles studio called Castle Rock came in one day in 1989 and asked about shooting the outside of the place for a sitcom. Somebody involved in the production had been there years earlier and wanted to use it as the exterior shot of a restaurant where the characters hung out. The owner, Mike Zoulis, didn't understand what this show was, but he figured it couldn't hurt and signed the release papers.

Seinfeld turned Tom's Restaurant into a

household sight, if not a household name. The RESTAURANT sign that wrapped around the corner building grew recognizable to millions as the place where Jerry, Elaine, George, and Kramer gathered to obsess over the minutiae of their lives. Though the fictional setting was known as Monk's Café on the show, word spread that the "real" Monk's sat on Manhattan's Upper West Side, where it had served Columbia students and staff for decades. The urbane New Yorkers who identified so strongly with Jerry and his friends now realized there was a place they could actually go to commune more deeply with their favorite characters, to eat fries in a place where those heroes of Manhattan living (sort of) hung out.

As the show grew in popularity, then exploded in syndicated reruns across the world, Zoulis saw more and more tourist traffic, from photo-taking outside its wraparound windows to Midwestern families seeking to sample some fries from "Monk's." Offers to franchise or sell the place poured in, but the Zoulis family declined. "We feel that we have a successful formula here," Zoulis told filmmakers Gian Franco Morini and Jesse McDowell, who gave the diner the star treatment in an unreleased 2014 documentary, *Tom's Restau-*

rant. "Maybe we're old-fashioned. Maybe we're afraid of change."

Maybe. They decided not to even pursue smaller tweaks to capitalize on their new level of recognition. Renovation? Nope. Maybe just a menu item or two, like "Elaine's Big Salad," or "Kramer's Burger"? No, thank you. "You can sit down, you can have a cup of coffee, you leave here with your wallet intact. What more could you ask for?" Zoulis said. "It's not like we were seeking fame and fortune."

Meanwhile, in Midtown Manhattan, *Seinfeld*'s original real-life crossover, Kenny Kramer, figured out how to get the role he'd wanted since *Seinfeld* began. That is, the role of himself.

He'd made peace with not being the Kramer America knew, even as the show became more popular. He met Michael Richards during the show's third season and liked him, even though others who spent almost every day on the set with Richards felt as though they didn't know him. The two bonded over being single fathers to teenage daughters. But as *Seinfeld*'s fan base grew and grew, Kramer couldn't shake the idea that there was some way for him to get a piece of this, even though he'd long ago signed away the rights to his name. In the spring of 1995, he wrote a proposal for a Kramer CD-ROM — then a popular emerging technology that stored computer programs, games, and other software on a compact disc — which would explain how to explore New York City without paying for anything. (He had done some voice-overs for X-rated cartoons on CD-ROM, and he thought the market showed promise.) But the companies he pitched said the project needed "entertainment value." That's when he thought about shooting some footage, and perhaps putting together a real-life tour of New York sites from *Seinfeld.*

He hired comedian Bobby Allen Brooks — also his neighbor — as his director. He passed a special exam to earn a city tour guide license. Then, in 1996, Kramer and Brooks launched Kramer's Reality Tour, which started with a stage show at the John Houseman Theater in Midtown, then proceeded to a three-hour bus ride past some of *Seinfeld*'s most recognizable landmarks: Tom's Restaurant, the New York Health & Racquet Club that served as the characters' gym, and Jerry's supposed building at 129 West Eighty-First Street (his address on the show, though the exterior shot features a building in Los Angeles).

Kramer even invited tour-goers to visit his own apartment at Manhattan Plaza, embracing his every Kramer-like quirk: sumo wrestling posters on the walls, two pairs of binoculars resting on the windowsill that he used to spy on the nearby headquarters of local news station NY1.

The demand was instant. The 800 number for bookings, which Kramer answered himself, rang eighteen hours a day. His website attracted hundreds of visitors every day. His first ten tours sold out. They ditched the CD-ROM idea as the tour took off.

Because of *Seinfeld*'s preoccupation with real-life inspiration, New York stories were at a premium in the writers' offices, and Spike Feresten showed up with a suitcase full of them.

He came to the show after five years on staff for David Letterman's late-night shows — first at NBC, then CBS. But he'd started his career in the office at *Saturday Night Live*. He had countless stories from two of New York's TV institutions *and* the Midtown neighborhood where both were based.

Among the ideas he pitched in his first season was one based on his time as a receptionist at *Saturday Night Live.* During his first year in show business, the legendary *SNL* creator Lorne Michaels was his boss. Feresten had idolized Michaels, and now he found himself down the hall from the man. Michaels needed only glance in Feresten's direction, and Feresten would flush.

Feresten found that aside from answering the main phone line in the office, another of his duties was to man the door at the *Saturday Night Live* after-parties. As he stood at the door late one Saturday, he spotted his boss dancing. What he saw, as he later told me, was Lorne Michaels dancing as if he'd never seen another human dance before. The man heaved and gyrated to a rhythm only he could feel. As Feresten recalls it, Michaels may have even been dancing with Sinéad O'Connor that night — if so, this would have likely been her first appearance on the show, in 1990, not her controversial 1992 performance in which she ripped up a picture of the pope on live television.

At that moment, Feresten realized Michaels was just another nerdy guy. It endeared Feresten's idol to him, and allowed him to look his boss in the eye with confidence.

In Feresten's eighth-season *Seinfeld* episode "The Little Kicks," the dance has more disastrous effects for Elaine: Her staff at J. Peterman, after seeing her dance the same way, loses respect for her. When Jerry and Kramer tell her she "stinks" at dancing, she videotapes herself to see — and wrecks the bootlegged movie Jerry was working on. Feresten even got to give Louis-Dreyfus a little dance lesson during production, schooling her in the singular Michaels method.

Feresten also brought his favorite Midtown lunch spot everlasting infamy via a *Seinfeld* script.

The script wasn't even fully formed when character actor Larry Thomas got a call for an audition to play a character known as "the Soup Nazi." He got no pages, just a general description of the character and instruction that he'd be reading on the spot.

It seemed worth a shot, given that it was a chance to be on *Seinfeld,* so he spent his prep time developing an idea of the character. He practiced imitating Omar Sharif in *Lawrence of Arabia.* He considered wardrobe: Should he wear a T-shirt, jeans, and an apron, as he expected most of the actors would, or should he go with this crazy thought he had to wear an army uniform?

He dug up some fatigues and a beret he had — actors have been known to have silly things in their closets — à la Saddam Hussein. When he and his wife looked at his reflection in the mirror, they both agreed: He had to go with this look. It wasn't an easy decision, since the rule of thumb was to go in full costume only for commercial auditions. In fact, Thomas had once auditioned for a part on *The X-Files* as a rabbinical scholar, and even though he'd simply chosen to wear a yarmulke with his regular clothes, the casting director had cracked, "Coming in costume, huh?" But the army uniform was so oddly perfect, and not a "costume" per se; after all, he was auditioning to play a soup chef, not a military man. It would just give Thomas a unique vibe, make him stand out.

He kept his regular mustache and the bit of extra stubble he'd developed over the weekend for the Tuesday-morning audition. He even wrote himself a line in case he had to improvise: "You, small fry, go to the end of my line or you get no soup."

When he arrived at the audition, he indeed saw a sea of T-shirts, jeans, and aprons among his fellow actors. The casting director handed him three scenes of Feresten's script. He felt great when he saw that the character barked, "No soup for you!" That meant he was on the right page with this character. Maybe it was obvious from the Soup Nazi name, but it still came as a relief.

Three weeks later, he was called back for a final audition in front of David and Seinfeld. He assumed he'd reprise the three scenes he'd seen at the first reading. He got there just as his audition time struck, and casting director Marc Hirschfeld rushed him into the room. There, Thomas found twenty people. Seinfeld, sitting at the end of the table, greeted him. Thomas stayed in character, as per advice he'd gotten in an acting class with Sheree North (who played Kramer's mother, Babs). If you're trying out for an evil character and you come in friendly, it's hard, North taught him, for producers to make the sudden switch. Now, with his cold demeanor and maniacal army uniform, Thomas would convince the producers that he was either perfect or too crazy to work with.

Thomas grunted in greeting, then turned to read his scenes with Hirschfeld. Seinfeld cackled in response to his line readings, even louder than Thomas talked. When Thomas reached the end of the third scene, he realized there was still a stack of paper in his hand. There was more given to him to read beyond what he'd already seen. With Seinfeld laughing so much, Thomas decided to ride the momentum and read it cold.

When he finished, he was asked to wait outside. They brought him back in, and Seinfeld said, "That was funny, but I don't get why the character is so mean and angry. Do you want to do it again where he has some good moments?" Seinfeld made a motion with his hand to indicate hills and valleys in a performance, a common shorthand in show business and a pet peeve of Thomas's. The actor didn't believe *every* character had to modulate. Some people were extreme. The Soup Nazi, of all people, would be mean all the time, he thought, at least in the moments portrayed on *Seinfeld.*

Still, Thomas tried it again, softening on occasion. Seinfeld barely laughed at all this time. The producers asked Thomas to wait again, and Thomas was sure he'd blown it. After he waited for a while, he was sent home without further news. He'd seen other guest stars in the episode get their casting news that day. He knew they were reporting back to the set at 1:00 P.M. to start work, so he figured his shot on *Seinfeld* was through.

Out on the street, he stopped at a pay phone and called his wife, an actress, to tell her how it had gone. He recounted how he'd gotten to meet Seinfeld, and how big a part it turned out to be. Even though he hadn't landed it, they decided to go to lunch to celebrate his big-time audition. As he headed to meet her, his pager went off: his agent. He returned to the pay phone and called; he'd gotten the part after all. "Go to work," his agent said.

After he called to cancel lunch with his wife, Thomas headed back to the *Seinfeld* stage. When he met up with Seinfeld again, the star said, "By the way, forget about the direction I gave you. For some reason, the meaner the funnier for this guy."

It turned out Seinfeld had deferred to Feresten on the casting. It had been down to character actor Richard Libertini and Thomas. Seinfeld had worried about Thomas's thinner résumé, which included only straight-to-video parts and a few tiny TV roles. When Seinfeld asked Feresten to make the call, Feresten chose the actor he called "the angry New York guy."

Thomas figured his gambit had worked — as an unknown quantity, he'd kept his edge over the better-known actors by committing to the character throughout the audition process. No one knew that Thomas was easygoing and gregarious outside the role.

When Thomas reported for duty, director

Andy Ackerman told him to keep the mustache and stubble. As rehearsals got under way, Ackerman and the producers weren't sure the episode worked. David watched a run-through, nervous. Thomas hit his delivery softer, harder, somewhere in between. Finally, something clicked, and it felt right.

After all that, even when they shot it, none of them realized they had created a national phenomenon. As with other memorable episodes, they just thought they'd gotten through another week and managed to be pretty funny.

The morning after the episode aired, the phone started ringing at the production office with media requests pouring in from the East Coast: "The Soup Nazi" was a sensation. New York media had caught on to the fact that the show was sending up Soup Kitchen International on West Fifty-Fifth Street, where Manhattanites lined up daily to suffer abuse from soup chef Al Yeganeh in the name of getting a cup of his heavenly broth. (It wasn't the first time Yeganeh had broken into pop culture; in the 1993 film *Sleepless in Seattle,* Meg Ryan's newspaper writer character pitches her editor a feature story on him, though she doesn't give him a name: "This man sells the greatest soup you have ever eaten, and he is the meanest man in America. I feel very strongly about this, Becky; it's not just about the soup.") After America learned of the Soup Nazi, reporters flocked to interview Yeganeh, only to suffer more abuse — and capture him cursing *Seinfeld* for branding him a Nazi.

On the other side of the country, thousands of miles from the real New York filled with Soup Nazis and dancing *Saturday Night Live* producers, an earthquake struck Los Angeles in the early-morning hours of Monday, January 17, 1994. Windows broke, parking structures collapsed, and freeway support columns buckled, their metal skeletons bulging and breaking through their skin. Fifteen seconds later, with two aftershocks, the Northridge earthquake had caused fifty-seven deaths, five thousand injuries, and $20 billion in property damage — one of the worst natural disasters in U.S. history.

Seinfeld was hardly the biggest concern among the casualties, but its set sustained enough damage to shut the show down for two weeks. Instead of shooting an episode called "The Pie" as scheduled, director Tom Cherones drove from his home in Sherman Oaks, through the damaged streets, to the Studio City set. The walls at each end of

213

the soundstage buckled outward, he later told me. The sets were scattered about the stage. The lights, thankfully, remained in place.

The *Seinfeld* crew considered getting a stage on the Paramount lot seven miles south, but CBS Studio Center promised to get the lot up and running again within two weeks. *Seinfeld* stayed put and waited.

As Studio Center rebuilt, the *Seinfeld* operation grew. It seemed like the perfect time to get a New York street set. Castle Rock would pay for it, so production designer Tom Azzari went to work designing it. Up until then, *Seinfeld* had borrowed "New York" streets on other lots, namely those of Warner Brothers and Paramount. Now, *Seinfeld* would have its very own $800,000 worth of "New York" storefronts.

That set, combined with Cherones's New York–based "second unit" — a team assigned to shoot exteriors of buildings and establishing shots in Manhattan — would come to represent *Seinfeld*'s unique version of New York City. (A Kramer body double was employed a few times to, say, run through the streets of New York or scale a wall.) It was full of real New York landmarks such as Tom's Restaurant, endless loops of taxi footage, and a Los Angeles apartment building at 757 South New Hampshire Avenue, complete with earthquake reinforcements, that served, improbably, as Jerry's apartment building.

With so many New York landmarks showing up on *Seinfeld,* the show became linked to the city it depicted, taking extraordinary amounts of credit and blame for Manhattan's real-life fate. New York media embraced it, celebrated it, composed overwrought editorials in its honor, and — in the ultimate form of respect for New Yorkers — picked apart the show's every misstep. The resulting media circus served to prove John Updike's observation true: "I am struck by how seriously — religiously, indeed — New Yorkers watch television," he once wrote. "In other parts of the country, television is taken as an escape from reality; in New York, all things being relative, it is considered a window into reality."

This television show did nothing less than play a "central role in the spectacular turnaround in the fortunes of New York City" after its crime-ridden, crack-epidemic-fueled low point in the 1980s, according to a *New York Post* op-ed. Famous New Yorkers responded accordingly. Rudy Giuliani recorded a cameo on *Seinfeld* at the height of his victorious run for mayor, taking time out from an intense real-life campaign in 1993 — in which he was promising a serious overhaul of city life to combat "panhandlers" and "squeegee men" — to comment on a fictional fat-free-frozen-yogurt scandal brewing on *Seinfeld.* (The episode, which ran just two days after Giuliani won, reflected his victory. The crew had shot two endings, and if he'd lost, he would have been replaced with actor Phil Morris — who later played the recurring character of lawyer Jackie Chiles — as a campaign worker for Giuliani's opponent, David Dinkins.) The Yankees welcomed the show's send-up of its owner, George Steinbrenner, even as a fumpfering idiot. (So did Steinbrenner himself, who'd once shot a cameo on the show that got cut: "I'm impressed with the detail, even down to the names in the Yankees' parking lot," he told *The New York Times.* "I was prepared not to like the show, but I came away laughing my head off.")

Seinfeld's popularity with New Yorkers lay in its ability to address the million tiny humiliations that are collectively called "living in Manhattan" — pleading with the Chinese-food delivery guy to cross his restaurant's boundary by *less than a block* to bring you food or having a conversation about the Mets' chances with a naked guy sitting across from you on the subway. But the love affair ran so deep because of the more fundamental New York–ness at *Seinfeld*'s core: As *New York* magazine later said, "All sarcasm, no politics, and, in a ground-rattling reverse, not a single character sought to ingratiate him- or herself to you. Instead, *Seinfeld,* that Cheez Doodle of urban fecklessness, turned the same face to the audience that New York turns to the country: *So? What's it to ya?*"

Not all New Yorkers embraced it: Locals thought *Seinfeld* so influential that some, like bohemian artist Penny Arcade, who came up in the city's downtown scene of the '70s and '80s, eventually blamed the show for making the city seem attractive and accommodating to suburbanites who then moved in, gentrifying, chain-restaurantizing, and sanitizing the character right out of Manhattan.

But this wasn't the worst thing *Seinfeld* would be accused of as it reached the heights of its popularity.

8
THE *SEINFELD* NATION

If you wanted a comprehensive list of all the fictional birthdays of *Seinfeld*'s main characters, Adam Rainbolt and Dave Antonoff could help you with that. Fictional phone numbers, job histories, movie titles, George's answering machine message, all the foods mentioned on the show, who won "The Contest," songs featured in episodes, even the sheet music for the bass line of the theme song — all of this was compiled on their "*Sein*FAQ" Internet page, another consequence of the special passion *Seinfeld* inspired in its now-massive fan base. They were among the first chroniclers of Seinfeldia, its self-appointed media.

Rainbolt and Antonoff "met" on the alt.tv .seinfeld message board where fans would post their feelings after each episode, and decided to work together to compile everything anyone could want to know about *Seinfeld*. The FAQ page was hosted on

GeoCities.com — a place where users could publish their own websites, categorized by region and subject. There, Antonoff and Rainbolt cataloged every bit of *Seinfeld* trivia possible.

Antonoff was the more obsessive of the two, taping every single *Seinfeld* episode on VHS, a magnificent feat during the time of complex VCR programming. Rainbolt was a *Seinfeld* fan with a knack for computers that was rare in 1994, the year he entered college. He'd grown up in rural Arizona playing with computers occasionally, but he found his calling in the Northern Arizona University lab full of boxy gray Macintosh IIs. The first popularly accessible web browser, Mosaic, had been released the year before, allowing personal desktop computer users their first easy, intuitive way to get online. Rainbolt declared his major in management information systems and decided to ride this Internet thing wherever it led.

When Netscape Navigator was released in 1994, it made surfing online — and, in particular, building online communities — even easier. As more users got online who weren't strictly tech-heads, the Usenet system — a discussion network allowing anyone with Internet access to post mes-

sages for public viewing and debate —
experienced an influx of "civilian" content.
Within Usenet, there were several categories
to denote content, including recreation
(rec.), science (sci.), and computers
(comp.). A catchall category known as alt.
included an unorganized heap of subjects,
such as television. If you wanted to find
Seinfeld discussions, for instance, you would
know to go to alt.tv.seinfeld.

Because Netscape had a built-in newsgroup reader, it made surfing these discussion threads that much easier for non-
programmers. FAQs soon popped up as a
way to simplify threads, tackling some top-
ics that tended to come up over and over.

Rainbolt liked screwing around online,
and he liked *Seinfeld,* even though he
"didn't even know what Jewish people
were," as he later told me. He saw the show
as a link to his grandmother, who had been
a nursing student in New York City before
she moved to Arizona. He'd started watching *Seinfeld* in its fourth season, like most
fans, and then caught up on the rest when
reruns started in syndication. He frequented
both the *Seinfeld* and *Mad About You* fo-
rums. When Antonoff posted a message asking for help with an FAQ, Rainbolt volun-
teered. Why not? He was a college student

with few responsibilities and lots of technical knowledge.

Rainbolt's tech knowledge and Antonoff's compulsiveness about the details of *Seinfeld* resulted in a particularly robust FAQ page that gained more attention than most. But there were plenty of other Internet pages dedicated to the show as well; it turned out that the Internet and *Seinfeld* were made for each other. The show generated so much online attention that *Yahoo! Internet Life* magazine documented the phenomenon in a March 1995 cover story. The headline declared: "On the Web, It's *Seinfeld* Forever!" Among the magazine's top ten *Seinfeld* sites were S-Man's Seinfeld Explosion, the creation of a fifteen-year-old superfan that included a weekly chat forum and, astoundingly for the time, a "sound collage" file of the best *Seinfeld* lines; a Scandinavian fan's site with an excellent video clip collection; *Entertainment Weekly*'s reviews of every episode that had run so far; an "automatic *Seinfeld* plot generator"; and an online tribute to George Costanza. The *Seinfeld* writers began checking message boards and other sites regularly to gauge fan response to episodes.

Even as online message boards expanded the scope of TV fandom, Internet connections started to invade more homes and make media executives nervous: Was this screechy modem thing possible competition, or not? But *Seinfeld* gave NBC suits hope that TV was safe for now. In fact, America Online's vice chairman, Ted Leonsis, said in an interview that his only competition was *Seinfeld.* When the show came on, he said, the network's numbers (an average of 450,000 people were online each hour from 7:00 P.M. to 11:00 P.M.) dropped. At the time, a dip in online engagement meant television was drawing people away; most viewers had not yet learned to interact with one another to discuss a show while it aired. *Seinfeld* drew 30 million viewers for a single half hour. With just 1.8 million users over the prime-time period, AOL pulled in numbers closer to MTV's or Larry King's. For the moment, AOL couldn't hope to dominate television. It would have to settle for running its *Jetsons*-themed ad spot, announcing "The Future — Now Available on America Online," during *Seinfeld.*

Those AOL ads weren't the only ones jockeying for an increasingly higher-priced slot during *Seinfeld. Seinfeld* wasn't just popular; it commanded the commercial realm like no sitcom before it. With the help of *Friends'* blockbuster debut as part of NBC's Thursday lineup in 1994, *Seinfeld* made "Must See TV" the rare slogan that meant something. It meant so much that the shows hammocked in the spots between those powerhouses included a notorious number of duds that still put up huge numbers. *The Single Guy, Caroline in the City, Suddenly Susan, Union Square, Veronica's Closet,* and *Jesse* were hardly classics, but could pull in nearly 20 million households, ranking in the top ten of all television shows at the time.

Thursday had become the most important night of the week for television programmers, a time when a large proportion of the young, wealthy demographic that advertisers coveted were watching. Movie studios in particular liked to buy up Thursday-night ad time to launch blockbusters on Friday nights, as did car companies pushing weekend sales.

As far back as 1982, NBC had branded the evening, particularly during its stronger seasons. The network promoted that year's lineup of *Fame, Cheers, Taxi,* and *Hill Street Blues* as "The Best Night of Television on Television." The marketing aimed to combat what then NBC president Grant Tinker often noted, that viewers were more loyal to shows than to networks. The night had become important to NBC as it rose from the last-place network in the late 1970s and early '80s to the first-place network in 1985 with Thursday favorites like *The Cosby Show* and *Cheers.* Most in the industry attributed this ascendance to Tinker's leadership, specifically his ability to nurture creativity — a reputation he earned as the head of MTM Enterprises, which he started in 1969 to produce his ex-wife's *The Mary Tyler Moore Show* and which went on to produce respected series such as *Hill Street Blues, St. Elsewhere,* and *Newhart.*

Brandon Tartikoff served as Tinker's second-in-command at NBC until Tinker's departure in 1986; then Tartikoff took over with a vow to uphold the quality and burnish the brand further, to take it, as he said, from "Kmart" to "Saks Fifth Avenue."

Seinfeld had helped do that, boosting the network's demographic reach in large cities, among upwardly mobile professionals, and among young audiences that advertisers craved. In the entertainment industry, such success led inevitably to imitators. Shows about young, single urbanites proliferated across networks, though that particular form of flattery came at least as much from other NBC series as from any other source.

David and Seinfeld noticed, carping that *Friends* had ripped off their show's concept — a group of single friends in New York City. And it was certainly true that from the beginning, *Friends* had *Seinfeld* DNA. Courteney Cox, who had played one of Jerry's girlfriends and went on to star as the uptight Monica on *Friends,* took charge at her new show by saying, "Listen, I just did a *Seinfeld,* and they all help each other. They say, 'Try this.' Or, 'This would be funny.' " She continued: "You guys, feel free to tell me. If I could do anything funnier, I want to do it."

But *Friends* differed quite a bit from *Seinfeld.* Upon seeing *Friends* as it developed, Littlefield thought, *This is a Shakespearean soap opera. It's a drama that's really, really funny, and with complex architecture. Seinfeld,* on the other hand, prioritized humor and disdained feelings. As *Friends* cocreator David Crane said, his show went for the emotion every time, rather than focusing on the minutiae of New York life and rapid-fire references to everything from John Cheever to babka. "That's why we were always surprised when people compared us to *Seinfeld,*" Crane said. Added Matt LeBlanc, who played Joey on *Friends,* "You cared about these people. You were invested in these relationships." *Seinfeld* was the opposite: You cared what happened to the characters because they were fun to watch, *not* because you cared a whit for their relationships or, God forbid, feelings.

Friends' producers felt equally resentful of *Seinfeld,* which they saw as an older brother who got to do whatever he wanted. When the *Friends* producers wanted to show a condom wrapper on-screen, NBC's standards and practices department balked; *Seinfeld,* on the other hand, had already aired its masturbation episode. "*Seinfeld* had different rules," Crane said. "Apparently, you can masturbate at nine but not at eight."

The double standard annoyed even network president Warren Littlefield: "That made me crazy," he wrote. "I had a lot of battles with broadcast standards over that. What could be more socially responsible than these characters practicing safe sex?"

Another show in the Must See TV lineup came closer to being *Seinfeld*-inspired, and got its good spot on the air because of it: *Mad About You,* starring Seinfeld's longtime friend and admirer Paul Reiser. "Paul Reiser, like Jerry Seinfeld, was a stand-up comedian, but Paul also had some serious acting experience, particularly his wonderful turn in *Diner,*" Littlefield later wrote. "In a sense, then, we were working an improvement on the *Seinfeld* equation by going into business with a comedian who could already act."

Littlefield thought *Mad About You* could make a good scheduling companion to his now-major hit, and it eventually got a prime Thursday spot. Audiences responded to it, even if it didn't permeate the culture as thoroughly as *Seinfeld.* The two shows had a symbiotic relationship: *Seinfeld* took a friendly swipe at *Mad About You* when Susan forced an exasperated George to watch the show with her instead of a Yankees game. And *Mad About You* got a *Seinfeld*-ian blessing in the form of a cameo by Michael Richards as Kramer — who, it turns out, lives in Reiser's character's old apartment. Given *Seinfeld*'s previous resistance to crossover gimmicks, this was a coup.

And in 1998 came yet another clear *Seinfeld* descendant on NBC, with only its approach to sexuality to set it apart: *Will & Grace* brought us a core cast of four cynical, self-obsessed New Yorkers with trivial problems as well; it's just that two of them happened to be gay men, two of them straight women. The show emulated *Sein-*

feld right down to its composer, hiring Jonathan Wolff to produce the theme and score. This time, he chose to play an exuberant piano solo instead of a spare bass solo. Even though Wolff had plenty of work before *Seinfeld,* he'd now become one of the hottest commodities in Hollywood, which is, as he told me, "a me-too town." He went on to score *The King of Queens, The Hughleys,* and *Reba,* among many others.

The networks would take any little piece of *Seinfeld* they could get.

NBC'S strong comedy lineup, led by *Seinfeld,* made everyone in Hollywood want to work with the network. Everyone now wanted to make "the next *Seinfeld.*" Even with barely any room left on the schedule to fill and agents warning their clients against trying to sell to the overstuffed network, NBC received a barrage of pitches. NBC became a brand name in itself, not merely a channel some shows happened to be on.

Seinfeld guest-starred on an episode of fellow NBC sitcom *News-Radio* as himself, the surprise radio-show guest who would help boost sagging ratings. He had gone from network pariah to the very embodiment of a ratings savior.

In 1996, largely due to *Seinfeld*'s success, NBC's revenues had ballooned to make it seven times more profitable than ABC — the only other network to turn any profit that year. The show contributed $200 million to that billion-dollar bottom line. A good thing, since General Electric, which had purchased NBC as part of its deal with RCA a decade earlier, required its companies to rank first or second in earnings in their respective industries, or be sold off. GE had jettisoned several of RCA's holdings but kept NBC, not only because it was the first-place network but also because an internal analysis showed revenue growth of 11.4 percent yearly between 1980 and 1984, despite the encroachment of cable and VCRs.

By 1997, *Seinfeld* had become the first television show to bring in more than $1 million per minute of advertising, something previously accomplished only by the Super Bowl. It could launch new shows for the network, keep weaker ones afloat, and help bring viewers to the network's news broadcasts, morning shows, and late-night lineup. The money pouring in allowed NBC to plan for its inevitable *Seinfeld*-free future, investing in cable networks, international markets, and long-term rights to broadcast the

Olympics. "It almost defies logic what the value of that program is," a media buyer told *Businessweek.* "*Seinfeld* is one of the most important shows in history." *Business-week* declared it a "TV supershow."

Seinfeld was now big enough that David — who once thought a down payment on a Lexus was as good as his career would ever get — bought himself a Porsche. Then he worried that it was too much and he didn't deserve it. So he returned it a week later and took a $16,000 loss.

With a huge swath of America now watching every week, even the famous were now fans. Director Stanley Kubrick had tapes of the show sent to him in England. Advice columnist Ann Landers, comedian Phyllis Diller, and author Dave Barry were among regular viewers.

The *Seinfeld* stars got to meet their idols as they became sought-after names for industry events. Louis-Dreyfus served alongside one of her role models, Teri Garr, on the Hollywood Women's Political Committee when it publicly supported first lady Hillary Rodham Clinton's health care reform efforts. Alexander became friends with William Shatner, whom he had admired as an actor and because Alexander was a hard-core *Star Trek* fan. Shatner told Alexander that his own experience on a hugely influential television show had embittered him at first; when it ended, he was angry that his career had possibly peaked with Captain Kirk, and he tried to distance himself from the character. It took him twenty years to finally embrace his fans from that time. "You might want to think about embracing it now," Shatner advised Alexander. George was going to be Alexander's Kirk, no doubt.

The show's famous fans now happily lined up for guest-star spots, too, often playing versions of themselves. Marisa Tomei romanced George. Mets player Keith Hernandez romanced Elaine. Raquel Welch played herself as a terrifying diva; Bette Midler played herself as the star of *Rochelle Rochelle: The Musical.*

Jon Voight appeared as himself in the episode in which George buys a used car that may or may not have belonged to the actor. Voight coincidentally crosses paths with Kramer, who can prove whether Voight is the car's former owner if he can get an impression of the actor's teeth marks to be analyzed and compared with a bitten pencil left in the vehicle. He decides to goad Voight into biting his arm.

Before shooting the scene, Voight gleefully declared to director Andy Ackerman, "I'm going to really bite him! Don't tell him."

When the cameras rolled, Voight did indeed grab Richards's arm and sink his teeth into it. Shocked, Richards screamed. Voight laughed. "Damn method actors," Richards muttered after the take was over. The famous were now regular folk on the set of *Seinfeld.*

Meanwhile, even the show's relatively minor characters became national sensations.

There was Jerry and Kramer's mail-carrier neighbor Newman, who became Jerry's nemesis. Wayne Knight, who'd appeared in such films as *JFK* and *Basic Instinct,* played him with evil aplomb and got to deliver one of the show's most popular catchphrases: "Hello, *Jerry.*" There was Elaine's monosyllabic boyfriend David Puddy, played by the hunky Patrick Warburton as either the dumbest or smartest character on *Seinfeld* — it was impossible to tell.

But George's and Jerry's parents rose to something far beyond recurring characters, ranking among sitcom history's most memorable parental figures and becoming career-defining roles even for actors with long Hollywood backstories.

Jerry Stiller joined the show in 1993 as Frank, the father figure who made us understand why George was who he was. Stiller found the *Seinfeld* family welcoming when he arrived on the set: On his first taping night, Alexander, Seinfeld, Louis-Dreyfus, and Richards surrounded him and wished him good luck. He felt a particular connection to the eccentric Richards. That day kicked off what Stiller would later call "the best years of my life as an actor."

Seinfeld came at a good time for Stiller, which is to say, at a bad time for him as an actor. He was sixty-five and short on the kind of work that could sustain him. He had just done a TV pilot called *Civil Wars,* from which his scene was cut. He and wife, Anne Meara, had just performed in a run of their longtime dual comedy act, featuring material they had once done on *The Ed Sullivan Show* decades earlier. He got a role in a staging of the comedy *Three Men on a Horse* with Tony Randall at the National Actors Theatre, for which he originally turned down the *Seinfeld* role. Then the play closed and he realized: His destiny was to play Frank Costanza — a role that had already been played on the show once by a different actor, John Randolph — after all.

Stiller thought he'd wear a bald wig for

the role, to match both George and Randolph, but soon that plan was abandoned. More important than the Costanza bald gene was the Costanza capacity for anger — Stiller would spend most of his time yelling and hitting Alexander.

Though director Andy Ackerman described Stiller as "the sweetest man on the face of the earth," anger was even more critical to the role of Frank than to the role of George. At first, Stiller resisted. Alexander suggested Stiller slap him in the face. "I can't do that!" Stiller said. Eventually, he did.

Richards lent his choreography expertise to Stiller: When the Costanzas planned their Festivus celebration, Stiller had to schlep an aluminum Festivus pole into Monk's Café. "Don't forget to drag it on the floor," Richards told Stiller, "so they can hear the sound."

Stiller had trouble remembering his lines, but the *Seinfeld* cast and crew developed patience with him because of how spectacular his performances were. In fact, what look like Frank's angry gestures are often Stiller's gestures of frustration with his inability to remember his lines. Everything about him looked pained, a perfect expression of Frank Costanza.

Stiller felt brave around these actors. And he had never seen himself as a courageous actor. He felt total freedom on the set. Stiller appeared on the show twenty-six times, doing plays on and off-Broadway, and getting a hip replacement, in between. He always looked forward to returning to work with his on-screen son. He loved to see the glint in Alexander's eye in response to Stiller's funny work in a scene.

Alexander wasn't the only one who cracked up over Stiller's antics. Louis-Dreyfus, too, was prone to breaking up in scenes with Stiller. In one scene, Frank had to challenge Elaine: "You saying you want a piece of me?" It took five or six times before she could get through it without doubling over in laughter. He could ask for no more as an actor.

Sixty-four-year-old Estelle Harris served as Stiller's irritable and irritating on-screen wife, Estelle Costanza — a defining role she played so well that Alexander felt, in scenes with his on-screen parents, that all he had to do was "stand in the middle." She came to *Seinfeld* with a résumé full of mother roles in films such as *Stand and Deliver* and the TV shows *Night Court* and *Brooklyn Bridge.* On *Seinfeld,* she got to use her nasal whine to its greatest effect as George's overbearing mother.

She made her first appearance on the show in the fourth-season episode "The Contest." Alexander was startled to see the five-foot-two-inch woman with a cloud of short red curls, who looked so much like his own mother. Her voice struck him as instant comedy. In the episode, she lands in the hospital, having thrown out her back during her aghast reaction to the discovery of George masturbating. "I go out for a quart of milk," she screeches, "I come home and find my son treating his body like it was an amusement park." She got even more screen time when George moved back in with her and Frank in Flushing, Queens, for a season.

The Costanzas' ethnicity went technically unspoken. Estelle constantly made paella. Their last name was clearly Italian. References were made to Christmas celebrations in the home. But when Harris — a Jewish New Yorker born Estelle Nussbaum — was cast as Estelle, Alexander knew for sure that he was playing a Jew because "she can't be anything but Jewish." Coming close to confirming this, Estelle Costanza once forbade Frank from buying a Mercedes because it's a German car. Stiller, also Jewish, described the Costanzas as "a Jewish family in the witness protection program."

The TV version of Mr. and Mrs. Seinfeld didn't have as much raw emotion to draw on for their characters. But they did provide a more normal model of aging parents than the Costanzas, with passive-aggressive guilt-tripping more their speed than screaming and violent outbursts. They also lived in a retirement community rife with political intrigue, hilarious bit characters, and the potential for entirely different sources of humor than *Seinfeld*'s standard apartments and coffee shops could provide.

Jerry's father, Morty, first appeared on the show in the first-season episode "The Stakeout" — like Frank Costanza, he was played by two different actors as the series evolved in its early years, free of mass scrutiny. At first, Morty was played by Phil Bruns. By the time he appeared again in the second season, he'd gotten more hair, distinctive dark-framed glasses, and a much jumpier persona, courtesy of Bruns's replacement, Barney Martin.

Martin, sixty-seven when he joined *Seinfeld,* was a former New York Police Department detective who launched his comedy career by giving funny presentations to deputy commissioners. He got his start in show business moonlighting as Jackie Gleason's stand-in on *The Honeymooners* in the 1950s and as a writer for *Name That Tune* and *The Steve Allen Show.* He eventually left police work altogether and went on to pursue a real acting career, appearing in the 1968 Mel Brooks movie *The Producers* (as a drunk in a bar) and the 1981 Dudley Moore comedy *Arthur.* In between, he enjoyed a robust Broadway career that included originating the role of cuckolded husband Amos Hart in the musical *Chicago.* Before *Seinfeld,* he appeared in character parts on shows from *The Odd Couple* to *21 Jump Street.*

Actress Liz Sheridan played Jerry's mother, Helen, from the beginning. At sixty-one, she came to the show with experience on sitcoms (*Alf* and *Family Ties*), dramas (*Cagney & Lacey* and *Remington Steele*), and soaps (*Santa Barbara*). She'd spent the early years of her career as a dancer in New York City, where she grew up, and she had a youthful affair with James Dean before he was famous.

Seinfeld was bemused when he heard about his on-screen mom's steamy past: "So, you were a friend of James Dean, huh?" he asked after he heard of her rumored paramour. She explained that, yes, she and Dean had been each other's first loves before he went off to become a star in the films *East of Eden* and *Rebel Without a Cause,* then died in a car crash at twenty-four.

From then on, Seinfeld would periodically ask her, "Got any good Dean stories?" She spoke of the January 1952 night when she and Dean first met. At the time, she was a dancer on *The Milton Berle Show.* She said Dean had lived on shredded wheat and tapioca pudding while trying to land parts. She recalled their shared love of bullfighting and the apartment they lived in together on the Upper West Side.

The actors playing Jerry's parents in particular gave Seinfeld a sense of his show's place in greater Hollywood history. Dean-like brooding may not have been *Seinfeld*'s thing, but his rebel spirit certainly was.

With even his TV parents becoming celebrities, Jerry Seinfeld was *everywhere,* the object of fascination and scorn. In 1993, he released his book *SeinLanguage,* a compilation of stand-up routines, and had to answer to rumors that he'd been paid $1.6 million for it. ("Ludicrous," he said, though he gave no alternative figure.) He parodied himself on HBO's showbiz-satire *The Larry Sanders Show.* The nation hung on Seinfeld's every word about his show, which he called "TV for the bored" in an interview with *USA Weekend.* "We'll do two more seasons," he teased a viewership now desperate for reassurances that there would be many years to come. "I will walk away from unbelievable bucks."

Seinfeld showed up in a tux for the Emmys and found his name mentioned as a possible Oscar host, but he continued to spurn Hollywood trappings like A-list parties. He didn't even love the idea of emceeing show business's biggest night. It was too controlled an environment for his taste. The Oscars weren't supposed to be good — weren't supposed to be *funny,* not really. People watch the Oscars because they're the Oscars, not for groundbreaking comedy from the host. In other words, Seinfeld still wasn't interested in gigs that didn't give him total artistic control.

The Emmys, however, wasn't an event he planned to shun. In September 1993, Seinfeld was up for an acting Emmy, an acknowledgment that he'd come a long way since he'd been so uncomfortable in the pilot. *Seinfeld* was nominated for nine major awards that night, and it won for Outstanding Comedy Series, beating *Home Improvement* and *Cheers* for what was its true breakthrough season, its fourth. Michael Richards won a Supporting Actor award, as usual beating out Jason Alexander as George. Larry David took home a writing award for "The Contest." In subsequent years, the show would find itself snubbed much more often than it was victorious; nominations were plentiful, but only Michael Richards and Julia Louis-Dreyfus took home major awards for the show. (Richards won three; Louis-Dreyfus won one.) *Frasier* beat *Seinfeld* for Outstanding Comedy Series every remaining year of *Seinfeld*'s run.

Seinfeld accepted the Golden Globe Award for Best Actor in a Comedy in January 1994, presented by actors Jeff Conaway and Tia Carrere. "Wow," he began his acceptance speech, "there's a lot of cleavage in this room. And that's why the Golden Globe award is the highest honor you can receive on a night like this." He did, however, add a touch of sincerity: "I love doing the show. It's really just having fun that makes it look like you're good. And I have to thank for that my wonderful pals, Michael Richards and Julia Louis-Dreyfus and Jason Alexander. And Larry David, who writes all the great stuff that we do."

Any doubt as to whether the show had arrived disappeared when Warren Littlefield showed up on set one day to cook breakfast for the entire cast and crew. There was the president of entertainment, flipping pancakes, making waffles and eggs, and sweating for their benefit.

Seinfeld, who was about to turn forty, continued to see the show as his primary relationship, but it wasn't his only relationship — a well-documented fact, according to the tabloid attention paid to the sitcom world's most eligible bachelor. Just as the show was becoming a sensation going into its fifth season, Seinfeld met seventeen-year-old high school senior Shoshanna Lonstein, a shapely brunette, in Central Park one spring day and started dating her. He had remained staunchly single throughout the show's run thus far because he always put his work first. Now that he was dating publicly, and had chosen a teenager as his paramour, the tabloids couldn't contain themselves.

Seinfeld had little choice but to acknowledge his new love publicly, calling her "the most wonderful girl in the world. . . . Shoshanna is a person, not an age. We just get along." More important, he said, the gossip pages' interest in his love life showed how far he'd come: "It's like winning an Oscar."

Julia Louis-Dreyfus won another dubious sign of success: her very own public spat with Roseanne Barr.

Louis-Dreyfus inadvertently parked in a spot designated for Barr's then husband, Tom Arnold, who at the time — March 1993 — starred in his own show, *The Jackie Thomas Show,* also filmed at CBS Studio Center. Louis-Dreyfus later said that she was instructed to park there by the parking attendants. Arnold left a note on Louis-Dreyfus's car: "How stupid are you? Move your fucking car, you asshole!"

Alexander, David, and Louis-Dreyfus confronted Arnold about the note, after which followed a Polaroid of someone's buttocks left on her windshield, and the word CUNT written in soap on her windshield. The incident went public, and Barr sort of apologized, but mostly, she called Louis-Dreyfus a bitch on *Letterman,* then added derisively, "They think they're doing Samuel Beckett instead of a sitcom." The *Seinfeld* cast tried not to talk about it in interviews afterward, hoping to take the high road, but sometimes they couldn't help themselves. "I am willing to make a bet that

243

she has never read anything Beckett ever wrote," Alexander said to *Rolling Stone.*

The subtext of that exchange perhaps explained the entire dustup best. *Seinfeld* was even more popular than *Roseanne* now, and more artistically respected as well. It was about New York elites and attracted the elite audiences that advertisers paid the highest prices for. It was the sitcom that had it all. The spat in the parking lot was pure Roseanne: She was proud of her working-class crassness and would shove it in the face of any elite who crossed her. It was also pure *Seinfeld:* Could the queen of populism possibly know Beckett as well as they did?

Barr wasn't alone, however, in her disdain for this show that 30 million viewers now watched every week. With great popularity comes great criticism, and according to some critics, society was unraveling at a rate directly proportional to Seinfeld's growth. "Call me a hopeless Puritan," wrote the Progressive's Elayne Rapping, "but I see, in this airwave invasion of sitcoms about young Manhattanites with no real family or work responsibilities and nothing to do but hang out and talk about it, an insidious message about the future of Western civilization."

Added Leon Wieseltier, literary editor of the New Republic, "Seinfeld is the worst, last gasp of Reaganite, grasping, materialistic, narcissistic, banal self-absorption."

Seinfeld had become *the* hot item for overanalyzers. Scholars opined that it represented modern male anxiety, Jewish cultural assimilation, the rise of irony and intertextuality, and the self-centeredness of the 1990s. *Seinfeld*'s real-life effects on fans made national news: When Florida high school student Dan Cassill fell into a coma after a 1996 car accident, he first awoke when his mother turned on his favorite show — and the media ate the story up. Jerold Mackenzie, a manager at Miller Brewing Co. in Milwaukee, lost his job for discussing "The Junior Mint" — specifically, the body part with which the name "Dolores" rhymes — with a female employee. He won a much-publicized wrongful termination lawsuit.

Thus began an almost comic roller coaster of melodramatic public and critical reaction to a show that nearly everyone had once been prepared to ignore. No sooner did one critic declare its return to form, hurrah!, than another would declare it better off dead.

■ ■ ■ ■

Even in the middle of the chaos and hype, there were occasional quiet, touching moments that reminded the cast and crew that they were just a lucky team of people working at what would likely be the best job of their lives. Seinfeld loved filming the seventh-season episode "The Rye." The elaborate staging involved pulling a rye up to George's potential in-laws' third-floor brownstone apartment with a fishing pole and required shooting on a large, outdoor set normally used for movies at Paramount Studios. The budget came in at almost a million dollars, as writer Carol Leifer remembers it, after accounting for the fake snow and the hansom cab Kramer drives. The cast and crew broke out into an impromptu fake-snowball fight.

Somehow it wasn't until that moment that Seinfeld stopped to realize, *Wow, this is almost like a real TV show.* The series had scraped by for so long on so little — so little attention, support, audience, budget — that the reality hit on time delay. The New York set looked so real, he thought, *This is where the adult shows are, the real shows like* Murphy Brown.

It proved difficult to shoot, but fun. They stayed on the set all night taping, and loved every minute — immersed in their work, immune to the churning publicity of the outside world. Shooting ended right before they broke for Thanksgiving, and as they wrapped, a truck pulled up to distribute HoneyBaked hams and turkeys to the cast and crew, courtesy of David and Seinfeld. That episode would become one of fans' favorites, and one of the best memories for those involved.

Even Frances Bay — the tiny, gray-haired woman robbed of her rye on the set that night — felt the instant celebrity that *Seinfeld* could now confer upon anyone in its orbit. Once the episode aired, all she ever heard was, "Oh, you're the Marble Rye Lady!" Her rabbi went out of his way to greet her now, she told *People* magazine, and he had a sizable congregation. This was no small show.

9
THE SHOW ABOUT SOMETHING

In 1994, even the news started seeming *Seinfeld*ian. Olympic figure skater Nancy Kerrigan was attacked by a man who clubbed her in the right knee as she left a practice facility in Detroit, an attack orchestrated by her competitor Tonya Harding and Harding's ex-husband, Jeff Gillooly. Major League Baseball players went on strike, putting a halt to the World Series. Newt Gingrich became the Speaker of the House of Representatives. And 95 million people watched former pro football player O. J. Simpson and his friend Al Cowlings lead Los Angeles police on a low-speed chase across the city's morass of freeways before Simpson was arrested on suspicion of murdering his ex-wife, Nicole Brown Simpson, and a visitor at her Brentwood home, Ron Goldman.

While some of these events had serious underpinnings and repercussions, everything could be seen through David and Seinfeld's skewed vision now. A conspiracy to club a figure skater's leg? Guys named Jeff Gillooly and Newt Gingrich? Millionaires on strike? Most of America glued to footage of a Ford Bronco on what appeared to be a leisurely drive, trailed by a cadre of cop cars? Had everything always been so absurd, or had Larry David and Jerry Seinfeld willed a new era of ridiculousness into existence? Somehow, a brave new order had emerged, in which the revelation of Kramer's first name — Cosmo — got the same amount of media attention as a devastating earthquake in Japan. One could wonder if the pundits who blamed *Seinfeld* for the degradation of society were onto something. Seinfeldia had seeped into real life just as much as real life had infused Seinfeldia.

In this spirit, *Seinfeld* celebrated its hundredth episode with a one-hour retrospective special on February 2, 1995. At the hundredth-episode party stood a centerpiece, a ten-foot-tall blowup of NBC executives' list of requested changes to the pilot way back when. Almost none of them had been made.

The show had courted strong reactions

from its earliest seasons; the difference then was that few watched, and fewer wrote in national publications about it.

Season four's "The Contest" marked a turning point. The network let the infamous masturbation episode air as written. Whether shocked by it, thrilled, or a little bit of both, millions had discussed it the next day, media attention had followed, and NBC remembered the power of television that sparked discussion. Nine advertisers pulled their spots from the broadcast, but in the end that loss was worth it. The episode was one of the highest rated of the season, and several advertisers who originally balked wanted to run spots when it re-aired over the summer.

From there, *Seinfeld* roamed ever freer in choosing its subject matter, whether sexual, politically incorrect, or otherwise controversial.

In the "Fusilli Jerry" episode, the script references "the Move," a sexual technique Jerry once bragged about to Elaine's boyfriend Puddy. However, Elaine notices that her new beau — Jerry's mechanic — uses the same move as her ex, Jerry. (Jerry's not happy: "It's like another comedian stealing my material." Elaine: "It's not even the same. He uses a pinch at the end." Jerry, on the other hand, favored a clockwise swirl.) In other episodes, Elaine bemoans her sax-player boyfriend who "doesn't really like to do *everything*" and George tries to persuade a girlfriend to let him eat pastrami sandwiches during the act.

In the fourth-season episode "The Handicap Spot," the foursome stops at a mall in the suburb of Lynbrook, New York, to buy a present on the way to an engagement party and can't find a parking spot. "Why don't you take the handicap spot?" Kramer suggests to George, who's driving his father's late-'70s Mercury Monarch.

"You think?" George asks. They'll be in the mall for only a few minutes, they're sure.

Elaine protests. "What if a handicapped person needs it?"

Kramer responds, "They don't drive. Have you ever seen a handicapped person pull into a space and park?"

Jerry answers with a tautology. "Well, there's spaces there, they must drive."

Kramer one-ups him on nonsensical logic. "If they could drive, they wouldn't be handicapped. . . . I got news for you. Handicapped people, they don't even want to park there. They want to be treated just like everybody else. Those spaces are always empty."

George concludes: "He's right. It's the same thing with the feminists. They want everything to be equal, everything. But when the check comes, where are they?"

Elaine won't let that one stand. "What does that mean?"

George ignores her and parks in the spot. They stay inside much longer than a few minutes, and return to find an angry mob trashing the car because a woman in a wheelchair was injured in an accident after having to park far away. This story line eventually culminates in Kramer buying the woman a replacement wheelchair that's used, and she ends up careening, out of control, down a hill.

This was exactly the sort of episode *Seinfeld* became known for — the kind no one was quite sure was okay to laugh at. But they laughed anyway, and talked about it the next day. As NBC found it increasingly difficult to hold on to its top ratings spot, it saw a savior in *Seinfeld* and its cultural antagonism.

Even *Seinfeld* had its limits, though. David and Seinfeld found their furthest edge when they attempted, and then scrapped, a script in 1990 called "The Bet," in which Elaine considered buying a handgun. The bet in question was about whether she'd go through with her plans to purchase a firearm for self-protection, based on the experiences of one of the show's writers, Elaine Pope. They got the script as far as a read-through. But several of those involved balked as they performed it for the first time, particularly at a line about Elaine shooting herself in the head and calling it "the Kennedy," gesturing to the entry point of the bullet that killed the president.

It offended director Tom Cherones (a former gunnery officer in the United States Navy) and the cast enough to stop things cold. The actors said they didn't want to do it. Cherones agreed.

The writer of the episode, Larry Charles, gave in. The episode was killed. (The script also, incidentally, revealed Kramer's first name to be Conrad, inspired by *Bye Bye Birdie*. His name would remain a secret until years later, when he was christened Cosmo instead.) David and Seinfeld rushed a replacement episode, "The Phone Message," in which George tries to erase an answering machine message he regrets. Guns, they realized, were just not funny.

Death, on the other hand . . .

In the summer of 1995, Larry David called Jason Alexander. "We've got a great arc for George," he said. "He's going to get engaged."

"To what character?"

"Susan."

"Who's playing Susan?" Alexander asked, though surely he knew.

"Heidi."

"Who's playing George?" Alexander cracked.

Alexander and Heidi Swedberg, who played George's ex, never worked on the same wavelength. While Alexander found it easy to play off of his regular costars, he always felt like he was fighting Swedberg in their shared scenes, even though he liked her as a person offscreen. He found her comic instincts to be "the complete opposite" of his own. "I always felt like I was punching into Jell-O," he later said. He'd do something in a scene with her, and it would fall flat. So in the next take, he'd do something else, and then David would tell him to go back to the original choice. Then in the next take, Swedberg would do something totally different. Alexander couldn't win.

"Don't you understand how perfect she is for you?" David continued. "You've driven her to lesbianism. You burned her father's shack down. You've practically shit on her, and nobody feels bad for her. They're all on your side. She's the greatest foil for you."

True enough, her character had been through even more than that thanks to George and his friends. Kramer threw up on her. She lost her job at NBC when George kissed her mid-meeting. Kramer stole her girlfriend.

Swedberg saw her role on the show as being the straight woman to the insanity. Susan was the stiffest of the stiff, unlike Swedberg herself, who rebelled against her uptight upbringing by threatening to join the circus when she was a kid in Albuquerque. Instead, she became an actress, took up the ukulele, and bought an Airstream trailer for her and her husband to hang out in — and keep in the yard at their Los Angeles home.

Her girl-next-door looks had gotten her onetime guest spots on shows such as *Matlock, Grace Under Fire,* and *Murder, She Wrote.* Eventually, those all-American looks also got her what was originally a bit part on *Seinfeld* as one of a group of fictional NBC executives who take George and Jerry's pitch for a sitcom. George's throwaway line that she had seemed to like him inspired producers to bring her back several times as George's on-again, off-again love interest. As a coworker on the set, Swedberg was an unassuming professional who caused neither trouble nor spectacle. She'd do her scenes, then retreat to a corner to read a book until she was needed again.

Now, Susan and George were the closest *Seinfeld* had ever gotten to a stable couple.

David had no idea where the plotline would end, but he was committed to seeing it through. About halfway through the next season, an episode required Jerry and Elaine to hang out with Susan, the first time either Seinfeld or Louis-Dreyfus had to work extensively with Swedberg. After the taping, the four lead actors gathered with David at Jerry's Famous Deli in Studio City, as usual.

"You know, it's hard to figure out where to go with what she gives you," Seinfeld said.

"Don't even talk to me," Alexander snapped. "I don't want to hear your bullshit."

Louis-Dreyfus added, "I just want to kill her."

And David said, "Wait a minute."

The conversation led to what Alexander called "the single coldest moment in the history of television": when Susan's death is met with what could generously be called an apathetic shrug . . . from her own fiancé. Warren Littlefield saw it as "the boldest comedy move I had ever seen," even though his kids' pediatrician wouldn't talk to him afterward.

One hopes this was as distant as George Costanza could get from his real-life inspiration, Larry David. "It would have been dishonest to make him upset, and that's why it's funny," David said afterward. "Somebody showed me something in some magazine where they wrote that this was a 'fuck you' to the network. Why would I do something like that? Why a fuck you, when all they did was let me do whatever I wanted for seven years?"

Everything *Seinfeld* did now took on grand significance.

Given the show's precarious early life — and NBC's specific concerns about its Jewishness — David and Seinfeld didn't go out of their way to send their main characters to synagogue or quote the Torah every week. But the Floridian parents, the marble ryes, the Jewish singles events — one couldn't miss that the title star of the show and more than half of its writers were Jewish. But as the series gained more viewers, the criticisms mounted: Too Jewish. Not Jewish enough. Even "too self-hatingly Jewish," according to *Washington Post* critic Tom Shales. Shales cited the show's parade of nefarious Jewish characters. Elaine's rabbi neighbor spills his confidants' secrets. Jerry and his girlfriend make out during *Schindler's List*. Elaine, a non-Jewish character, discovers her "shiksappeal" that attracts Jewish men.

In 1996, scholars at a Stanford University Jewish Studies symposium debated the show's merits for their own culture. Any Jewish identity in mainstream culture was a positive development, said Richard Siegel, the executive director of the National Foundation for Jewish Culture. For author of *New York Jew* Alfred Kazin, however, neither *Seinfeld* nor novelist Philip Roth made the cut in terms of representing true Jewish culture. To him, a representation wasn't sufficiently Jewish unless it dealt with a relationship to God. Stanford religious studies professor Arnold Eisen agreed, comparing *Seinfeld* to "bagels and lox, which are no longer Jewish." In an interview at another time, Rabbi Jonathan Pearl of the Jewish Televimages Resource Center complained that *Seinfeld* became "unfunny" whenever it dealt with Jewish issues.

Alexander, who's also Jewish, didn't disagree when it came to one fifth-season episode called "The Bris." He hated the character of the mohel who circumcises

Elaine's friend's child. Alexander said, "You have to go a long way to hit my Jew button. To me, this was anti-Semitic in a hurtful way." He told David he'd have to boycott the episode and persuaded David to soften the portrayal. (In the end, the mohel was merely incompetent, rather than blatantly offensive.) Alexander was never comfortable with the episode, but he could live with it.

Still, the show did bring bits of Jewish culture to the masses in America, many of whom — particularly in the Midwest — barely knew what Hanukkah was.

Writer Steve Koren worked a story line into one of his first scripts about a kid trying to kiss Elaine at his bar mitzvah because he's "a man now." Unlike at *Saturday Night Live,* however, Koren knew this wasn't enough to support an episode. He was right: Seinfeld liked the concept but said, "What else, what else?" Koren came up with several versions of the story, but none quite worked. He had that story on the bulletin board in his office for a year before he realized: The kid renounces Judaism for Elaine.

With that, the bar mitzvah kid made it into Koren's favorite of the episodes he wrote, "The Serenity Now." It was, if anything,

Seinfeld doing the exact opposite of renouncing Judaism; for one of the few times in its run, it was unequivocally embracing its Jewishness, no matter whom you asked, with a traditional Jewish ceremony front and center for all of America to see.

Cultural diversity overall was *Seinfeld*'s blessing and curse. Seinfeld was outspoken about prioritizing comedy over all other concerns, including the show's representations of all races. But several plotlines took on racial issues: George desperately searches for a black friend to prove to his African American boss that he's not racist. Kramer has visiting Japanese tourists sleeping in his chest of drawers. ("Jerry, have you ever seen the business hotels in Tokyo? They sleep in tiny stacked cubicles all the time. They feel right at home.") Jerry buys Elaine a cigar-store Indian figure and thus inadvertently offends a woman he wants to date. Elaine dates a guy she thinks is black, enjoying the cultural cachet; it turns out he isn't, and he had referred to their relationship as "interracial" because he thought she was Hispanic.

While *Seinfeld*'s neighbor in fictitious New York, *Friends,* ignored minority characters almost entirely despite being set in

America's most diverse city, such plotlines allowed *Seinfeld* to include many guest actors of color. Some of those notable portrayals were small, such as the black family whose *Breakfast at Tiffany's* viewing George crashes. Some were large: Phil Morris made several memorable appearances as a bossy send-up of O. J. Simpson lawyer Johnnie Cochran with the recurring Jackie Chiles character. (Barking in Cochran's then-famous cadence at Kramer for soothing the injury for which he's suing a fast-food chain: "You put the balm on? Who told you to put the balm on? I didn't tell you to put the balm on. Why'd you put the balm on? You haven't even been to see the doctor. If you're gonna put a balm on, let a doctor put a balm on.") *Seinfeld* was also one of the few New York–set shows at the time with nonwhite actors consistently appearing in prominent onetime roles and smaller recurring roles: Sid, the parking guy in "The Alternate Side" (played by Jay Brooks); Larry, the cook at Monk's Café (Lawrence Mandley); charity worker Rebecca De Mornay (named after the white actress, but played by black actress Sonya Eddy); and Mr. Morgan, one of George's bosses (Tom Wright).

But anytime a minority ended up the butt

of a joke, it could turn problematic in a way that the show's white characters' foibles never did. The Chinese restaurant host who doesn't know the difference between "Costanza" and "Cartwright" and the gay Latino armoire thieves did nothing to assuage criticisms of *Seinfeld*'s lack of diversity. Even Chiles came in for criticism that he reinforced racial stereotypes, although he was clearly based on a public figure.

Adding fuel to the fire, in 1997, performance artist Danny Hoch spent a huge portion of his touring act calling Seinfeld "the enemy." The lengthy monologue recounted Hoch's experience in a 1995 guest role on the show, in which he refused Seinfeld's requests to play a pool boy as a heavily accented Latino.

Before being cast on *Seinfeld,* Hoch did a stage show in which he told the history of his Brooklyn neighborhood. He played ethnic characters with accents — Cuban, Jamaican, Trinidadian. (His ancestors, however, were Jewish.) He'd long resisted sitcom work, but he figured an appearance could bring audiences to his one-man show. But when he received the script for "The Pool Guy," he worried about how it might go. According to his account, he called and asked one of the producers, "This isn't your stereotypically Spanish-speaking pool guy, is it?" He was assured the character could be "whoever you want it to be."

When Hoch got to the table read on set, he did his lines as a "higher strung" version of himself. Afterward, at rehearsal, he found himself alone with Alexander, Louis-Dreyfus, Richards, Seinfeld, and director Andy Ackerman. Ackerman or Seinfeld asked him to do the part in a Spanish accent. He refused. "The role is stupid and it's a clown and I have no problem doing it and it's funny," Hoch said. "But I can't do the Spanish accent because it's one-dimensional. Why does it have to be in Spanish? Why can't it be Israeli?"

Seinfeld answered, "Because it's funnier that way." After talking to David on the phone for about ten minutes, Seinfeld returned. "It's just a half-hour comedy show," he pressed. "What's the big deal?"

"It's a big deal to me because there's too many friends of mine who are highly trained actors that are Cuban and Puerto Rican and Dominican," Hoch said. "All they get asked to do are one-dimensional roles, and here I am, not even Latino, and you're asking me to play a clown, and I can't." Alexander and Louis-Dreyfus supported him, he said, encouraging him to follow his instincts.

Richards warned him that he'd be replaced if he didn't go with the direction.

When Hoch returned to his Los Angeles hotel that night, he got a message from the production office: They'd find someone else. He flew home and was never paid for his work on the show. They got a different, white actor to play the role instead, with no accent.

The incident made its way into Hoch's next show, and he began telling the story to audiences throughout the country. This served as part of the inspiration for a story line on a ninth-season episode in which Sally Weaver (played by Kathy Griffin) becomes famous when she builds a one-woman show around calling Jerry "the devil."

That plot wasn't just based on Hoch's rant, though. It also mixed in an incident from Griffin's own life. She had previously appeared on *Seinfeld* in the seventh season as Susan's old roommate. She asks Jerry to deliver a doormat as an engagement gift to George and Susan. While filming the episode, Griffin, a stand-up, wanted to get Seinfeld's autograph for a party she was attending that night at a friend's house to watch the Golden Globes. But when she approached him to ask, he was in the middle of telling director Andy Ackerman all the things he still wanted to change about that week's script. As Seinfeld got more worked up, Griffin realized she'd picked the worst possible moment — but was now stuck a few feet away, holding a pen and paper. Finally, he turned to her and snapped, "You had a question?"

She stammered, "Oh, yes, Jerry, glad to be on the show. My friend Dennis is having a Golden Globes party tonight, and I thought it would be really great since you're nominated for a Golden Globe, if you could write a little note to the party, like, 'Dear Dennis's party, Vote for me, Jerry Seinfeld!' "

"What?" She could feel herself flush at his confusion. "I'm going to the Golden Globes, I'll just see you at the party."

She explained that, no, she'd be at someone's private home, as she was not invited to the ceremony, but she thought it would be fun if . . .

"That's about the last thing I have time for right now," he said before he walked away.

The script girl cast a sympathetic eye at Griffin. "He's cranky," she explained.

After about an hour of work, Seinfeld was leaving to get ready for the Globes. As the crew wished him good luck, he turned to

Griffin. "And you. You wanted me to sign something?" He did it this time, and Griffin was the hit of her party.

Griffin could tell Seinfeld tried to be extra-friendly to her the next day, acknowledging on some level that he'd been testy. Still, like Hoch, she told the entire story as part of her act, which became her first stand-up special on HBO the following year. She was cast in NBC's new Brooke Shields sitcom *Suddenly Susan* soon afterward. Then she heard that Seinfeld had seen her bit. Could he somehow get her fired? Didn't he rule that network now? Soon, Griffin's agent called her and said, "Jerry Seinfeld is sending you something."

Terrified, she waited for the package, sure it would be a box of excrement, if not a letter of termination. When it arrived, it was a box of SnackWell's cookies — a low-calorie treat once consumed on *Seinfeld* — with a note. "I was, up until your recent monologue on some obscure cable channel, unaware that you had ever appeared on my number-one hit television series that is named after me," Seinfeld wrote. "I nonetheless very much enjoyed your little skit. . . . Enclosed please find a box of SnackWell's for you to enjoy with my compliments."

He had even been having a tape of her stand-up played during the audience warm-ups on *Seinfeld*'s studio-audience nights. A year later, Seinfeld invited her back on the show to play some strange amalgam of Sally Weaver, Danny Hoch, and herself.

Despite the criticism *Seinfeld* weathered at its heights, it also won accolades, particularly for its treatment of gay issues. The fourth-season episode "The Outing," in which George and Jerry try to persuade a college newspaper reporter who overhears a misleading conversation that they're not gay, won an award from the Gay and Lesbian Alliance Against Defamation. David and Seinfeld almost abandoned an earlier version of Larry Charles's script for the episode due to fears of offending the gay community, but during the discussion, Charles uttered what would become one of the show's stickiest catchphrases — "not that there's anything wrong with that." Once David and Seinfeld asked him to put that in as a recurring joke, it became a satire of homophobia, skewering straight, liberal men's desire to emphasize their heterosexuality while maintaining their image as enlightened beings. It was a perfect depiction of '90s political correctness.

This came at a time when gay characters were never main characters, and were mostly relegated to quirky, cult shows (*Northern Exposure*), cable (*Dream On*), soap operas (*One Life to Live*), reality shows (*The Real World*), silly dramas (*Melrose Place*), and teen shows (*My So-Called Life*). They were on the sidelines of the sidelines, and almost always treated with deadly seriousness. They were either a "very special episode" topic or, on the vast majority of shows, ignored. Bringing a gay discussion into the mainstream with humor constituted a major breakthrough.

Later that same season, *Seinfeld* casually brought another gay discussion into an episode: George ran into Susan, then his ex, at the video store and discovered that she was dating a woman. Peter Mehlman, who cowrote that episode — in which George praises Susan for her "hip" choice and frets that he's driven her to lesbianism — didn't feel like the show deserved a GLAAD award for such things. But he was proud to be on a show that took on issue after issue; he loved to argue that *Seinfeld,* of all shows, was hardly a "show about nothing." It was, in fact, among the few comedies that were about *something.*

■ ■ ■ ■

As *Seinfeld* reached new heights of popularity, David didn't feel the same way about it that Seinfeld did — it wasn't David's "primary relationship." David married his talent manager, Laurie Lennard, on the spur of the moment during a trip to Las Vegas in March 1993. Soon, the couple was expecting their first child, and they moved into a new house in Malibu that had narrowly escaped destruction by a brush fire the day before. There was no denying it anymore: David couldn't claim to be his former sadsack, unlucky self.

But that didn't mean he wanted to continue dedicating so much time and energy to *Seinfeld.* The whole thing was exhausting. He'd gone grayer and balder in the time the show had been on the air, which led him to choose a more neatly trimmed hairstyle, with rampant sideburns the only hint of his former wild look. Meanwhile, the script schedule fell further and further behind as each season progressed. The set construction crews and extras made massive overtime pay for rush jobs and last-minute rehearsals. Often rehearsals and rewrites took up weekends. "People won a lot of acclaim and a lot of awards for Larry's work," writer Alec Berg said of the scores of scripts credited to staffers but heavily revised by David. "That's the job of executive producer." David, however, wasn't sure how much longer he could handle that job.

The cast and crew were supposed to have the script on Tuesday to start work on Wednesday. But more often than not, they'd get it on Friday, come in on Saturday to rehearse and shoot the show on Tuesday, only to start all over again the very next day. Production designer Tom Azzari and director Tom Cherones would show up in David and Seinfeld's office on Fridays to say, "We start Monday, boys, and we don't have a set. Can you tell us what we might have so we can build it?" David and Seinfeld would make their best guesses, the crew would build over the weekend, and sometimes it would get used, sometimes it wouldn't. If it didn't, it would go in the warehouse where they kept all of their extra set pieces, never knowing what weirdness might pop up on this show next.

Things began to change on the *Seinfeld* set. The change started with the departure of director Tom Cherones in the sixth season. Seinfeld wanted to switch things up in the director's chair just as they did yearly with the writing staff. In fact, Cherones was surprised he'd lasted so long.

Thanks to *Seinfeld*'s success, he had no trouble finding work. He went on to direct a season of *Ellen,* several episodes of *Caroline in the City,* and four seasons of *NewsRadio.*

Larry David had met Andy Ackerman while helping out with a Fox pilot called *Sammy and Friends* that David's wife, Laurie, produced. The pilot production took a lot of work — recasting, rewriting. Even down to the last night of the shoot, Ackerman and David were rewriting while filming until 3:00 A.M. Ackerman was a huge fan of Larry David and *Seinfeld,* and as they parted ways that early morning, Ackerman figured it couldn't hurt to throw out what he saw as a joking offer: "If you ever need any help on that other little show of yours, give me a call."

Three weeks later, Ackerman got a call at home from David. "You sound like you're interested in doing the show," David said. "I want you to meet Jerry and talk about this."

Ackerman scheduled the meeting, then hung up and screamed to his wife, Betsy, "You won't believe who just called!"

Ackerman met David and Seinfeld at a diner for breakfast. Finally, Ackerman asked, "What are you saying? Is this real?"

"Yeah," Seinfeld said, "we'd like you to do the show."

Ackerman took over directing for the eighty-sixth episode of *Seinfeld,* in which Kramer mentors a beauty-pageant contestant. On his first day, Ackerman sat down to conduct the table read, opened the script, and felt a shock of panic. He managed to look calm, maybe even bored, from the outside. But he realized what an important moment it was in his career.

Soon the cast started reading, and because they required little direction by now, he calmed down. He saw how professional everyone was on *Seinfeld,* unlike shows he'd worked on in the past, like *Cheers* and *Wings,* where everyone always goofed around. At *Seinfeld,* he never had to wait for anyone to get their head in the game, or to get to the set on time. He was in heaven, working with actors who wanted to rehearse. He didn't have to grab people away from the foosball table and summon them to where they were supposed to be, like he had on other shows.

Ackerman had worried about fitting in, but he found his comfort zone. The actors welcomed him. David challenged him. When Ackerman fell into "sitcommy" staging, he said, David would say, "I feel like I've seen that before." Ackerman appreciated the fresh perspective David and Seinfeld brought to sitcoms.

He felt like David and Seinfeld had no idea of the effect they now had on culture; they were too focused on just getting through each week. He told them how great the show was, and they said, with seeming sincerity, "Really?"

Then things *really* changed when Larry David decided to leave the show in 1996, before the eighth season began.

David had worried since 1990 that the show had no more stories left in it. Every year, around the thirteenth or fourteenth episode of the season, halfway through, David told Seinfeld he wasn't sure he wanted to return for another year. Every year, Seinfeld talked David into staying. This year, however, David was ready to do something, anything, else. And he didn't need the show, financially. He hoped that everyone else who worked on the show would feel the same way, but it turned out he was the only one. He remained friendly with Seinfeld and the cast and crew, however, even as he announced his departure.

David's final episode reflected his sensibility like few others: His last script was the one in which he killed George's fiancée, Susan, with no remorse. His final scene has the four main characters stifling their relief in reaction to the doctor's sad news. Andy Ackerman and Jason Alexander would have to figure out how to inject the episode with just enough pathos to sell it to America — and return the following fall to make more comedy. They tried several takes to get it just right. Alexander struggled. He huddled with Ackerman and David to talk it through.

Finally, Alexander just put in take after take to play every level possible. One fell in the right spot, with enough feeling to go over in America's living rooms but not violate David's sacred edict against hugging and learning. Not every viewer would love the episode, but most of America would continue watching the show.

Larry David had done 134 episodes. Seinfeld was sure that on some level, David hadn't wanted to do any more than the pilot. Seinfeld announced to the writers, cast, and crew that David wouldn't return, but the show would. The actors worried about continuing without David's guidance,

Alexander in particular, since his character was based on David. But they also had faith in Seinfeld, and knew he wouldn't continue if he didn't think the show could maintain quality.

David had taught Seinfeld, through example, how to run a show, and he had taught the writers everything they needed to know. When a writer's name was on a script, he or she got to participate in casting, shooting, editing, and sound mixing, a unique experience for sitcom writers. (On other shows, they just wrote, period.) Now that experience would be put to good use.

David planned to write a film script now that he was free of *Seinfeld*. He sat in his office on the Castle Rock lot, trying to write, alone, and panicked: He had done the wrong thing. He missed his friends. He thought about everyone at *Seinfeld* getting ready to do the first episode of the new season. What had he done? Why wasn't he with his friends? Why was he such an idiot? How could he have left the biggest show in the country to write this stupid script? What was he, nuts?

He grew depressed. They were filming now, he knew it. They were doing it without him. How could they do that? How dare they do that?

Eventually, he got through it.

But he did return several times that year to voice Steinbrenner. Even so, he didn't feel like he belonged there anymore. For the first time, David did Steinbrenner lines that he hadn't written. Driving through the gate to the studio, he'd have to give his name to the guards, and they'd have to call out to the office to ask if he was allowed on the set. *Don't you understand?* he thought. *See that show? I created that thing!* Years later, when writer-producer Aaron Sorkin left the show he created, *The West Wing,* David advised him never to watch his own show after leaving. "Either it's going to be wonderful and you'll be miserable," David told him, "or it won't be wonderful and you'll still be miserable." Sorkin took his advice.

With the start of the eighth season, Seinfeld became head writer and executive producer, the double title previously held by David. Seinfeld was the only one who could take over David's roles. For the next season, he would have even more control than he had before: He would be a lead actor, executive producer, and the head of the writing staff. *Seinfeld* was now an autocracy — an autocracy Seinfeld needed a lot of help to run, though, and the writers would have to step up like never before . . . or run the show they loved into the ground.

10
THE LARRY DAVID–SHAPED HOLE

The TV writing team of Alec Berg and Jeff Schaffer had paid a fair amount of dues. They had worked on a failed sitcom starring Tobey Maguire called *Great Scott!*, a comedy version of *Hard Copy* called *Exposé,* and a sitcom starring Jeff Garlin called *My Kind of Town* that its producers sold as "*Seinfeld* with a gun."

Luckily, their bosses at *Great Scott!* were now on staff at the real *Seinfeld.* Tom Gammill and Max Pross encouraged them to submit some ideas during *Seinfeld*'s seventh season — when David was still there — but the exercise felt "like sending a letter to Santa," Schaffer said. "You don't think anything's going to happen." Just as they were about to move to New York to work on Conan O'Brien's new late-night show, they got a call from Gammill and Pross asking them to come in and pitch in person. They canceled their moving van, which had been scheduled for that very day, and went to the meeting.

They found Gammill and Pross on the lot around the corner from the *Seinfeld* office, sitting on the front porch of the *thirtysomething* house. It was a three-story, Craftsman-style home set where the show had shot its exterior scenes. To its left was another house set from *thirtysomething.* Nearby were a tower from *Falcon Crest* and a graveyard from several John Wayne films. They sat on the porch smoking cigars, as they often did when they were brainstorming. Between puffs, Gammill and Pross told Berg and Schaffer to go meet with David and Seinfeld in their office.

In the meeting, Berg and Schaffer found themselves inadvertently spending a lot of time complaining about working for *My Kind of Town.* How could those guys even *think* that dumb show was anything like *Seinfeld*? It was embarrassing! They realized how horrible it was to spend an interview complaining about their jobs, but they couldn't stop themselves. And David had his own version of this, which was to complain that he had no idea how to run such meetings, even though he'd now been in charge of a major television show for some time. They made a good match.

Berg and Schaffer were hired. They took a pay cut compared with their O'Brien deal, but they felt it was worth it. In fact, during their first season at *Seinfeld,* when they turned a script around extra-fast on a tight deadline, David and Seinfeld handed them a check, a bonus for stepping up. They would become part of a second wave of writers hired near the end of David's time on the show who would find themselves pitching in way more than they'd initially expected — essentially, helping Seinfeld to fill the void now left where the Wizard of Seinfeldia once pulled all those levers behind the curtain.

Seinfeld couldn't have been more different from Berg and Schaffer's previous experience with traditional sitcoms. At *Seinfeld,* they learned that what they thought was the whole script for an episode was only the first act. David and Seinfeld kept compressing their ideas down, over and over, to pack ever more into their twenty-two minutes. And then once they turned their scripts in, they'd watch the pages go into David and Seinfeld's office, behind closed doors. Five or so at a time, over minutes or hours, the pages came out with David's changes and notes scrawled on them, handed to the writers' assistants, who were sitting just outside the office waiting to retype the pages.

Berg and Schaffer, or whichever writers were responsible for the script that week, paced outside to glimpse the pages of notes. If they saw few changes, few enough to go to the table read with basically what they'd written, they knew they'd nailed it. For Berg and Schaffer, their first score was "The Label Maker," a 1995 episode in which dentist Tim Whatley regifts to Jerry a label maker Elaine gave him. They believed, for the first time, that they might survive at *Seinfeld* when Jason Alexander said to them, "I heard you guys really hit it out of the park." Then, a few minutes later, they started panicking about their next episode. Would they ever be as good again?

When David left, their lives changed drastically. David had been the guy who'd step in to fill a void if an episode fell through. David had worked all hours, all days, while the writers at least had their weekends. With David gone, there was simply a large black hole where he'd been, sucking everything into its orbit.

Everyone would have to deliver now, all the time.

The comic book character Bizarro first appeared as a "supervillain," a mirror image of Superman who is pure evil, in 1958. He meant the opposite of everything he said and had powers opposite of Superman's (freeze vision instead of heat vision, flame breath instead of freeze breath). The comic strip's author, Alvin Schwartz, said: "I was certainly inspired to some degree by C. G. Jung's archetype of 'the shadow' — and Bizarro reflected that." By 1961, the character proved popular enough to get his own fifteen-issue comic-book run, *Bizarro World;* he would appear in other Superman-related comics, in various forms, in the following decades.

"Bizarro World," or Htrae — "Earth" spelled backward — was a cube-shaped planet that served as home to Bizarro and his posse. There was a Bizarro Lois Lane, with whom Bizarro had Bizarro children. The Bizarro Code commanded: "Us do opposite of all earthly things! Us hate beauty! Us love ugliness! Is big crime to make anything perfect on Bizarro World!" (The Bizarros tended to speak like Frankenstein.) A Bizarro bond trader did well with this pitch: "Guaranteed to lose money for you."

When twenty-five-year-old Dave Mandel joined the *Seinfeld* staff in 1995, overlapping for one year with David, he got to use his comic-book fanaticism for good, delving into the Bizarro concept from Superman for one of his most memorable scripts. In "The Bizarro Jerry," Elaine befriends three guys who are "the opposite" of Jerry, George, and Kramer. They are polite, cultured, and considerate. Though the show had dabbled in self-reference before, this plotline relied completely on the audience's knowledge of the main characters; it directly commented on the show, even pointing out the characters' worst qualities. Mandel liked the idea of seeing *Seinfeld*'s characters from the outside via their Bizarro doubles' perspective: What would other New Yorkers think of them? The answer: They would not think highly of our "heroes." It was the first time the show acknowledged the massive flaws of its main characters.

Once Mandel had written the episode, it seemed remarkable that this concept hadn't come up earlier in *Seinfeld*'s run. Seinfeld loved Superman, and the show had a knack for creating alternate versions of real-life people — Kramer, Joe Davola, the Soup Nazi, J. Peterman. One could see these as exaggerated — and in several cases, evil — versions of their earthly counterparts. Seinfeldia, the place where *Seinfeld*'s reality and fiction mix and mingle and allow its fans to interact with it, is *Seinfeld*'s Bizarro World, *Seinfeld*'s Htrae.

If nothing else, the Bizarro plotline on *Seinfeld* proved Mandel had found the show where he truly belonged.

When Mandel first got an offer to join *Seinfeld*'s writing staff in its seventh season, he didn't have a place to live in Los Angeles, and he didn't know how to drive, having spent most of his life in New York City. Coming west meant leaving a job as head writer at *Saturday Night Live* — where he had worked his way up the ranks for the previous three years — and Becky, the woman who had been the love of his life since he met her seven years before. A chance to join *Seinfeld,* however, was worth all of this to him.

He found a Los Angeles driving school to give him lessons on his way to the *Seinfeld* lot and a house from which he could drive to and from work without ever getting on the freeway. And then he dug into his new role.

When he got to write the "Bizarro Jerry" episode, it all paid off. He got to incorporate his love of comic books into a script. He got to write Becky into the episode. Becky had grown up on a farm in Maine and always hated her hands. In the episode, Jerry dates a woman who has "man hands." This was a *Seinfeld* writer's version of a love poem, a grand gesture. In 2007, Dave and Becky were married.

The new wave of writers stepping up as David exited in season seven also included *Saturday Night Live* veteran Steve Koren, a friend of Mandel's. Koren's New York sensibility would be a huge help on the show, Mandel told him, suggesting he submit some story ideas from New York City while still at *Saturday Night Live*. Koren loved *Seinfeld*'s approach to making the smallest things funny. Next thing Koren knew, he got an offer to join the staff of the No. 1 comedy in the country, just after being promoted to head writer at *Saturday Night Live*. He was coming off the best year of his career so far, getting several sketches onto *SNL* in any given week. His last show, with guest host Jim Carrey, had contained three of his pieces, a huge deal for a writer who started out doing one-line jokes for the fake news segment, "Weekend Update." What the hell was he going to do? It was difficult, but obvious: He could keep doing what he was doing, or he could learn something new. Of course he would join *Seinfeld*, and start from the bottom.

Over the summer, Koren moved to Los Angeles — something he'd always said he'd do only for *Seinfeld* or *The Larry Sanders Show* — and studied up on *Seinfeld.* He'd watched, of course, but he hadn't caught every episode because he was so busy with *SNL.* Seinfeld put him up in a temporary apartment, and the show staff sent over tapes of every episode so far in the seven seasons on air. He knew they liked his story ideas — that was how he'd gotten the job — but he needed to learn how to execute them, how to weave them into the complicated structure that *Seinfeld* had invented.

Once he met the team, he felt more at ease. Veteran Peter Mehlman helped him learn the ropes, as did Schaffer and Berg and, of course, his old friend Dave Mandel. If he pitched what sounded like a good idea, often they'd say, "Oh, here's what you can do with this." Even so, Koren was terrified: As a man of modest means, with no family money or savings to fall back on, he'd been in a state of panic since he began his career as a television writer. His panic was acute now that he was away from New York and in TV's most intense sink-or-swim environment. He knew that in comedy writing, the elation of getting a job is quickly replaced by a sinking feeling: *I'm going to lose this job if I can't deliver.*

The difference between *Saturday Night Live* and *Seinfeld* became clear to Koren: *SNL* was a hundred-yard dash, and *Seinfeld* was a marathon. A marathon every week. At *SNL,* about a quarter of the sketches pitched might get onto a show; but at *Seinfeld,* as Koren learned, "If it ain't working, your episode is not going to happen."

Soon every tiny incident in his life became story fodder. He left the show office to buy candy at a nearby convenience store, and as he surveyed the offerings, a beautiful woman approached him, saying, "Mike! Mike!" She walked right up to a befuddled Steve Koren until she was about two feet away. "Oh, I'm so sorry," she said. "You're not my boyfriend."

When Koren returned to the office, he told the story to the other guys. "I can't believe that a guy who looks like me somehow managed to get that girl," he said. Boom: George story.

Dan O'Keefe joined the team around this time as well. He was a freelancer and didn't have to come on site, but he hung around the offices anyway and eventually wrote the 150th episode, "The Pothole." In his late twenties, he couldn't believe his luck, getting hired onto the best show in television. He'd watched the show since he graduated from college, in 1990. After that, he'd gotten a job as an editor of the *National Lampoon,* but when the entire staff got fired, he thought better of his print media plans. Though he hadn't been allowed to watch television growing up, he knew people at the Letterman show who did pretty well, so he looked for TV jobs in Los Angeles.

Once transplanted from the East Coast, he worked for *The Tonight Show with Jay Leno* and *Married with Children.* His girlfriend had stayed back in New York for a while, but decided to join O'Keefe in L.A. A week after they moved in together, *Married* got a new showrunner, which meant the staff was cleaned out so she could bring in her own writers. He was out of a job. He tried to get another TV gig, but came up empty-handed. He thought, *Maybe law school?* He was reluctantly looking into taking the GREs when he managed to beg his way, through friends, into a chance to send some story ideas in to *Seinfeld.* He spent six months going to Kinko's daily, faxing in his ten pages of ideas, five ideas per page. Soon he was allowed to at least hang out at the offices, if not write his own entire episode yet.

He would pitch to no less than Jerry Seinfeld, who scared the shit out of him. Seinfeld was friendly, but he was the gold standard of comedy. Seinfeld pitched his own jokes to the writers' room in addition to presiding over it. If O'Keefe managed to get Seinfeld to laugh at something he'd said that day, he'd go home and tell his girlfriend about it.

He didn't have a steady paycheck just yet, but he was living on laughs from Jerry Seinfeld.

Peter Mehlman was inching close to the end of his rope on *Seinfeld* after working there for four years. At this point, only Seinfeld himself had logged more time in the writers' office than Mehlman had. He'd outlasted wave after wave of new writers while he turned in some of the show's most distinctive scripts. Now he was surrounded by a bunch of Harvard boys in their twenties. At forty, he felt ancient.

Around this time, he wrote a whole script about how people who went to Harvard always manage to drop that fact into conversation within five minutes of meeting you. He liked the boys, he really did. He thought

Dave Mandel, in particular, was brilliant. The script had nothing to do with them personally. But Seinfeld didn't get it, so it didn't matter anyway. It never got made.

He did write an episode called "The Yada Yada," though, and suddenly everyone was saying "yada yada." He hadn't invented the phrase "yada yada" — an editor had said it to him once at a meeting — but he did invent a term in the episode, "anti-dentite," which described Jerry's feelings toward his dentist, Tim Whatley, whom he suspected had converted to Judaism just so he could do Jewish jokes. Mehlman thought "anti-dentite" should have caught on as much as "yada yada," but it didn't.

He did still love *Seinfeld*'s instant ability to affect culture. One day you were writing something that just made you laugh, and the next day the nation was saying it over and over. That never got old.

"The Yada Yada" got Mehlman an Emmy nomination. That was good news. He was tired of the show not winning Emmys. He was tired of not winning Emmys.

Everyone, including his "Yada Yada" co-writer Jill Franklyn, told him that *Ellen*'s "Puppy Episode," in which that show's main character comes out of the closet to represent its star, Ellen DeGeneres, also coming out of the closet, would be tough competition, given its newsworthy implications. Even before the nominations were announced, Franklyn and Mehlman fretted over the threat of "The Puppy Episode." Mehlman theorized that "The Puppy Episode" would be in a different category, because it was an hour long. He was wrong.

Mehlman was so set on winning an Emmy, he couldn't help but talk about it as Emmy night approached, he later told me. He confessed to Julia Louis-Dreyfus, as they chatted over the food on the craft services table, how much he wanted to win. "Of course," she said. "If you didn't, you'd be an idiot." Louis-Dreyfus knew; she had only just won her first Emmy the previous year on her fifth nomination.

On the way to the 1997 Emmy ceremony, Mehlman's limo got lost, speeding fifteen miles in the opposite direction from the Pasadena Civic Auditorium before it turned around. When he arrived, he realized he'd forgotten his Emmy tickets. He talked his way in anyway, and rushed to take his seat next to Franklyn, who sat next to Martha Stewart, who was reading a book and eating a plum.

Early in the evening, Franklyn and Mehlman's category was announced to the television audience of 18.8 million people. They lost to *Ellen*'s "Puppy Episode." Mehlman slumped in his seat as he imagined his friends at his funeral saying, "He was never the same after losing that Emmy."

Other things annoyed him, too. Like the fact that *Seinfeld,* after it won an Outstanding Comedy Series Emmy in 1993, kept losing to *Frasier.* When did *Frasier* ever have an episode worth remembering, worth talking about even the very next day? By 1997, when "The Yada Yada" lost, Mehlman had had enough. "It's like we lost to Ellen coming out of the closet," he cracked to a reporter, "and we lost to Frasier never coming out of the closet." What was the point of being on a show like *Seinfeld* if you didn't say stuff that was completely offensive?

In the summer of 1997, Carol Leifer had left *Seinfeld* to create and star in her own show on the WB, nearly a decade before Tina Fey would usher in a wave of female creator-stars in sitcoms. Leifer was a pioneer, and she felt the weight of it. Jerry Seinfeld came to her pilot taping to show his support. As she neared a nervous meltdown while preparing to shoot, imagining dire consequences to her career should this project fail, her old friend visited her backstage. "Carol," he said, "there's not just one thing."

She took a breath. He was right. Having your own show *seemed* like the big break, the only thing that mattered. But that was only in the moment. If it didn't work, other things would come along. Both of them knew that the heights of creativity and total enjoyment didn't always come together, especially once agents and networks were involved.

Seinfeld was one of what she called her "go-to Yodas," along with Jay Leno. He was sage. He was right. There was not just one thing. And if anyone knew about fluke second, third, and fourth chances, it was the man who cocreated *Seinfeld.*

Many people who would go on to bigger fame had also passed through the guest-star revolving door at *Seinfeld,* no small number of them as Jerry's endless parade of beautiful girlfriends. Teri Hatcher, of "they're real, and they're spectacular," was now a full-fledged geek-boy crush as the female half of *Lois & Clark.* (Surely, *Superman* fan Jerry would be among her admirers.) Bryan Cranston — aka Jerry's dentist, Dr. Tim Whatley — had appeared in *Saving Private Ryan.* Jon Favreau, who played a clown who argued with George at a party, had starred in *Swingers, Very Bad Things,* and *Deep Impact.* Jerry's "loser" girlfriend, Christine Taylor, appeared in *The Wedding Singer* and on *Friends.* Courteney Cox — another Jerry paramour, the one who pretended to be his wife for a dry-cleaning discount — was now famous as one of the *Friends. Seinfeld* had become a star maker.

The next generation of writers flowing into the *Seinfeld* offices were hoping for similarly big breaks, too.

Jennifer Crittenden arrived in 1996, at the beginning of *Seinfeld*'s eighth season, from two years at *The Simpsons,* to take up where Carol Leifer had left off in the female-writer role. The twenty-seven-year-old wasn't fazed by being so outnumbered by guys — that was the norm in comedy rooms, including at *The Simpsons* and at *Letterman,* where she had her first job. She didn't feel like she was treated differently by the other writers, and they didn't expect her to write only for Elaine. By now, she felt at home among the supersmart, funny Harvard types who populated such shows' writing offices.

She did feel a little self-conscious of her gender when, after every episode taping, the writers would all go back to Seinfeld's office to smoke cigars before heading out to

Jerry's Famous Deli together. The smell of cigars made her sick. She tried to smoke once but couldn't stand it. Skipping out on a smoke was the kind of thing a guy could get away with without a second thought, whereas she worried it made her look a little "girly." The guys also sometimes asked her to write their brainstorming notes on the whiteboard because she had the nicest handwriting.

What really amazed her, though, was how fast things moved at *Seinfeld* in comparison with *The Simpsons*. Because *The Simpsons* was animated, and animated shows had much longer production cycles than sit-coms, the staff there could go over and over the scripts, comb through details, do endless rewrites. At *Seinfeld,* she kept thinking, "When are we going to go over this?" The next thing she knew, a show had gone from the whiteboard in the office to the air. It made her nervous, even though everyone seemed on top of things. Even Seinfeld seemed calm, despite his total responsibility.

Spike Feresten came to *Seinfeld* in this later wave of writers, fresh off five years at *Letterman.* He'd left the New York–based talk show because he wanted to be in Los Angeles, where most TV action took place.

He hadn't watched much *Seinfeld* because he worked late on Thursdays. But he had a chance to pitch *Seinfeld,* so he bought a paperback of Seinfeld's book, *SeinLanguage,* to get the comedy rhythms down, then pitched to Larry David in 1995, during the show's seventh season, at David's house.

When Feresten got the job and got to the lot, he was shocked to see how small the operation was: The writers' offices were just a tiny cottage among the studio buildings. Letterman had fourteen stories on Broadway.

Though the size didn't impress him, Feresten was intimidated because of his lack of experience writing half-hour comedies. When Seinfeld asked him, "Why do you want to work on this show?" he was astonished that the question could be asked with such earnestness.

"You guys don't know what you are to the world yet?" Feresten said. "This show is a revelation!" Like Ackerman, Feresten felt like David and Seinfeld didn't realize what a phenomenon their creation had become.

Feresten was relieved to learn that what *Seinfeld* needed most from its writers was real-life experiences that would make good story lines. They should pitch odd little things that had happened to them, and let the characters perform what they had *wanted* to do in the situation, but, most likely, hadn't. Feresten loved to go out, walk around, experience things, and write them in his notebook.

He had plenty of experiences stored up from his New York life as well, which was a hot commodity at *Seinfeld* because many of the writers had been away from the city for years at this point. He'd lived with a girl-friend who had asked if her friend, the wig master from *Joseph and the Amazing Technicolor Dreamcoat,* could stay with them. There was an episode. (If you don't see the humor inherent in that situation, you haven't lived in a cramped New York apart-ment with the wig master from *Joseph and the Amazing Technicolor Dreamcoat.*) Fe-resten had parked his Jeep in a cheap Up-per West Side garage and found used con-doms in the backseat when he went to pick it up. Episode. He found out that Holocaust survivors got priority when it came to secur-ing tennis court time. Episode, with some changes: Survivors of the shipwrecked *An-drea Doria* would get dibs on apartments. *Seinfeld* wasn't quite ready to poke fun at Holocaust survivors.

To get those fresh New York stories without spending years working for *Letterman,* the writers took two field trips east during the show's final two seasons to stay at the Four Seasons in Manhattan for a week or so and walk around the city for a few hours each day, taking notes.

Feresten famously wrote the episode "The Soup Nazi," but he also wrote the memorable episode "The Muffin Tops." For the week the episode was shooting, he had originally written a script based on the fact that back in New York, he used to have a police scanner in his apartment; tuned to the right frequency, he could hear his neighbors' conversations on their cordless phones. He and his friends would kick back with margaritas and listen. It seemed an obvious story line for Kramer. But on Tuesday, the night before the table read for that script, *Frasier* did the same story line. The writers came in Wednesday morning in a panic: They had to think of a new idea.

As everyone pitched, Feresten remembered that he once had a girlfriend who would only eat the tops of muffins — that became Elaine's story, and eventual attempt at a business. ("Top o' the muffin to you!")

One of the writers also mentioned the bus tours of New York City now being led by

Kenny Kramer, Larry David's old neighbor. If Kenny was going to profit from Kramer's Reality Tour, *Seinfeld* could certainly use that as a Kramer story to weave into the "Muffin Tops" episode. They began with the raw material they mined from Kenny Kramer's tour and passed it through their Bizarro transformer: "That was one of the certain joys of that show," writer Alec Berg said. "When the show started interacting with the world, we'd start interacting with that interaction."

Berg and his partner, Jeff Schaffer, had also heard about a comedian buying a friend's story to tell as if it were an anecdote from his own life when he was going on a talk show. The resulting *Seinfeld* plot: Elaine's eccentric catalog-magnate boss, J. Peterman, had been outed in a recent episode as quite a bit more boring than his persona would imply. He purchased stories from Kramer to use as his own in his autobiography. In "The Muffin Tops," when the book came out, Kramer would capitalize on this by offering his own (ultimately doomed) "Peterman Reality Tour" of sites from his own stories, as co-opted by Peterman. In the end, though, he'd have to use the tour bus to transport muffin stumps to the dump for Elaine.

Stealing from real life had made *Seinfeld* magic again.

Former *Seinfeld* writer Andy Robin — still recovering from his disappointment over "The Junior Mint" script — now wrote for *The Martin Short Show,* a *Seinfeld/Larry Sanders Show* hybrid in which Martin Short played a talk show host named Marty Short. But Robin still wasn't happy. He considered applying to med school and making a clean break from this career altogether. But then he started thinking: Maybe he had gone about this TV writing thing all wrong.

First, he noticed that many comedy writers had partners, which seemed to make the process a lot more fun. So he got in touch with his college friend Gregg Kavet, who worked at a consulting firm in Boston.

The two had written together a lot at the *Harvard Lampoon,* though Kavet had abandoned writing for a quieter office life while Robin went off to New York for *Saturday Night Live.* Kavet didn't think he could handle the pressure of having to be funny all the time. But Robin called to talk his old college dorm-mate back into comedy: "We wrote together really well in college, and it seems that teams work better than an individual out here. I've got all these great contacts, and before I leave and they're gone, we should try to pitch something."

Seinfeld was, as it happened, the only show Kavet watched regularly. He couldn't pass this opportunity up. He agreed to help his old friend remotely. They'd work on ideas over the phone; Robin would pitch them to David and Seinfeld; and Kavet would fly out for casting and shooting their scripts.

Robin also realized he had rejected his own ideas too quickly when he last worked on *Seinfeld.* Maybe if he brainstormed them out a little bit more with Kavet, he could give them some shape and gain some confidence before they pitched them.

Robin called Seinfeld and asked if he could come back to pitch. *The Martin Short Show* was on the same lot anyway. Soon he was back at *Seinfeld* for good, this time with Kavet along. Kavet came in handy for *Seinfeld,* not just because he was funny — but also because he'd been working in an office until very recently, which gave him story ideas for George's and Elaine's work lives. George's desire to nap under his desk, for instance, came from one of Kavet's former coworkers.

Kavet and Robin's first episode together

was one of Robin's favorites, "The Jimmy," in which Elaine agrees to go on a date with a guy who talks about himself in the third person; she thinks he's setting her up with someone else.

Perhaps it was because Robin had matured a few years and found his groove with TV writing, but he found that working for just Jerry, with no Larry David around, was less scary. When David was there, Robin never knew how much his script would be changed during the rewrite. On one hand, he hoped David and Seinfeld would like his work and not change a thing, but on the other hand, he hoped they would fix his mistakes.

Seinfeld, however, was harder to pitch to. With David, all you had to do was catch him in a good mood and give a decent performance. Seinfeld was tougher to find in a calm enough moment for a pitch, and even harder to keep interested for very long. He was always distracted by the million parts of his job — writing, memorizing lines, producing the entire show. Once you nailed it with Seinfeld, however, the resulting script tended to be smooth sailing.

Making Seinfeld laugh became the primary goal of the young writers' lives. They would have been thrilled to get a Seinfeld laugh at any time in their lives, but now, with him as the sole voice of authority on which scripts were made, it became crucial. Dan O'Keefe once made Seinfeld double over cracking up at one of his pitches and counted the moment among his life's greatest achievements. He told a story about a hippie chick he'd dated who liked to burn a vanilla candle whenever they had sex, which made him hungry — this became "The Blood," in which George tries to talk a girlfriend into letting him eat a pastrami sandwich as part of sex. But the line that got Seinfeld was George telling his girlfriend during sex that he had to go because he had a bus transfer that was good for only another hour, when, really, he wanted to go eat.

For O'Keefe, this was his peak, at age twenty-eight. He was sure of it. Even the birth of his first child would not rival the moment Jerry Seinfeld doubled over during his pitch.

Steve Koren once pitched a long list of ideas to Seinfeld and the other writers, really selling them. Seinfeld laughed and laughed. At the end, he chuckled some more. "Boy, I really appreciate that pitch," Seinfeld said. "You put a lot into it." Koren thanked him. "Unfortunately," Seinfeld continued, "I'm not going to use any of these stories. But, God, I have to tell you, I appreciate the effort." Everyone, even Koren, laughed even harder. Then one of his fellow writers said to Koren: "The Serenity Now thing. Tell Jerry that one." He did, and, finally, he had a winner.

As Seinfeld took over sole control of the show, it moved away from its everyday-life, observational, "show about nothing" bent and toward a more absurd, cartoonish approach. It lost David's complexity and darkness and gained more of Seinfeld's light-heartedness. Seinfeld had always loved the simple slapstick of Abbott and Costello, a predilection that showed in the newer episodes. *Seinfeld* also took a turn toward the sensibilities of its young writers, many of whom were in their twenties. Some of Jason Alexander's anxieties were realized: "It felt like it shifted from a show where George was the most compelling character to a show where Kramer was the most compelling character," he said. "He had a youthfulness, an innocence, that writing staff knew how to write. And Michael was so easy to write for. 'Kramer comes in.' You're done."

Other parts of the production changed as well. Because the music wasn't one fixed, melodic theme, it began to morph with the show's mood, becoming, as Wolff described it, "more aggressive, a little more annoying." The vocal portion grew more nasal, the bass edgier, the entire composition calling more attention to itself. It had gone from music that said, "I hope it's okay that we have this weird music on this quirky show," to music that said, "We are the top show on television with the coolest music. What's it to you?"

New director Andy Ackerman added his own new twist to the show's distinctive look. In the eighth-season episode "The Pothole," for instance, he obsessed over one simple scene in which Jerry accidentally knocks a girlfriend's toothbrush into the toilet. Ackerman could shoot it the normal way: a profile of Jerry looking down at the toilet. But he thought: What if we could see that from the toilet's point of view? Cherones had long ago set *Seinfeld*'s look as more cinematic than the average sitcom. The toilet POV made sense in this world.

Ackerman mounted the camera on a short tripod, underneath a toilet with a glass bottom. It took a few takes to get the brush to fall in just the right spot, but the results were true visual humor: The toothbrush drops, then Jerry's horrified face appears overhead. The crew spent about four hours

305

total on what could have taken a few minutes, if shot conventionally on an average sitcom. For other episodes, Ackerman used cranes and Steadicams, far beyond the equipment any other stage-bound sitcom at the time would dream of. That's what being the No. 1 show on television was all about.

Ackerman's no-holds-barred visual comedy heightened what was becoming a manic, wacky version of *Seinfeld.* Instead of the five-page scenes of traditional comedies, or the four-page scenes of early *Seinfeld,* now the scripts — which sometimes ran fifty or sixty pages — contained one- to three-page scenes, tops. In other words, the cuts were even quicker, to go along with the fast-paced, cartoonish plotlines the new, young staff spun: Elaine meets the "Bizarros"; Elaine's new boyfriend won't let her talk during the song "Desperado"; Jerry and Kramer switch personalities when they switch apartments. A story line revolved around Kramer getting a new showerhead, so Richards could do elaborate physical bits, miming hurricane-force water pressure. One ninth-season episode, "The Betrayal," ran in reverse.

Everyone on set felt Larry David's absence; they were a little bit lost without his clear vision and guidance. But in some ways, his departure freed up new energy. The writers took on more responsibility for their own episodes and for the production, since Seinfeld had to split his time between writing and performing. Mom and Dad were gone and the kids had the run of the house, as Ackerman once described it.

A new writing and producing system emerged. The show had never had a traditional writers' room like other sitcoms, where all the staffers would gather every day to brainstorm jokes and story ideas, then send one writer off to assemble it all into a script. The *Seinfeld* writers had always operated independently, pitching to David and Seinfeld alone, writing alone. Now, with David gone, Seinfeld developed a new procedure with, essentially, multiple writers' rooms. There was an idea room, where plotlines were pitched, accepted, and rejected in a group setting. There was an outline room, where the group would brainstorm the steps of an entire episode. After that, the script's writer or writers would go off to compose. When they turned the script in, it would go to a rewrite room, where the writer and a few colleagues of his or her choice would work out revisions. At every step of the way, at least two or three writers were doing the job that one Larry David used to do.

Robin enjoyed the rewrite sessions with Seinfeld, a process the writers hadn't previously experienced when David was around. That was where the real comedy happened, and Seinfeld seemed to like the idea of combining different "flavors" of writers in each session, based on their strengths: "I think we need a bit of Koren in this script," or, "Let's get Robin in here." They got to spend hours in a room watching Jerry Seinfeld at work.

It was not easy, though. Seinfeld and the writers worked what somehow felt like more than twenty-four hours a day, more than seven days a week, to make the transition from the time of Larry David to the time without him, beginning with the show's eighth season, work. They did not recognize weekends. They had nothing in their lives besides the show. All they did was scour their lives — their past lives, the ones where they did things other than write television — for ideas. The time Koren spent worrying about losing the record of his high score on the local Frogger arcade-game machine when the machine was carted off. (George would buy the machine to prevent it from happening.) Or the conversation Koren had with Mehlman about Mehlman's hatred for *The English Patient.* (Elaine would inherit that.) Once they found them, they hoarded them until they had enough for an entire episode.

They would work for something like fifty-six days in a row without a break. That was what it took to replace Larry David. They'd take a day off, then do another forty-four days in a row. If the Super Bowl was on, they'd work all morning, take a break to watch the game, then go back to work.

No one, however, complained about the long hours, least of all Seinfeld, who would cheerfully show up for an 8:45 A.M. rewrite session on a Sunday. Of course, Seinfeld constantly working meant that his writing staff was constantly working. No one wanted to be the person who wasn't around, so they were all around, always. Crittenden often sat in her office for hours, thinking of script ideas, something she could have just as easily done at home. But she wasn't about to look like the slacker, even if that meant less time at home with her husband. Robin, the only other married writer, often went home to have dinner with his wife, then came back to the set. No one had kids.

The new *Seinfeld* writing system did not operate perfectly. With all the writers helping Seinfeld to run the show, competition was fierce to be among those helping *the most*. Factions formed: There was a Berg-Schaffer-Mandel alliance, and a Kavet-Robin-Feresten contingent. The other writers felt they had to pick sides.

Sometimes they chose by accident. Mandel often helped Crittenden make her story lines converge at the end of her scripts; he also contributed material to them: the idea that David Puddy could be a recovering germophobe; and the idea that George wanted an apology from James Spader's character, who is going through Alcoholics Anonymous's twelve steps; and the idea that Elaine's doctors were conspiring against her by noting how "difficult" she was on her charts. Crittenden couldn't deny the boost these story lines gave her scripts, and she couldn't help but drift toward Mandel's side of the office as a result.

But the choosing just added one more layer of stress to the writers' overwhelming work lives.

All of this stress, plus his recent Emmy Snub, plus his irritation at being surrounded by twentysomethings all day prompted Peter Mehlman to at last put an end to his time at *Seinfeld*. He left at the end of the eighth season.

He'd come back to write one more episode with Mandel, "The Betrayal" — the episode that ran in reverse, revealing that the gang ended up on a disastrous trip to India because Elaine wanted to spite her nemesis, Sue Ellen Mischke, by actually showing up at Sue Ellen's overseas wedding. Elaine was convinced Sue Ellen had invited her only because she figured Elaine would never go to the trouble to attend. Mehlman liked the episode because, despite its high concept, it started with the kind of small impetus he loved on *Seinfeld.* That is, spite.

When Mehlman went out into the "real world" beyond *Seinfeld*'s office walls, he found that everyone in television wanted "the next *Seinfeld,*" but they didn't want to take any of the chances necessary to make such a thing. They wanted *Seinfeld* money, but they seemed to resent *Seinfeld* itself for breaking the rules of television. He would go in to pitch ideas to executives and hear, over and over, "That character's not really likable." He'd thought *Seinfeld* had done away with likability.

Seinfeld had even ruined his mother for all other sitcoms. Whenever she watched anything else, she said, "How does anybody think this is good?"

■ ■ ■ ■

Despite Larry David's departure, *Seinfeld*'s ratings rose in the first several episodes of the eighth season. The show had more pop culture juice than ever, landing Yankee Derek Jeter, game show host Alex Trebek, and talk show host David Letterman to guest star in the same November 1996 episode, "The Abstinence."

Seinfeld agreed to a ninth season in January 1997, but only if his castmates also signed on. That was a much bigger "if" than it had been in previous years. The cast said they'd come back for the right pay, and they were in a position to demand almost anything. Their contracts were expiring and the show was still printing money for NBC. The network now made $550,000 per thirty-second ad spot on the show, the highest rate in prime time. That meant more than $200 million in earnings that season after ad agency commissions. Even after paying production company Castle Rock its licensing fee, the network made $150 million per year on *Seinfeld.* And the series was worth even more than that to NBC: It could launch other shows that aired near it or were promoted during it.

Seinfeld had agreed to a salary of $1 million per episode for his dual roles as star and executive producer. He made an additional $40 million the previous year from syndication of the show, and the cast didn't get a cut of that — a major sticking point for their negotiations. Alexander, Louis-Dreyfus, and Richards had made $125,000 per episode the previous season; NBC now reportedly offered the costars $500,000 per episode.

They strategized as a team. They had researched the numbers and knew the stakes. They had asked for a cut of syndication profits and hadn't gotten it. It was getting harder for the three supporting players to hope the show would last much longer, Alexander later said, at least from a business standpoint. They had played their characters so well that they'd inevitably have some trouble transitioning to the next phase of their careers. That was an excellent problem to have, but they wanted their fair share of the millions being made. As Alexander later described his feelings: "I want to leave the most successful television show in history knowing that I never have to work again."

Given all of this, when they broke down how much the network profited on the show and figured in how much of that was due to them — as part of an equation that included Seinfeld, David, the writers, the guest stars, and the crew — they came up with a counteroffer: $1 million per episode.

NBC executives refused to even discuss it. In fact, the high-stakes negotiations dragged on for four months in the middle of production of the eighth season. The network stonewalled, according to Alexander, ignoring the actors and their representatives from December 1996 to April 1997. While the cast remained cordial with everyone on set and continued to laugh together nearly every day, a sense of tension lurked in the atmosphere. Seinfeld was both their costar and their boss, a fact they were suddenly reminded of because of his awkward position. He tried to stay out of the discussion. The crew knew only what they heard around town and read in *Variety,* which was that the three cast members seemed to be jeopardizing the show's future for an obscene amount of money. This didn't make anything easier on set.

Finally, according to Alexander, with just a few weeks left before NBC had to finalize its fall lineup, Seinfeld stepped in and demanded NBC strike a deal with his costars. The network offered what Alexander described as his rock-bottom price: $600,000 per episode and a cut of future DVD sales. The cast signed on for a ninth season. But negotiating seasons beyond the ninth would only become more difficult as time went on.

When *Seinfeld* returned for a ninth season, most of the cast and crew felt the show's days were numbered. The writers were working most of their waking hours and jostling for power; Seinfeld was writing, producing, and starring; and the main cast members just barely got what they felt they deserved to be paid. Now was the time to push the show's limits, to try every story that seemed funny, no matter how crazy.

The writers went as meta as possible with story lines like hack comic Kenny Bania becoming a "time-slot hit" at the club just because his act follows Seinfeld's — a dig at the parade of lesser shows that became hits because they aired in the spaces between *Friends, Seinfeld,* and *ER.* (That fall: *Union Square* and *Veronica's Closet.*) The episode "The Voice" came directly from an office joke in which Feresten used a silly voice meant to imitate the sounds his girlfriend's stomach made.

Berg, Schaffer, and Mandel wrote "The

Voice" together when they were most pressed for time and story ideas. Usually Berg and Schaffer wrote as a team and Mandel wrote alone, but then they realized that they could pool their story lines if they worked together. "The Voice" was one of Mandel's favorite episodes among his scripts, but it divided fans. Critics were watching the show closer than ever for chinks in its armor, and many picked up on this second episode of the ninth season as indicative of a downward trend in quality. Mandel thought maybe they were just reacting to the episode's extra "silly" factor.

Ratings were up at *Seinfeld,* but four episodes into the ninth season, the *New York Post* ran a poll asking readers whether *Seinfeld* was as good as it used to be, and more than half said it wasn't. Seinfeld called the paper to promise that the sixth episode would have the series back on track. (That would be "The Merv Griffin Show," in which Kramer would reconstruct the classic talk show's set in his apartment after he finds its furniture in a Dumpster, then play host to his own version.)

Variety's Phil Gallo, however, was not impressed: "Having raised the bar to stratospheric heights — is there another show that has added new phrases to the American lexicon year after year? — it feels like a dog's age since the last multiplot show clicked on every cylinder. . . . In its quest to be about nothing, *Seinfeld* writers have stretched the tangents too far. The conversations don't have the logical randomness that defined the show in its earlier days when Kramer was the curious interruption to the neuroses of George and Jerry, two characters who have drifted into a meandering void." He concluded: "If *Seinfeld* ends this year, it might well be on a whimper, no longer fodder for the water cooler and described thus by its longtime fans: 'It was a great show that poked fun at all things urban and yuppie and then yadda, yadda, yadda, it was off the air.' "

The writers, however, were proud of their work. Most of them were too busy with the show to hear about the backlash.

At the show's Christmas party that December, Seinfeld and Louis-Dreyfus shared some tequila, and then climbed into the rafters above the set. The vantage point afforded them a different perspective on Jerry's living room — Seinfeld felt, at this point, that this was *his* living room far more than that place where he lived in real life. Instead of seeing the room the way they usually did, from the back, with the audience before them, they could see everything at once: the sofa, the table, the bookcases, the kitchen, and the key area between the couch and the counter where most of the action happened, which the cast variously called the Canyon of Heroes, the Wheelhouse, and Power Alley. From here, though, they could also see all the lights, pulleys, and cranes above it. The cast had recently met in secret to discuss the idea of ending the show. As the two of them looked down on their lives for the past nine years, they realized it might be time.

Each year around Halloween, network president Warren Littlefield would visit Seinfeld's office and officially ask him back for another season of *Seinfeld*. Seinfeld would think it over for a few months, and talk to his castmates, and around Christmas, a deal would get done.

This time, in December 1997, in the middle of the ninth season, a deal was still not done. And for good reason.

11
THE END

By December 1997, after more than eight years starring in and running *Seinfeld,* Jerry Seinfeld was spent. He wanted to stop making the biggest comedy of the '90s, which was within his rights, though it wouldn't be easy. He was not just the figurehead of that product of his and Larry David's imagination, Seinfeldia. In the real world, where millions of dollars meant something, he was also the linchpin in the most profitable network lineup in TV history.

He wanted to go out on top, he said. And he was there: *Seinfeld* had helped make its network, NBC, No. 1 for three years running. The show had helped NBC reach $1 billion in profits the previous year, with $200 million of that from *Seinfeld.* The show had become the '90s equivalent of *I Love Lucy* or *The Honeymooners, All in the Family* or *The Cosby Show.* And though *The Honeymooners* remained the gold standard

319

for *Seinfeld* — he wasn't sure yet whether his show would hold up for decades the way *The Honeymooners* did — there was way more money at stake when it came to *Seinfeld.*

Bob Wright, the president of the network, called to say that he and Jack Welch, the chairman and chief executive of NBC's parent company, General Electric, would like to have brunch with Seinfeld and his managers, Howard West and George Shapiro. For two weeks beforehand, they negotiated everything, down to what Seinfeld would like to eat — oatmeal? French toast? When the day came, they all gathered in Wright's apartment on the thirty-eighth floor of Trump Tower in New York City. Wright sat at the head of the table, with Welch and West flanking him. Across the table sat Seinfeld and Shapiro. Three waiters attended to them as they overlooked Central Park on a sunny, clear, early-winter day.

West was in heaven, talking to his business hero, Welch, about everything but *Seinfeld.* Then it came: The GE-NBC guys started talking *Seinfeld* research, complete with charts. *Seinfeld,* Welch insisted, hadn't reached its peak. The NBC guys felt like they'd nailed this. "You know, Jerry, I go all over the world," Welch said. "People only want to know about one thing — Jerry Seinfeld and his show."

But as it turned out, the sales pitch wasn't enough. Seinfeld noted that there was only one way to find out where the show's true peak was — by hitting the downturn, something that didn't interest him. Seinfeld wished it were a "regular show," he later said, "like a grocery store. You don't close it. You leave it open. 'We're making money here!' But the show had its own rules, so I felt like I had to play by them." As Seinfeld continued to demur about doing another season, Welch said, "Jerry, come here," and took the comedian off to the side for a private conversation. Welch wrote something on a slip of paper and handed it to Seinfeld: $5 million per show, up from the $1 million he was currently making. Another season of twenty-two episodes could net Seinfeld $110 million. That was Welch's offer.

Seinfeld declined.

He felt that, with episodes like "The Betrayal" — in which the action unfolded in reverse — and "The Bizarro" — in which the characters met their opposites — *Seinfeld* had "broken enough china in the china shop. . . . There wasn't much left to break down, and I didn't want to twist a dry sponge." He'd sensed for years that he was running out of material because he spent so much of his time making the show instead of living a normal life. He once went into a deli on the Upper West Side and saw little credit card–type things for sale that apparently allowed people to buy phone time. He had no idea what they were, and he hated feeling so disconnected from the sort of minutiae that had inspired his show, and his act, to begin with. He thought of the Beatles, who dominated entertainment for nine years, then stopped.

Seinfeld's ninth season would be its last.

Shapiro, West, and Seinfeld left the meeting and went for a walk around Central Park. Seinfeld stopped at a bench at Eighty-First Street and Central Park West and said, "Guys, when I was twenty-one, I sat on this same bench." There, he told his father he was going into stand-up, just before he moved into his first apartment. His father gave his blessing to Seinfeld's career choice, saying he wished he could have gone into comedy himself.

"For me, this is all about timing," Seinfeld told the *New York Times* on Christmas Day. "My life is all about timing. As a comedian, my sense of timing is everything. . . . I wanted the end to be from a point of strength. I wanted the end to be graceful." He added that the show was "the greatest love affair of my life. . . . We felt we all wanted to leave in love."

Though Seinfeld's costars would collectively lose an estimated $40 million without another season (presuming they signed for the same salary as the previous year), the cast supported the decision. Every year for the previous four years, around the holiday season, they met in Jerry's dressing room to talk about how they felt about another season. When they did this before Seinfeld's meeting with Welch and Wright, they all said they felt like calling it, as Alexander and Louis-Dreyfus later recalled.

Louis-Dreyfus was tired of juggling the intense shooting schedule with her two young sons at home. They knew they could keep making funny episodes, but they didn't feel like they could surprise the audience anymore. Plus, they agreed, it would be classy to go out on top. "It seemed artistically right," Alexander later said. Seinfeld told his writers that nine was his lucky number, so he just had to go out with his ninth season. "There's just something perfect about nine," he said.

Media chatter about the show's impending end exploded. Camera crews and photographers lingered outside the studio gates at all hours, hoping to feed demand for even the tiniest hints of *Seinfeld* "coverage." *People* magazine planned an entire special issue. One of the magazine's reporters camped out at music director Jonathan Wolff's office because Wolff was one of the few people in the world with a full set of *Seinfeld* videotapes — a standard contract stipulation for him. Wolff set the reporter up in a spare room, where Wolff's staffers would stop in to watch an episode or two with him.

Newspaper columns obsessed over the hole the loss would create in NBC's mighty Thursday night. The network still had *ER*, now TV's top show, on that night. But that show was up for renegotiation in February, and could consider offers from other networks. Warner Brothers could ask for more than $10 million per episode for *ER*, which it produced, rather than the $2 million it was currently receiving. At the time of Seinfeld's announcement, *Mad About You*'s stars, Helen Hunt and Paul Reiser, hadn't decided whether to do another season of their hit show — a decision that seemed even more potentially perilous for NBC given Hunt's probable Oscar nomination for her recent role in the film *As Good as It Gets*. Every permutation of the possible schedule meltdown fascinated media reporters and competing networks alike. Fox Television had to deny reports that its president, Sandy Grushow, sent Seinfeld a thank-you note for quitting.

Perhaps the *New York Post* put it best in its front-page headline: "Plucked Peacock: NBC Badly Hurt After *Seinfeld* Calls It Quits." "Plucked Peacock" would be a nickname that stuck, even fifteen years hence, as the network's luster faded.

Grushow wasn't the only person (allegedly) thrilled at the announcement: Al Yeganeh, the owner of Soup Kitchen International, rejoiced over *Seinfeld*'s demise. The show had ruined his life, he told the *Post* when a reporter visited his West Fifty-Fifth Street restaurant. The Iranian immigrant — who'd kicked Jerry Seinfeld himself out of his store after the "Soup Nazi" episode aired — was besieged with media requests all over again. Yeganeh told the Associated Press that Jerry Seinfeld was just "an idiot clown." Reporters swarmed to Soup Kitchen International, and one unlucky one, WABC-AM's Babita Hariani, asked Yeganeh to repeat the Soup Nazi's catchphrase, "No soup for you!" Yeganeh threw a headset at her and chased her out of his establishment. The entire incident was broadcast on the air.

In the second week of January 1998, Seinfeld stood in front of a two-hundred-person studio audience for the first time since his announcement. A lesser-known comedian did the audience warm-ups, but Seinfeld usually mingled briefly with the crowd before the show. "Five million bucks a week?" the comedian said. "Is he crazy?" He may have been, but with the demise of *Seinfeld,* everyone in Hollywood wanted a ticket to the crazy man's taping. "Welcome to the last helicopter out of Saigon," he added. The cast shot their 169th episode of what they now knew would be 180 total. The episode was "The Cartoon," in which Elaine obsesses over an inscrutable *New Yorker* illustration.

End-of-*Seinfeld* excitement built. *Seinfeld* writers were snapped up by studios handing out holding deals — which give studios first rights to anything they produce over a specified period of time — to anyone who might give them the next *Seinfeld.* Syndicator Columbia TriStar locked down the largest single deal in syndication history by selling the show to WNYW for $300,000 per week as the "supply" of *Seinfeld*s became suddenly finite. A thirty-second ad spot during the finale now cost $2 million; by comparison, the same spot in the 1998 Super Bowl went for $1.3 million, and in a regular 1997–98 *Seinfeld* episode for $575,000.

Even the possible scheduling shuffles *Seinfeld*'s absence would cause the following fall riveted readers. Fox had a rumored plan to move its animated hit *King of the Hill* from Sunday to Thursday to anchor a one- or two-hour comedy block that could rival NBC's. ABC could move *The Drew Carey Show* from Wednesdays to Thursdays in an effort to take advantage of NBC's weakness.

The most speculation focused on which show would inherit *Seinfeld*'s slot on NBC, as if it were the 9:00–9:30 P.M. time period itself that made the show so magical. *Frasier* could move from Tuesday into *Seinfeld*'s Thursday spot on NBC, but that would break up the network's other successful comedy block. Or *Third Rock from the Sun* could move there from Wednesday. *Friends* could move to *Seinfeld*'s slot, but then what would NBC put at 8:00 P.M.? *Variety* reported that the sitcom *Just Shoot Me!* was "in the lead" to take over *Seinfeld*'s slot. *Broadcasting & Cable* suggested that other contenders included a new sitcom from *Frasier*'s creators, starring Nathan Lane; and established shows like *Mad About You* and

Veronica's Closet. In the end, *Frasier* got the spot.

The media coverage then swirled toward what might happen on the finale itself. Perhaps Jerry and Elaine would get married. Perhaps George would get a clue. Perhaps they all would grow a conscience, or grow up. A *New York Post* "fax poll" found that two-thirds of readers — or at least those who bothered to send their thoughts through their fax machines — thought the show should go on without Seinfeld, as a spin-off that featured his three friends. "We think it's all a trick, and he'll be back," said one waitress at Tom's, voicing the sentiments of a nation.

On the alt.tv.seinfeld newsgroup, a variation on the Tom's waitress theory popped up: The joke of the finale would be that it wasn't the finale, and the show would, in fact, carry on. Others on the site thought that perhaps the whole cast would move to California because Jerry would get another shot at a TV show, or that Kramer would swallow an irreplaceable key to Jerry's apartment, or, in a strangely specific theory, that the last line of the show, uttered by George, would be, "What am I going to do now?"

On his GeoCities page, Adam Rainbolt,

the cocreator of the *Sein*-FAQ page, posted polls to gauge audience reaction to each remaining episode. He asked users to give the week's half hour a letter grade between A and F, the way *Entertainment Weekly* critics rated shows and movies. Rainbolt also posted unauthorized excerpts from magazine coverage of the finale. He even considered recapping the remaining episodes, but then thought, *Who would want to read about what just happened on a show they already watched?*

Jason Alexander thought the show's only hope might just be a non-finale. A regular episode, as if it were no big deal. The pressure was just too much for any script to handle. Lucky for him, the finale script wasn't his problem. It was Larry David's.

The *Seinfeld* writers bid good-bye to their dream jobs by collaborating on the show's penultimate episode, "The Puerto Rican Day Parade." Several of them had pitched the idea of a "one-set show" — similar to "The Parking Garage" or "The Chinese Restaurant" — that would take place in a traffic jam. O'Keefe, for instance, had pitched the idea of a Yankees Stadium traffic jam, Mandel pitched a Puerto Rican Day Parade traffic jam, and others had pitched backups at other major New York landmarks or events. Seinfeld settled on gridlock related to the Puerto Rican Day Parade, a New York event known for its ability to snarl traffic and co-occur with — some would say *cause* — mayhem in the surrounding areas. Every writer would get a credit on the episode. They would all work together one last time, on a production that would be almost as elaborate as the finale.

They each took their allotted scenes home to write. As Jeff Schaffer typed away at night, sending Kramer into a stranger's apartment during an open house to use the restroom, he realized: These were the last *Seinfeld* words he would type. This was it.

They shot at Universal Studios, which had a bigger New York street set than the one on *Seinfeld*'s lot, with several intersecting blocks. Everyone threw bits of story into the hodgepodge they'd created, in which almost anything could happen: The foursome was stranded in a traffic jam due to the parade. They abandoned the car, and split up to try their luck separately navigating the city to get home. The debacle culminated in Kramer accidentally setting a Puerto Rican flag on fire, then stomping it in an innocent effort to put it out; this did not go over well with parade-goers.

The episode was shot on location in five days, with no studio audience. This gave it a surreal quality: The finale felt nothing like a regular weekly episode, and "The Puerto Rican Day Parade" took place off the home set, so the episode the week before — "The Maid," an unmemorable half hour in which Jerry sleeps with his cleaning lady — was, the cast and crew realized, the last normal episode. They'd left their old lives behind before they realized it.

National Puerto Rican Coalition president Manuel Mirabal wrote to NBC before the episode even aired, after hearing about the episode's title. He asked that the network allow Hispanic consultants to review it for offensive content before it went public, but NBC declined. "We don't consult a rabbinical council when we do a show about Jews," writer Alec Berg later said.

When the episode ran, it was the show's highest-rated yet.

Things would get more incendiary from there.

David returned to write the actual finale. It was always David's show, and he had left it on good terms; it made sense to bring him back to end it. But that also meant taking on all of the pressure of delivering on the hype's promise. He spent a month crafting the show's good-bye script. He started his brainstorming by thinking about how much he'd miss the characters, so he figured he'd want them to end up in a place where he could imagine them being when the show ended. He asked himself, "Where could I send them for a year or two with the possibility of them coming back?" First he thought of Biosphere 2, but that seemed a little too out-there.

So instead, he settled on prison. He had heard about the "Good Samaritan law" in France that required onlookers to rescue anyone they see who is in danger if it's reasonable for them to do so. He figured he — and, thus, the *Seinfeld* characters — could get in a lot of trouble under such a law. They could go to jail for a year, and when they got out, everything would be pretty much the same. Perfect. Of course, he knew that if one of his writers had pitched him the idea back in the day — that the characters would stand by while someone got mugged, then make fun of him — he would have said, "No, it's too mean." But it seemed like the best way to get them arrested, but for something not *so* bad, like, say, murder. He also liked the idea of a trial that would bring back a parade of the most memorable former guest stars to "testify" to the ways the foursome had wronged them.

The writing staff had no idea what to expect from the finale. They had no idea what was in the final script until the table read. Each got a script with a watermark bearing his or her name. They had to turn their scripts in after each reading or rehearsal. The script came in at more than a hundred pages (as opposed to a regular week's, which would've been closer to forty-five or so). The shooting schedule stretched to eight days, instead of the usual three.

Secrecy enveloped the episode in the weeks before its May 14, 1998, airing. In fact, the *Seinfeld* crew kept everyone so in the dark that it was "frustrating some at NBC and leaving eager viewers to soak up morsels of information from the Internet," as *USA Today* reported. David and Seinfeld gave the finale a fake title, "A Tough Nut to Crack," to throw off snooping reporters and fans. Anyone involved in the finale had to sign a confidentiality agreement, and the actors beyond the core cast had to work without a full script. Seinfeld really liked the idea of using ink that could not be copied, because it had such spylike implications. The production staff looked into it, but it didn't turn out to be practical on that scale. (Go figure.) Instead, they went with shredding each set of scripts after every rehearsal, then making new photocopies for the next. Mandel saved a handful of shredded scripts in a glass box as a memento of the week.

Filming would take place over the next week and a day following the table read, on several locations and soundstages, before culminating in a studio-audience taping on April 8.

On March 31, the cast gathered with David for their last table read, and that's when emotions started to flow. They were sitting in their well-worn places for the last time, crunched together at the end of the long, folding tables set up in front of the empty area where the audience would later sit. Seinfeld compared it to no less a life-changing experience than birth or death. "You're going to hear me say 'thank you' a lot during the week," he said to his costars. "Here's the first one."

For the first time since the first episode, their parts were announced before the reading: "Michael Richards in the role of Kramer, Jason Alexander as George, Julia Louis-Dreyfus will be playing Elaine. And Jerry Seinfeld as Jerry." Louis-Dreyfus started crying before they read a word.

After the table read, a rehearsal began with some supporting characters. As David and Seinfeld stood on the sidelines, they discussed an editorial in the *New York Times* that credited their show with New York City's turnaround in the '90s. "The image of the city is this fun, silly place," thanks to the show, Seinfeld explained to a *Rolling Stone* reporter visiting the set for a cover story. As a native New Yorker, Seinfeld still couldn't help being a little impressed with himself for making the *Times* op-ed page: "The lead editorial!" He'd already sold his Hollywood home and was looking forward to moving back where he belonged. "I've had enough of Los Angeles," he said. "I always say that Los Angeles is like Vegas, except the losers stay in town."

David, listening to Seinfeld being interviewed, offered some appreciation for his longtime partner. "I am watching the greatest interviewee ever," he said. "This is a beauty."

"Larry always marvels at my ability to just come up with horse-shit for these interviews."

"I've probably read over two hundred interviews," David said. "Each one is different: always something new about the show, about life, about something. I'm amazed. I stand in awe. The greatest bullshitter on this planet."

"It's good bullshit," Seinfeld said. "Good, salable bullshit."

Old friends of the show milled about on the set that week, even if they weren't involved in the production. Throughout the week of filming, the atmosphere was a party, joyous. Kenny Kramer had VIP access, and roamed about from the craft services' food table to the stands.

Writer Peter Mehlman was no longer working for the show, but his new office was still on the lot, so he stopped by. He attended the table read for the final episode, and thought it held up pretty well. Sure, it was a little more blatant, a little rawer, than anything the show had done before. But no matter what this finale did, he figured, it couldn't live up to its hype. It had an hour-plus to fill and tens of millions of viewers waiting for it. What could it do?

Alexander liked it, too, because it allowed for a reunion-type atmosphere. Characters like the Soup Nazi, the Low-Talker, and so many others had made such a huge difference in the show but had disappeared from the set before anyone knew how important they'd be. This allowed them all to return for a thank-you.

For director Andy Ackerman, the finale was a logistical nightmare, mainly due to the extraordinary amount of press attention. (There were even press helicopters hovering as the crew shot on location.) *Rolling Stone* and Katie Couric were on set for sanctioned coverage. At every location, there were more press and paparazzi trying to get even a scrap of information. A few photographers scaled the studio wall near New York Street. A security guard was stationed on the set around the clock because random items were starting to disappear.

That week, Richards found himself newly preoccupied with the intricacies of his character. He asked himself, "How does Kramer function in a courtroom? How does he behave in jail? How does his view of life change from behind bars, if at all?" He'd always been asking questions like, "How does Kramer relate to a woman? What is his whole deal with a woman?" throughout his nine years as the character. But this episode tested his limits because of its outlandish story line.

When the writers saw the final product coming together, they loved it. O'Keefe later told me he thought it was a "conscious return to the roots of the show."

On April 8, 1998, at 6:30 P.M., the cast of

Seinfeld gathered in front of their final studio audience to film their 180th episode. The audience members had all signed secrecy affidavits. Backstage, the four stars held hands as the introductions began, just as they did before every taping, a tradition they called the "circle of power." Seinfeld got misty-eyed. "I want to say something," he said to his costars. "For the rest of our lives, when anyone thinks of one of us, they will think of all four of us. And I can't think of three people I'd rather have that be true of." Louis-Dreyfus and Alexander wiped away tears, while Richards grunted emotionally.

They took their places on the courtroom set. "Do you know what these four people were?" raved Phil Morris, who played attorney Jackie Chiles, in his opening statement scene. Louis-Dreyfus covered her giggles by looking down in mock distress. "They were innocent bystanders. Now you just think about that term, 'innocent bystanders.' Because that's exactly what they were. How can a bystander be guilty? Have you ever heard of a guilty bystander?"

They filmed until past 2:00 A.M. The final shot was as it began: Jerry, doing stand-up. This time, for the final scene, his stand-up routine would be in prison. Only one prob-

338

lem: The scene, a late addition, had no script. This episode was the first time his stand-up had been incorporated into an episode since the seventh season. Seinfeld had thought others were handling it amid the finale hoopla; everyone else figured that since it was a stand-up scene, Seinfeld would write his own jokes. The writers and producers assembled and started throwing jokes out until a few stuck. Finally, they wrapped.

Seinfeld said another tired thank-you to his castmates and crew. Alexander and Louis-Dreyfus both thanked Seinfeld back: "Because you don't hear that enough," Alexander said.

Mehlman left as soon as the shoot was over. He had created a new sitcom for ABC, called *It's Like, You Know.* The first table read for the pilot was the following morning. He tore himself away from the festivities and said good-bye to David and Seinfeld. "God, I feel like I'm sending my kid off to college," David said.

Seinfeld added, "Here it is, take the baton, run with it." Mehlman couldn't have felt better.

Ackerman had a hard time leaving the set that night. He stayed for hours after most people had left, lingering with just his wife,

Seinfeld, Dave Mandel, Alec Berg, and Jeff Schaffer. They hung around until 5:00 A.M., sitting on the diner set. Finally, they each grabbed a keepsake from the set and left, heading out into the foggy, damp morning. Schaffer would never tell what he took.

On May 14, 1998 about a hundred protesters gathered outside, NBC's glistening corporate tower at 30 Rockefeller Plaza in Manhattan, holding posters branding Seinfeld a "racist." They waved Puerto Rican flags and chanted: "NBC, don't you know, Puerto Ricans are no joke!" The previous week's episode, featuring the Puerto Rican Day Parade, had ignited controversy among Puerto Rican activists who said it was an "unconscionable insult" that "crossed the line between humor and bigotry."

Of course, something bigger was distracting most of America from the issue. As the protesters milled in Midtown, actors Dave Chappelle and Tom Hanks wrapped shooting on a scene at Café Lalo for the romantic comedy film *You've Got Mail,* then rushed to a bar around the corner to catch the *Seinfeld* finale. Another thirty blocks uptown, actress Susan Sarandon, novelist Frank McCourt, and the actor who played *Seinfeld*'s "Soup Nazi," Larry Thomas, gathered at a red-carpet event at Tom's Restaurant. *Maxim* magazine had rented the diner out to celebrate the *Seinfeld* finale's airing that night. And 2,800 miles west, the cast and crew of *Seinfeld* were watching the broadcast in a private screening room on the Warner Brothers lot in Los Angeles.

The seventy-five-minute final *Seinfeld* episode aired that evening, laying to rest all the crazy theories floating about. *Seinfeld* loomed so large over the television landscape that other networks took the rare step of going *Seinfeld*-meta in tribute. TV Land, a network built on syndicated reruns of sitcom classics, broadcast only a closed office door featuring a note that said, "Gone watchin' SEINFELD." ABC's *Dharma and Greg* aired an episode called "Much Ado About Nothing," which included a line about how everybody in the country was watching the *Seinfeld* finale. Competing, it seemed, was futile. The episode even showed on big screens live in Times Square. "I'm sad to see it go," one fan told *People* magazine as he watched there. "But that's what reruns are for."

Seinfeld appeared on *The Tonight Show with Jay Leno* later that night to discuss the show's end as the audience chanted, "Jerry! Jer-ry!" In response, he quipped, "What the hell, I'll do one more season. Come on, let's go."

NBC's finale extravaganza attracted 76 million viewers. (It was the third most-watched sitcom finale in TV history, after *M*A*S*H* and *Cheers*.) Everyone involved with the show was happy with the results — until they started hearing the public reaction the next day. *Seinfeld* would go down in history, it turned out, as having one of the most memorable, most watched, and most hated finales.

Entertainment Weekly critic Ken Tucker wrote: "Talk about sour grapes: Returning cocreator David turns spiteful, unforgiving moralist, making Jerry, George, Elaine, and Kramer pay for all their years of 'selfishness, self-absorption, immaturity, and greed.' . . . Retribution prevailed: It's as if David forgot that in nearly every episode invoked, the gang was made to suffer for whatever wrongdoing they committed. It's not as if Jerry got off scot-free for mugging that old woman for her marble rye; as if George didn't pay for going cheap on those wedding invitations. This crew led miserable lives, and we relished their exceptional pettiness. That they should be punished for all the vicarious fun we had at their expense is David's way of saying we never should

342

have made these cruel losers Must See–worthy."

The *New York Observer*'s Ron Rosenbaum went further: "The ludicrously humorless, pathetically strained and witless final episode was confirmation beyond my wildest dreams of just how insanely overrated the show has always been. It was more than the most titanic flop in comedy history — although it certainly was that. It was the culmination of one of the greatest episodes of mass-media-induced mass hysteria in recent American history. One that the sycophants, perpetrators and promoters of the hype should all feel thoroughly ashamed of, in the awful light of the morning after one of the worst hours of television since the cathode-ray tube was invented."

Not everyone hated it, though. Online chatter favorably compared the final episode's plotline to Albert Camus's *The Stranger,* while noting hints of Sartre's existentialist classic *No Exit.* And Caryn James wrote in the *New York Times:* "The hilarious final episode was everything *Seinfeld* was at its best: mordant, unsentimental and written by Larry David. . . . Wildly self-referential and slightly surreal, the final episode revels in petty details, turns clichés on their heads and reveals why *Seinfeld* worked so well."

The news came out the next day that eighty-two-year-old Frank Sinatra had died at his Beverly Hills home during the finale. His wife and emergency crews were able to rush him to the hospital faster than they normally would have because the streets of Los Angeles were so clear. Everyone was home watching the *Seinfeld* finale.

The real-life version of Jerry Seinfeld publicly killed off his notoriously single "Jerry Seinfeld" character a year and a half after the show's demise. Seinfeld, now forty-five, proffered a Tiffany diamond ring and proposed to his new girlfriend, twenty-eight-year-old publicist Jessica Sklar, in an amber-lit booth of the trendy Balthazar restaurant in SoHo in November 1999. The two had become a brief tabloid sensation in the fall of 1998 when she left a wealthy new husband to pursue a relationship with Seinfeld. The two had met at a ritzy Reebok Sports Club near Seinfeld's Upper West Side apartment just before her June 1998 wedding to Broadway theater heir Eric Nederlander and a month after the *Seinfeld* finale. She went through with the wedding, then left her new husband for Seinfeld three weeks after the ceremony.

By October, gossip pages couldn't get enough of Jerry-and-Jessica spottings, shopping at fancy food store Zabar's, cheering on the sidelines of the New York City Marathon, and cuddling in corners of the gym. The *National Enquirer* blared, "Seinfeld Steals Another Man's Wife," and *People* magazine asked, "Master of Whose Domain?" As Nederlander filed for divorce, he took public shots at his ex and her famous new beau: "I was manipulated, misled and completely caught off guard by Jessica's infidelity," he told the *New York Post* in 1998. "Jerry and Jessica have no respect for decent values. They deserve each other." They seemed publicly unfazed, vacationing together in Hawaii and Aspen and Sicily.

When news of Seinfeld's engagement broke, Tom's Restaurant owner Michael Zoulis spoke for the nation. Upon hearing the news from a *People* magazine reporter, he cracked: "It's about time." Just a year later, Jerry Seinfeld was not only a husband but also a father. Jessica gave birth to their daughter, Sascha. Soon after, Seinfeld went back on the road, returning to stand-up.

Seinfeld toured Australia — a hotbed of *Seinfeld* fandom — and Europe before coming back to Broadway in his hometown. On

August 9, 1998, he performed live on television from the Broadhurst Theatre in an HBO special, *I'm Telling You for the Last Time,* a final run-through of all his previous material before he retired it and came up with an entirely fresh routine.

HBO knew where its bread was buttered. It touted the special: "You thought the *Seinfeld* finale was the year's must-see TV event? Wait until August 9, when Jerry Seinfeld returns to television to star in his first stand-up TV special in over a decade." The cable network's prized shows *Sex and the City* and *Arli$$* were pushed back an hour from their normal time slots to make room for the Seinfeld special. "For the past nine years, Jerry Seinfeld has played a stand-up comedian on the most acclaimed sitcom of the decade," an HBO marketing memo said, "but not once has the real Jerry performed a full-length stand-up routine on TV."

When the day came for the broadcast, picketers once again gathered to protest the "Puerto Rican Day Parade" episode, this time outside the Broadhurst. Audience members who'd paid $75 a ticket streamed in, along with celebrity guests such as Chris Rock and Richard Belzer. After the taping, Seinfeld and his longtime manager, George Shapiro, went to Coney Island to ride the

Cyclone roller coaster, a ritual for them after performances. Jerry Seinfeld was now out of the sitcom business and back in the stand-up business.

His costars were moving on, too. Louis-Dreyfus decided to take some time off to spend with her husband and two young sons. Jason Alexander had a two-year deal with Studios USA to produce new series. Richards teamed up with *Seinfeld* writers Spike Ferestcn, Gregg Kavet, and Andy Robin to create a pilot for *The Michael Richards Show,* which featured the actor as a Kramer-like detective in Los Angeles.

Feresten felt some trepidation but agreed to the project anyway. "I just felt an obligation to these people," he said. "Launching a show is really hard. It doesn't matter who you are. The idea wasn't quite right. It was too soon to bring Michael back." Kavet felt it would have been better the way they had originally pitched it, as a single-camera comedy, but NBC had balked. It lasted two months, from October to December 2000, before being canceled.

The actors moved on from *Seinfeld,* but *Seinfeld* continued to live on — in fact, it lives on to this day. From the minute it ended, its influence and reach only began to grow. Unmoored from that weekly prime-time series called *Seinfeld,* the idea of *Sein-feld* spread further and mutated faster. It became *Seinfeldia.*

Writer Fred Stoller and the monkey he befriended on the set. COURTESY OF FRED STOLLER

Actor Steven Hynter, who played comedian Kenny Bania, and writer Fred Stoller on the set. COURTESY OF FRED STOLLER

Writer Fred Stoller and
actor Wayne Knight,
who played Newman.
COURTESY OF FRED STOLLER

Julia Louis-Dreyfus, Jerry Seinfeld, Michael Richards, and Jason Alexander in the
emotional final moments of shooting, taken by David Hume Kennerly. GETTY IMAGES

Julia Louis-Dreyfus, Jerry Seinfeld, Larry David, and director Andy Ackerman at the final table read. GETTY IMAGES

In 2012, Jason Alexander hands out samples of the Original SoupMan soup, the inspiration for the episode "The Soup Nazi." GETTY IMAGES

Kenny Kramer poses amid his merchandise at the Brooklyn Cyclones's *Seinfeld*-themed game in 2013. PHOTO BY JENNIFER KEISHIN ARMSTRONG

Seinfeld fans Matt Bergstein, Emily Donati, Evan Chinoy, and Jerry Kallarakkal at the Brooklyn Cyclones's *Seinfeld* night in 2013. PHOTO BY JENNIFER KEISHIN ARMSTRONG

"Soup Nazi" actor Larry Thomas poses with fans at the Brooklyn Cyclones's *Seinfeld* night in 2013. PHOTO BY JENNIFER KEISHIN ARMSTRONG

Jerry Seinfeld, Jason Alexander, and Larry David while shooting the final *Seinfeld*. GETTY IMAGES

Nearly 5,000 fans came out to watch the *Seinfeld* finale together in St. Louis. GETTY IMAGES

Monica Shapiro and Richard Yates, with Monica's brother-in-law, Richard Levine, and sister, Sharon Yates. Monica was one of the inspirations for the character of Elaine; her novelist father, Richard, was the model for Elaine's father, Alton Benes. COURTESY OF MONICA SHAPIRO

Jerry Seinfeld and Bob Wright, the former NBC president who tried to talk Jerry into doing a tenth year of Seinfeld for $5 million per episode, at the 2004 release party for the show's DVDs. GETTY IMAGES

NBC programming executive-turned-filmmaker Jeremiah Bosgang chats with Jerry Seinfeld in Bosgang's independent feature *Show Me Your Potatoes*. COURTESY OF JEREMIAH BOSGANG

Michael Richards, the guest-star chimp, and Jerry Seinfeld.
COURTESY OF FRED STOLLER

12
SEINFELDIA EMERGES

Rick Lipps had just made the biggest bet of his young career. During the first syndication cycle of *Seinfeld* in 1995, he served as the general manager of KLBK, the CBS affiliate in Lubbock, Texas, a nondescript town in that squared-off part of the cowboy hat atop the state's head. He bought the show for about $90,000 per episode, beating out the other stations in his market for the new golden goose of off-network reruns. The show's distributor, Columbia Pictures Television, had given him a shiny Montblanc pen that cost hundreds of dollars just to sign the contract. He treasured the pen for years after.

Even as he signed, he reassured himself: This was a slam dunk for the 10:30 P.M. slot to swap in for *Late Night with David Letterman,* a chronic underperformer in his market. *Letterman* came in fourth in the ratings in Lubbock, beaten by NBC's *The*

Tonight Show and syndicated episodes of *M*A*S*H* and *Cheers* on other stations.

For the three months in the spring of 1995 leading up to that contract signing, Lipps had considered snagging *Seinfeld* for his station. Now that he'd gotten it, Lipps was still fretting, even while his colleagues rejoiced.

Rick Lipps needed to pick hits.

Lipps couldn't rest easy, even though *Seinfeld* was popular and had the sexiest demographics in television — young, hip, upwardly mobile audiences loved it. But Rick Lipps had made some big slips. He'd paid top dollar for *Growing Pains,* a pleasant, popular family show he'd seen as a sure thing, only to watch it tank in the afternoon. *Roseanne* and *Empty Nest* had washed out in the market as well.

Lipps's career remained in its formative stages. He was in his late twenties, now at his second job managing a local station in the bottom half of the nationwide media market rankings. He'd come to Lubbock from a job in Monroe, Louisiana — a town with about a quarter of Lubbock's population — and this could be a make-or-break job. Lipps had grown up in the tiny Southern Illinois town of Mt. Vernon, sixty miles east of St. Louis, where routes 57 and 64 meet, watching TV but never imagining he'd be part of it. After Lipps graduated from Florida State University with a biology degree, a roommate's dad hired him as a cameraman for one of the local stations he owned. From there, he built a career.

Now he found himself throwing millions of dollars around in hopes that enough people in Lubbock, Texas, wanted to watch reruns of this so-called "show about nothing." And syndication decisions could determine the success or failure of a station manager, who could lose a job because of a bad deal. A misstep could mean pulling a show off the air but continuing to pay the fees for the duration of the contract.

Three months later, terrible news: Bank of America sold KLBK to a company called Petracom in August 1995. A new network-affiliate agreement was part of the deal, and it required all stations to run *Letterman.* With about a month before the new season started, Lipps needed a new place for *Seinfeld.* He couldn't afford to let it sit on the shelf while he paid the show's lofty fees. But now *Seinfeld* would be stuck with the only other available time slot, 4:00 P.M., between Maury Povich's show and *Jeopardy!* — not a big-bucks spot in terms of advertisers. What local car dealership wanted to pay top dollar for a time when primary breadwinners were still at work? Worse, the lineup had zero flow, as they called the compatibility among shows scheduled in a block. A tabloid talk show, a sophisticated sitcom, and a game show? Who wanted to watch all that in a row? Of the 194 markets that carried syndicated *Seinfeld* reruns, only two scheduled it earlier than Lipps's station had. All others placed it in the half hour before prime time, or in late-night.

The policy switch came as a symptom of a larger sea change in affiliate-network relations spurred by the Fox network's 1994 bid for legitimacy. That year, Fox paid $1.6 billion to run NFL games and the Super Bowl for the first time, a move CEO Rupert Murdoch believed was necessary to establish his network as a major power. At the time, most of its affiliates were lower-powered UHF stations instead of VHF, like most of the major networks' affiliates. After the NFL deal, Fox dropped many of its old stations and acquired dozens of new stations on the VHF dial, which would give them more pull with advertisers. To do this, Fox made an unprecedented type of deal to purchase a $500 million minority stake in New World Communications, a production company and owner of several stations. The deal meant a dozen stations across the country, most of them previously affiliated with CBS, flipped to Fox overnight.

Fox's sudden major moves set off a chain reaction of effects throughout the television industry. One of them was that networks gained more power over the affiliates, Lipps felt. Since the advent of television, affiliates had been treated as customers of the networks, wined and dined and wooed with swag while retaining control of their stations. Now, networks were increasingly bossing the affiliates around, using their symbiotic relationship to force changes. Networks, for their part, didn't feel like they could trust their affiliates anymore — suddenly, stations across the country were flipping to Fox for the right price. The networks felt backed into a corner. They reacted with new rules that forced their power onto their affiliates, the television-system equivalent of the national government trumping states' rights.

In the case of Lipps's purchase of *Seinfeld,* that turned out okay in the end — and hinted at the power *Seinfeld* would have in syndication. The show didn't rake in major profits in its riskier time slot — the price was too high for that — but it did something else. It won the slot and took viewers from

Oprah. Its "halo effect," as Lipps character-
ized it, helped lift the station's entire
afternoon heading into the local evening
news. It was like Must See TV all over
again, with local afternoon programming
benefiting this time.

Seinfeld's small victory in the Lubbock
market demonstrated exactly what was
special about the show. It pulled off surpris-
ing feats in other markets as well. As soon
as reruns started airing at 11:00 P.M. on
WPIX in New York City, for instance, *Seinfeld* started beating all three local newscasts
on the other major networks in the market,
a historic accomplishment. When it went off
the air, its influence refused to abate. The
more it played in reruns, the more it perme-
ated culture. Viewers could now watch it, if
not *any* time, at several times, on several
stations that had purchased those pricey
syndication rights.

Even as fans grumbled over the finale,
they found comfort in watching *Seinfeld*
after work, with dinner, during sleepless
nights. Soon they forgot about that finale
and retreated into the repetition, the routine, the night-after-night way the show just
became part of their lives. Despite its cyni-
cism, its aversion to hugging and learning,
it started to feel like a family member,

thanks to the ways it brought people to-gether to watch and bridged generations. Maybe you didn't have much to talk about with Dad, but you could instantly spark a laugh or a happy exchange by dropping a "yada yada" or a "not that there's anything wrong with that."

Seinfeld's syndication success took on enough significance that several inconsisten-cies in the show's casting were reshot or redubbed for the reruns — an unusual, and possibly unprecedented, move for a sitcom at the time. This was possible because the show was still in production when the first syndication deals were struck. Larry David and Jerry Seinfeld, who knew how much their fans fixated on every detail of the show, reshot any earlier inconsistent scenes that they could. For the second-season episode "The Revenge," actor Wayne Knight redubbed scenes that featured the voice of his character, Newman — originally voiced off camera by Larry David. Once he became such a well-known recurring character, it made sense to give him the voice viewers would recognize when they rewatched in syndication.

The fourth-season episode "The Handi-cap Spot" got entire new scenes in syndica-tion: When Jerry Stiller joined *Seinfeld* in

1995 as Frank Costanza, he replaced John Randolph, who'd made just one appearance. After Stiller's hiring, the crew reshot Randolph's scenes with Stiller and subbed them into the syndicated version. The first-season appearance of Phil Bruns as Jerry's dad, however, couldn't be reshot with his replacement, Barney Martin — Jerry's apartment set had changed significantly, and Jerry had aged enough to make any changes look too obvious.

Fans online seemed to relish the changes, enjoying sharing this bit of trivia with other fans to prove their insider knowledge. Only a few grumbled online that the changes showed a lack of faith in audiences' intelligence. For the most part, viewers seemed to like this attention to detail, this attempt to make sure *Seinfeld* was as "real" as possible.

As *Seinfeld* reruns spread across the TV dial in the United States and across the world, the show gained new generations of fans, and its influence on television grew. In the years that followed *Seinfeld*'s finale, TV remade itself in *Seinfeld*'s image. Just seven months after *Seinfeld* ended, *The Sopranos* premiered on HBO and became the new *Seinfeld* — that is, the show that America was proud to obsess over, an entertaining, but still smart, series that proved TV wasn't just for idiots. It also owed at least a little creative debt to *Seinfeld* — after those lovable idiots were tried and convicted for their lack of morals, a show about a sympathetic family man who kills people for a living wasn't as much of a stretch. (In 2013, *The Sopranos* and *Seinfeld* would occupy the first and second spots at the top of the Writers Guild of America's list of TV's best-written series.) *Sopranos* creator David Chase said the concept came to him as "a mobster in therapy, having problems with his mother" — an idea one can imagine showing up in a *Seinfeld* script.

With *The Sopranos,* HBO became a beacon of the coming "Golden Age of Television." As Seinfeld later said: "The idea that you have two guys who have never written a show, being run by a network executive that had never had a show, leading to a show that has a unique and unusual feel — this is a model that all the networks subsequently ignored and never did again, except for HBO. That's a network that hires people that they like and says that's the end of their job. We like you; do what you think you should do, and it leads to much more distinctive programming."

Of course, *Seinfeld*'s influence showed most obviously in the next decade's sitcoms. Though *Seinfeld* ended up in a strange netherworld between the traditional taped-before-a-studio-audience approach and a more filmic, on-location approach to production, its quick scene cutting and multiple locations made an impression on viewers and future comedy producers. In the following years, sitcoms dropped their laugh tracks and embraced "single-camera" shooting — that is, the filmic approach that *Seinfeld* secretly pioneered.

Specific shows took on even more *Seinfeld*ian characteristics. When NBC remade the British sitcom *The Office* for an American audience, it was because *Seinfeld*'s awkward humor and unlikable characters had paved the way for a similar sitcom from abroad. In 2006, comedian Tina Fey created her own show, *30 Rock,* stuffed full of surreal antics, dovetailing story lines, and absurdist bits that made almost every character at least as weird as Kramer. Even shows in much different genres carried *Seinfeld* DNA: *Lost* obsessed Internet-fueled fans with its every interlocking detail. In all of these shows and others of the era — *The West Wing, Arrested Development, Veronica*

Mars, Six Feet Under, The Wire — the narrative complexity that *Seinfeld* pioneered became the norm.

And despite all that artistic advancement in television, *Seinfeld* would continue to hold its own against the onslaught of sophisticated shows over the decade and a half after it concluded its run. As TV audiences — with hundreds of cable channels, plus online and streaming services to choose from — fragmented down to slivers of the ratings *Seinfeld* once pulled, TV's last Great Big Hit would remain more universally quotable than its heirs like *South Park, Entourage, Modern Family, Parks and Recreation, Louie,* and *Girls.*

By 2013, *Seinfeld* would become the most successful show ever in syndication. Networks buy reruns in packages sold in "cycles," and *Seinfeld* was the first show in history to get to a fifth cycle, taking its rerun sales through 2017 — nearly twenty years since its finale. As of 2014, it still played in 90 percent of TV markets across the country, on top affiliates such as WPIX in New York, KCOP in Los Angeles, and WCIU in Chicago. Its syndication ratings at the time remained in the top five among adults twenty-five to fifty-four, along with more recent hits such as *The Big Bang Theory, Two and a Half Men, How I Met Your Mother,* and *Family Guy.*

It had brought in more than $3 billion in revenue since its network run ended, with a million viewers still tuning in every week-night for TBS's reruns, in 2013. The repeats did so well for WPIX that in 2014, the station bought out the ad space on several of the city's subway cars; it ran ads that made the train interiors look like riders were hanging with Jerry, Elaine, George, and Kramer at Monk's Café. In 2014, WUTV in Buffalo, New York, tried to move *Seinfeld* reruns from 10:30 P.M. to 4:00 A.M. to make way for the much newer *Hot in Cleveland* in the prime syndication spot. Outraged viewer response caused the station to move it back two months later.

New generations continued to discover the show, as did countries across the globe. The actors found themselves recognized around the world: Alexander was approached at a market in Budapest during the World Cup, and on the streets of Ramallah. Richards went to Bali and, he later claimed, found fans who spoke in a language he didn't understand, except for one word: "Kramer."

Anything known via *Seinfeld* now stood a chance of being recognized not only across

America but across the world. Demand increased for real-life appearances by *Seinfeld*-related characters, from the "real" Kramer to the guy who played the Soup Nazi. Fans clamored for a cast reunion. Scholars studied the show. Artists paid tribute to it. Bloggers dissected it.

Seinfeldia grew far beyond what its original architects had imagined.

13
THE BIZARROS: THE SEQUEL

As Calypso music played, Kenny Kramer bounded onto a tiny stage in the cramped Producers' Club Theaters on West Forty-Fourth Street in Midtown Manhattan, almost as recognizable now to locals and *Seinfeld* fans as the man who played the sitcom character he'd inspired. On this temperate and sunny May Saturday afternoon in 2014, he was kicking off his seventeenth year of playing the "real Kramer" to crowds willing to pay $37.50 for a tour of *Seinfeld*-related city sites and a brush with a guy who knew a guy who made a TV show. This seemed perfectly reasonable to the dozens of us who had shown up that day.

Kenny Kramer dresses nothing like the character based on him. His signature uniform is a backward baseball cap, long gray hair, *Magnum P.I.* mustache, flowy white shirt, and black pants. Grinning and taking the microphone, Kramer seemed to relish the role as if he'd just been cast in it. He had room for sixty-one tour-goers, but sixty-five had shown up; his solution was not to turn people away but to give prizes to those willing to sit on each other's laps once we all boarded the bus. Four volunteers obliged in exchange for KRAMER'S REALITY TOUR coffee mugs.

Welcome to the capital of Seinfeldia, where Kenny Kramer is, of course, mayor. (More on that in a bit.)

About half of those in the audience indicated with a show of hands that they were visiting from Australia. Kramer nodded: He'd done very well on an Australian tour, performing a stage-only version of his act, a retelling of *Seinfeld* history, heavy on the Kenny Kramer and the charming jokes. In that country, he said, he's even recognized on the street. Australians account for about 20 percent of his business these days.

He launched into his retelling from there, augmented by breaks for video clips, funny old footage of Larry David with a halo of frizzy hair, or bits of interviews in which David talks about Kramer. Kenny explained that he still lived a few blocks away, in Manhattan Plaza, where he'd met David nearly three decades earlier. He paid regular rates now, not the subsidized rates for struggling artists ($62 per month in the '80s when the two lived there). He met David for the first time, he recalled, while organizing a talent show among residents of the complex. He knocked on David's door and asked him to do ten minutes of stand-up material for the event. If David agreed, he'd get paid $150 for his trouble. "Everybody was excited about this except Larry David," Kramer joked.

"If I did it, and I wasn't good, I was worried they'd kick me out of the building," David explained in a video clip, "because they'd see I wasn't a real comedian." But Kramer wore David down.

The two bonded over their mutual Yankee fandom. David had an encyclopedic knowledge of baseball that Kramer admired, and an unusual dedication to the Yankees for a guy who grew up in Brooklyn, which was then Dodgers territory. Kramer liked to listen to David kvetch about Yankees owner George Steinbrenner's decisions.

During his show, Kramer slayed the audience with tales of David's early stand-up career, particularly his confrontations with audiences. "I think you're a bunch of assholes," Kramer imitated David saying. "You can sit there for the rest of your life and I won't tell you another joke." David would also sometimes come to the microphone, Kramer said, look around at the crowd, and say, "Eh, I don't think so."

After *Seinfeld* became a hit and David moved out to Los Angeles, Kramer lost his everyday connection to David, but, he said, they remained in touch. When Kramer visited the set for the taping of the episode "The Pilot," he recalled, there were then *three* Kramers present: Himself, Michael Richards, and Larry Hankin, who played the actor playing Kramer in the faux pilot, *Jerry*. Once again, Kramer recalled, he asked David and Seinfeld if he could play *this* Kramer. Once again, they said no.

When he finished telling stories, Kramer next directed us to another room he'd dubbed "KraMart," where we could purchase all manner of souvenirs. But he didn't *just* direct us there. He showed us each and every treasure available, somehow making the tchotchke tour enjoyable. A VANDELAY INDUSTRIES bumper sticker. A KRAMER FOR MAYOR baseball cap. (A must-have, he said, since "I have a shitload of them left.") A REAL KRAMER T-shirt featuring himself. A blanket bearing the image of Cosmo Kramer.

Over the years since it began, Kramer's tour has grown from needing a thirty-one-seat van to requiring a sixty-one-seat luxury coach. He has managed to make the operation into his entire living, supplemented by corporate speaking gigs (he bills himself as a "demotivational speaker") for up to $25,000 a pop, and theater tours. In the years just after *Seinfeld* ended, he did college speaking appearances that paid up to $150,000 each, but budget cutbacks have brought offers down to the $7,500 range — hardly worth his time. He has turned down offers for radio shows and TV roles. He runs tours weekly between May and September, then takes off to Cabo San Lucas, Mexico, for the winter.

When he's off tour duty, he can seem a little tired of talking about *Seinfeld* — say, in an interview — even though he's game to do it. He perks up more when he can talk about a different part of his life: his run for mayor of New York City on the Libertarian ticket in 2001. "Tired of career politicians ruled by special interests, patronage, and cronyism?" his mission statement said. "Then Kenny Kramer is your candidate." Despite that weak nod toward a clear philosophy, Kramer ran mainly as the guy who inspired the guy on *Seinfeld*. He wasn't terribly serious on the campaign trail. He proposed giving cell phones to the mentally ill people wandering the streets talking to themselves — if it looked like they were on the phone, they wouldn't scare visitors as much. Or the city could pair people who talk to themselves, he suggested, with people who hear voices. When asked during the candidates' debate what he would do if he became mayor, he had a simple answer: "I would go out and buy a suit and necktie."

Then airplanes slammed into the Twin Towers that September, and New York City was suddenly the most serious place on earth. Kramer was already on the ballot — in fact, primary day for Democrats and Republicans fell on Tuesday, September 11 — but his approach fell out of favor. He understood that giving money to Red Cross trumped giving money to his campaign.

He's since settled for life as a civilian, and as a major force in Seinfeldia. He and the other Bizarro versions of characters from the show continue to keep its spirit alive, giving tours, doing public appearances, and even reviving one of Seinfeldia's chief industries, the clothing-order business of one Mr. J. Peterman.

John O'Hurley was hosting the game show *To Tell the Truth* in 2001, a perfect use of his blend of glittery charm and smooth authority. He invited his *Seinfeld* character's inspiration, John Peterman, on as a celebrity guest. On the show, Peterman and two "liars" would try to convince the players that they were the real J. Peterman. This process did not acknowledge the confusing mess *Seinfeld* had made of the word "real."

As Peterman remembers it, when the taping ended, he joined O'Hurley at the actor's house for dinner. As the two public faces of J. Peterman stood in the backyard at the fire pit, overlooking the glittering San Fernando Valley, Peterman and O'Hurley discussed the public failure that had befallen the clothing company in the three years since *Seinfeld* ended.

After hitting a sales peak of $75 million and opening retail locations across the United States, J. Peterman had filed for Chapter 11 bankruptcy in January 1999 and was purchased by the Paul Harris Company. Peterman attributed the failure to pursuing too much expansion — a chain of stores, expanded catalog offerings, $198 reproductions of the necklace in *Titanic* — which he had originally thought the company could handle because of the *Seinfeld* exposure. One of the final pieces of catalog copy written for the company, but never published, said everything: "As my boat sank into the

Sambezi I watched all my luggage float downstream over Victoria Falls. But the day wasn't a total loss. The trek back to the hotel gave me time to think about things. How much does a man need, really?"

Because of the company's *Seinfeld*-fueled fame, its disintegration attracted more press than that of another company of its size would. Hundreds of newspapers and magazines chronicled its bankruptcy proceedings and the Kentucky office's closing. The *Harvard Business Review* published a thorough case study on the company's rise and fall. In *The New Yorker,* a humor piece imagined used office equipment being sold via Peterman-esque dramatic vignettes. "Is it possible to love a water cooler? Somewhere it is 1947. The country is back to work. The war is over. The 'boys' are home. Everyone's wearing hats, even children. People eat lunch at Automats. Things are 'Martinized.' Cars are huge. Gravy is put on everything. And water coolers. Down at the end of the hall. In every office in America. Big, blue-green glass bottles holding clean, cold, crisp water. And by its side a long metal tube dispensing delicate conical paper cups so small you have to fill one six or eight times for a satisfying drink. No matter. We've found one exactly like those old ones. Only in plastic. And empty. But you can fill it. How, we don't know. But good luck to you. Price: $450."

Peterman began drafting plans to launch a new Internet venture using the name "John Peterman," which was still legally his. But the Paul Harris Company itself went bankrupt a year later, and Peterman now had the chance to buy his own company back — if he got enough investors.

"We're putting the company back together," Peterman told O'Hurley as they stood in the actor's backyard. "Do you want to invest?"

He agreed. Thanks to O'Hurley's and others' contributions, Peterman continued to sell huaraches, paille-maille dresses, and the like. ("Soft leather Mexican huaraches comforting your delicate feet through Japan's greatest garden on a sun-drenched breezy afternoon. Glorious.") Peterman kept things simpler this time: catalog and online only, sales of about $20 million.

Since its debut on *Seinfeld,* Festivus had infiltrated reality far beyond its bizarre origins in writer Dan O'Keefe's family. Companies sold Festivus poles and beer flavors. Virginia congressman and House majority leader Eric Cantor threw Festivus fund-raisers, and many more celebrations sprung up throughout the country in homes and on college campuses. In 2012, Google gave *Seinfeld* fans their own electronic "Easter egg": The search engine programmed its results screen to display a Festivus pole down the left margin of the screen to anyone looking for "Festivus" from then on.

But in 2013, Festivus reached new levels of absurdity when Fox News launched its War on Festivus, apparently a new tactic in the network's nine-years-running campaign to convince America that there is such a thing as a "War on Christmas."

Atheist activist Chaz Stevens built a six-foot-tall Festivus pole made of empty Pabst beer cans at the Florida state capitol building in Tallahassee to protest a privately funded Nativity scene on display there. "Is this how PC we've gotten in our society, really?" Fox News host Gretchen Carlson raged. "Why do I have to drive around with my kids to look for Nativity scenes and be like, 'Oh, yeah, kids, look. There's baby Jesus *behind* the Festivus pole made out of beer cans!' " She called the holiday "fake" several times during the segment, but, as O'Keefe could attest, that wasn't quite right. (Besides which, what makes a holiday "fake" or "real"? The mind reels at the philosophical implications.) "I mean, the episode was funny," Carlson added, wandering off the edge of reason, "but not Festivus." The same Christmas season, Fox News anchors also flipped out over an online essay that suggested Santa didn't have to be white.

O'Keefe couldn't believe, as he told *Mother Jones* magazine at the time, that "anyone gave a flying fuck" about Festivus. He wasn't sure how it became an atheist flash point, since his father, who invented the holiday, was raised Catholic and briefly studied to be a Jesuit priest; his family celebrated both Christmas and Festivus. "By the time I met my father," he said to me later, "he was at least agnostic."

O'Keefe's father died at eighty-four, just a year before the uproar, content in the knowledge that he had done something few can claim: He had invented a holiday. A *real* holiday.

The line for soup stretched around the block in Albuquerque, New Mexico. Larry Thomas signed photos and soup ladles and anything else with a flat surface, chatting with fans and barking, "No soup for you!" over and over. Two hours in, however, the flow of fans stopped. Thomas hadn't expected to be done already.

When he looked up for the first time since he'd settled in at his signing table, he saw a couple locked in an embrace, making out. Hundreds of appearances as the Soup Nazi, thousands of strangers yelling, "No soup for you!" at him, and somehow, this had never happened. No one had ever thought to reenact the scene in which Jerry and his girlfriend get kicked out of the soup shop for kissing in line and missing their turn.

Thomas picked up the cue, roaring: "You're making out in my line? Nobody kisses in my line!"

The couple jumped up and down with excitement. Thomas was equally excited: "You guys are true originals," he told them. "You made my day."

Like everyone in line before them, the couple got free soup, Junior Mints, muffin tops, and a photo op with Thomas, who'd now been playing the dictatorial food stand proprietor for seventeen years. This particular appearance came as part of a 2012 road tour, in which Thomas traveled across the country in his white chef's coat, with a truck full of soup. He was back in what had turned out to be the role of his life, making stops in Albuquerque, Chicago, New York,

Philadelphia, and other cities to promote *Seinfeld* reruns.

Playing the Soup Nazi had long ago morphed from a onetime guest appearance (pay: $2,610) into a living for the actor. Even after the episode's surprising success, the career path to lifelong Soup Nazism did not immediately present itself when the show first ran. Through syndication, however, his staying power became more apparent. While on a touring production of a female version of *The Odd Couple* starring Barbara Eden in 2001, he and his onstage brother, David Castro, visited a Subway sandwich shop in Fort Lauderdale, Florida. "You look like the Soup Nazi," the sandwich maker said to Thomas.

"He is," Castro answered. "We're doing a play at the Parker Playhouse."

The sandwich maker couldn't contain his excitement. He ran out of the store to grab a friend hanging out at another place in the strip mall to bring him back and show him: The Soup Nazi! In their Subway!

As the two actors headed back to the playhouse, Castro, who was living in El Salvador at the time and thus not privy to *Seinfeld* fever during its original '90s run, said, "I had no idea your thing was like that! How do you handle it?"

"Like President Clinton said," Thomas replied, "I don't inhale it."

He knew he had done better work in his life than what was on display during that one *Seinfeld* episode. But he was also realizing that he wasn't going to shake this Soup Nazi thing, and he had come to terms with it. This reveals an impressive reserve of equanimity on Thomas's part: Many actors before him had lashed out at those who wanted to keep them stuck in the role that made them famous. Julie Kavner, the voice of Marge on *The Simpsons,* refused to ever do the voice in public. *Hill Street Blues* star Daniel J. Travanti avoided any mention of the show or his character in interviews just a few years after it went off the air. James Spader wouldn't discuss his breakout role as smarmy, rich jerk Steff in the 1986 film *Pretty in Pink.* Fred Gwynne shot down all questions regarding his part on *The Munsters.*

Thomas had learned to embrace his Soup Nazism with an extra helping of good cheer. When people pointed this out to him, he would say, "For me, the Soup Nazi is so cool that I feel honored to be attached to it in any way. I guess when your character is cooler than yourself, why be Larry Thomas when you can be the Soup Nazi?"

By 2012, he spent most of his time traveling to promotional appearances, corporate events, and autograph conventions. Autograph conventions were a particular boon to him, since they favor stars who are famous enough to draw fans willing to pay $20 for an autograph, but not so famous that they won't sit in a suburban conference room all day, signing their names and chatting up fans. He was a perfect fit. The convention circuit — at least a dozen of these things happen every month across America — could keep any such person willing to travel and schmooze in decent money. Thomas spent a lot of time in booths across the country signing autographs, surrounded by figures of late-twentieth-century pop culture: the guy who played Robin on the 1960s *Batman* TV series, the guy who played Peter Brady on *The Brady Bunch,* second-tier cast members from *Buffy the Vampire Slayer,* the guy who played the principal in *Back to the Future,* Lou Ferrigno of TV's *Hulk.*

Thomas knew every quirk of fan behavior. So many times, fans wanted to do *something,* to ritually reenact the *Seinfeld* episode they knew him from, but they weren't sure how to approach it. So many times, he sat at a table signing autographs, and a guy stepped up to say *something,* but struggled under the pressure to come up with something good.

Instead, the guy would end up standing and staring at Thomas, mute. Finally, Thomas would say, "Hey, how are you doing?" The guy's mouth would start to move, but nothing would come out. Thomas would help him out by barking, "No soup for you!" Thomas had come to understand that fans just wanted an experience, something special, but they weren't always sure what to do. That's why he loved it when the couple kissed in front of him.

Thomas had long ago gotten over qualms about playing the same one-note character for decades. Being the Soup Nazi on demand paid his bills, and he couldn't say the same for acting roles. If he put in a few *Seinfeld*-related appearances, he could take a low-paying role in an independent film to satisfy his artistic impulses. Before *Seinfeld,* he had spent fifteen years doing what he called " 'beg, borrow, and steal' theater." He appreciated being known for *something.* And he preferred playing the Soup Nazi to scraping together onetime guest spots on television.

As the Soup Nazi, he got to travel around the world to delight the show's international fans: In Oslo, Norwegian fans at a soup-company promotional event yelled, "No soup for you!" in perfect English. He has sold autographed photos and soup ladles to fans in Bosnia, Croatia, the Netherlands, Australia, England, and Venezuela. He was invited to autograph conventions in Iran, Bangladesh, and the United Arab Emirates.

By continuing to play the Soup Nazi, Thomas even got one of the highest-profile gigs possible: appearing with Seinfeld in a 2012 Acura commercial during the Super Bowl. After the shoot, when Seinfeld thanked him for doing it, Thomas said, "Well, health care and pension points." Seinfeld, who had likely stopped worrying about his health care and retirement funds through the Screen Actors Guild some time before, looked a bit mystified.

The job had its challenges. In 2013, for instance, Thomas saw a T-shirt online bearing an image of him with a rifle for a campaign against New York's gun laws. The NO SERBU FOR YOU! tagline was directed at the New York Police Department, which the company's owner, Mark Serbu, was refusing to sell his equipment to, given the state's ban on certain assault rifles.

Thomas got in touch with Serbu and asked the gun merchant to pull the image off his websites and Facebook page. Serbu apologized and offered Thomas compensation, but Thomas felt too strongly in favor of gun control to sell out for a couple grand. Serbu suggested Thomas put out a press release denouncing the use of his image to make up for the breach — and, not coincidentally, get some "controversy" press for Serbu's company. Thomas went along with this much of the plan. He called a contact at the *New York Post,* and as soon as the item ran on Page Six, it made national news. The *Huffington Post,* TMZ, and MSNBC called to interview Thomas; Serbu switched the image to his own face. Everyone came out happy.

Al Yeganeh, Thomas's real-life inspiration, appeared to spend most of his post-*Seinfeld* fame struggling to capitalize on his renown while still resisting the source of it. In 1997, he signed a deal to open soup kiosks in New York and Canada, but the plan never came to fruition. A year later, he sold a line of frozen soups on the Home Shopping Network, netting 1,600 orders in just the first eight minutes.

But by 2004, Yeganeh's original Fifty-Fifth Street shop in Manhattan had closed; he reopened on Forty-Second Street a year later and expanded to forty locations, but

Soup Kitchen International struggled and folded. By 2010, he'd reopened his Fifty-Fifth Street spot as Original Soup Man — renamed from Soup Kitchen International, and a nod to his identity as the "Soup Nazi." Though Yeganeh continued to denounce the show and its star when given a chance, his Original Soup Man company, using the tagline "Soup for You!," had expanded to thirteen locations by 2013. His lobster bisque, chicken noodle, and other flavors of soup were available for order online and at grocery stores. The company also operated food trucks around the country, and Yeganeh opened Al's Famous New York Delicatessen & Restaurant in Atlantic City.

Only once did Thomas get the urge to make like Yeganeh and deny his Soup Nazi connection. He was riding the Los Angeles subway, playing solitaire on his phone, and a few young men were looking at him. Finally one said, "Did anyone ever tell you that you look like the Soup Nazi?"

He was in the middle of a really good game, so he said simply, "Yeah, I get that all the time." He went back to his phone and won.

14
THE LEGEND OF THE CURSE

Larry David had become the ultimate cult celebrity, his name uttered like an incantation to invoke in-the-know-ness. All of America had come to love *Seinfeld,* as improbable as that seemed back in 1989, and the show was adding fans every year following its syndication across the country. By 1998, the way to separate yourself from the ignorant masses of fans, to indicate that you were a *true* fan, was to drop David's name into your cocktail party banter about *Seinfeld.* You weren't one of those idiots who knew only of Jerry Seinfeld — you knew who'd *co*created *Seinfeld,* maybe even *truly* created *Seinfeld,* or at least all that was innovative about it. You knew David was the one who came up with the idea of intertwining all four characters' plotlines at the end of each episode, the one who uttered the commandment, "No hugging, no learning," the one who was "the real George." You pored over profiles of David in the *New York Observer* and *The New Yorker.* You knew, for God's sake, what a *showrunner* was.

Curb Your Enthusiasm started as an HBO special in 1999, a mockumentary in which Larry goes about his daily business, preparing for a stand-up concert film, with extensive footage of him working on his act at small clubs. It did well enough that the cable network signed David to star in a ten-episode series, as a fictionalized version of himself, in January 2000. The improvised sitcom premiered on October 15, 2000. Cheryl Hines played Larry's wife, Cheryl; comedian Jeff Garlin played his manager, Jeff.

If a show could be more about nothing than *Seinfeld,* this was it. The series mimicked *Seinfeld* in several ways, obsessing over the minutiae of daily life — the difference was its far less affable, often bumbling, and irritable protagonist. One could see it as a sort of sequel to *Seinfeld,* following George Costanza after he got rich and famous making *Jerry* the sitcom and settling in Los Angeles. Indeed, there may be no bigger contributor to Seinfeldia's longevity than the links between *Seinfeld* and *Curb Your Enthusiasm.*

The newer show's title addressed such

comparisons head-on, urging viewers not to get their hopes up too much about the show just because of its relationship to *Seinfeld.* The approach mostly worked. *Curb Your Enthusiasm* stoked many critics' *Seinfeld* adoration anew, winning dozens of Emmy nominations as it progressed past its first season. Richard Lewis, Alanis Morissette, Ted Danson, and Mary Steenburgen were among the famous names to show up to play versions of themselves on the show. But its viewpoint, dyspeptic in comparison with *Seinfeld*'s, put some off. "David's anger . . . is merely the anger of frustrated entitlement," the *New Republic*'s Lee Siegel wrote. "[He] has perfected *Seinfeld*'s superior, uninviting stare into a cold, cruel sneer. The reason that so many people like it is that they want it to like them."

Several former *Seinfeld* writers — including Alec Berg, Dave Mandel, and Jeff Schaffer — brought their lists full of unrealized *Seinfeld* story ideas when they joined the *Curb* staff. Some had held on to them for quite some time: An eighth-season episode, "The Palestinian Chicken," contained a nugget of story that Steve Koren had intended for *Seinfeld,* thirteen years earlier — about a chicken restaurant so delicious that the characters are all willing to endure its discomfiting pro-Palestinian artwork.

Curb's infamy made for a funny reversal: Suddenly people were asking Jerry Seinfeld what Larry David was like in real life. Was he as cranky and obnoxious as the way he played himself on TV? Seinfeld would say, "I find his character on *Curb* to be the most reasonable and logical person. And I've never understood why people think of him any other way. To me he is one of the most intelligent and perceptive people, and our minds are very synchronous. So I think he is very much like that character. Maybe not as nice all the time."

"What am I doing here?" Jerry Seinfeld asks an audience at the tiny Comedy Cellar, a club in New York City's West Village tucked underneath the Olive Tree Cafe. "I made it! I had my own show! What did I do? I'm back here now." He was, in fact, making good on the promise of his HBO special. He was starting over, working on new material and testing it out in front of every comedy-club brick wall he could find.

"I've got like two bits," he told the camera crew following him for a 2002 documentary called *Comedian,* the distinctive comedy-club smell of wood, alcohol, and cigarettes permeating the air. "The rest is shit."

He told his friend and comedian Colin Quinn that he wasn't even sure he'd know when his routine was working anymore, it had been so long since he'd built it from scratch. "When you're killing, and while you're up there killing, you're miserable," Quinn answered. "Then it's back to where it used to be: When you're like, 'Eh, big deal, I made these idiots laugh.'"

Seinfeld was met with standing ovations just for showing up, but he insisted that his life as a comedian hadn't gotten any easier since his earlier days. Sure, they knew who he was and were primed to like him. But in the end, he still had to be funny. That was, after all, the beauty of stand-up: Whatever happened was between the comedian, the audience, and the microphone, and the only thing that made it work was laughter.

This return to the basics did not go perfectly for the $5 million man. He found himself in the middle of a story onstage at Gotham Comedy Club, only to lose track of his thoughts. He paced, he checked the notes sitting on a nearby bar stool. "And now my point here . . . Goddammit." After several rounds of nervous, supportive laughter, the room grew quiet. "And I didn't even want to say what I just said," he told them, irritated at his gaffe. "That's the ugly part."

385

"Is this your first gig?" a British woman asked from the audience.

"As you can see," he said, "this is quite painful."

If his mere rustiness didn't ground him after the lofty heights of *Seinfeld,* the democracy of comedy clubs did. When he performed at Governor's in Levittown, New York, at a time when the *Seinfeld* finale was still fresh in most Americans' minds, the club owner came to Jerry's dressing room. "I need you offstage by nine fifteen," he told the comedian. Seinfeld was a little shocked — here he was, a big star, coming to this tiny club in this Long Island town to polish up his brand-new act. Then he realized this was why he'd gone back into stand-up: to be treated like any old comedian again, not the major star of the most major TV show. "Stand-up is a life of just brutal reality," he said, "which is the opposite of the life I had been leading in L.A. and that I missed."

Of course, Seinfeld continued to take advantage of his stardom when there was a new project he wanted to do, like *Halloween,* his 2002 children's book. It was the ultimate trendy celebrity side project at a moment when everyone from Spike Lee to John Lithgow was also doing it, though Seinfeld maintained his distinctive comedic flavor in kid-friendly form: "Bing-bong, come on lady, let's go! Halloween, doorbells, candy, let's pick it up in there." He enjoyed his growing family life, too, as wife Jessica gave birth to their second child, son Julian Kal, in 2003, and their third, son Shepherd Kellen, in 2005. Though Seinfeld would never quite be a regular dad: All three kids' arrivals were announced on the air by morning-show host Regis Philbin.

As the years since *Seinfeld* passed, it became clear that part of Seinfeld's job would always be stoking the fires of *Seinfeld* mania. From 2004 to 2007, he and his fellow cast and crew gathered to record commentary tracks for the in-demand *Seinfeld* DVD sets. He shot several webisodes in 2004, sponsored by American Express, titled "The Adventures of Seinfeld and Superman," with Superman voiced by Patrick Warburton, *Seinfeld*'s Puddy. He played "himself" in a 2004 episode of *Curb Your Enthusiasm.*

Seinfeld was a dream résumé line, and it got the former *Seinfeld* writers meetings with networks that they had long wished for. Though they soon realized that nothing would ever compare with their experience on *Seinfeld,* their years of being on a top show that got no network notes. They found themselves summoned to networks to deliver "the next *Seinfeld*" only to be met with the same confusion and blank stares that David and Seinfeld once encountered in their early TV days. The *Seinfeld* writers found themselves trying to explain jokes, to no avail, and rebutting objections to the exact sorts of stories and characters everyone loved on *Seinfeld*. "Well, what about likability?" the executives would say. "Something with more emotion?"

"No," the writers countered. "We're going to love the person for being neurotic."

"But we'd really like this person to say, 'I love you,' at the end of the scene." Hugging and learning were back.

Spike Feresten, meanwhile, landed his own talk show on Fox in 2006. It became the network's longest-running attempt at a talk show thus far, because it lasted more than one season; it ultimately lasted three. Feresten had learned everything he knew about being a performer from watching Seinfeld; and everything he knew about running a show from watching Seinfeld. It helped that Seinfeld himself appeared as a guest in the pilot.

But no matter what happened, Feresten was known foremost as "the guy who wrote the Soup Nazi episode of *Seinfeld.*" Larry Thomas, who played the Soup Nazi, did promo spots for the show in character.

Writer Andy Robin chose the most unexpected path: He went to medical school and became a doctor. He continued to write on the side, but he didn't have to write something unless he wanted to. He didn't have to pitch anything to anyone. He could just go about his business, healing the ailing of Rhode Island, three thousand miles from Hollywood, never thinking of "The Junior Mint" again.

Just four years after *Seinfeld* ended, *TV Guide* named it the best show of all time, holding it in higher esteem than *I Love Lucy, The Honeymooners, All in the Family,* and *The Sopranos.*

And yet the "*Seinfeld* curse" clung to its former stars. Alexander, Louis-Dreyfus, and Richards all attempted starring in their own sitcoms, but struck out within their first seasons. In 2000, *The Michael Richards Show* featured the former Kramer as a private detective and was created by three former *Seinfeld* writers, Feresten, Kavet, and Robin. But it lasted only eight episodes on NBC. Alexander played a motivational speaker in *Bob Patterson,* which premiered to negative reviews and faded out after five episodes — though it also faced the impossible task of being a comedy that debuted ten days after September 11, 2001. Alexander's 2004 show, *Listen Up!,* about a sportswriter, fared better with critics and viewers, but still wasn't able to stay on the air for longer than a year. Louis-Dreyfus headlined an innovative sitcom called *Watching Ellie,* which premiered in 2002 and showed the title character, a cabaret singer, in real-time, twenty-two-minute segments of her life. It lasted sixteen episodes.

Larry David called talk of the curse "the most absurd, silliest, stupidest thing to say. . . . It's so annoying to hear something like that. There was no curse. It's crazy. So there were two TV shows attempted that didn't work? *Big deal.* How many TV shows work?" And as Alexander said, "It's not a *Seinfeld* curse. It's a success curse. There's a reluctance on the part of the audience and producers to put you into another role. . . . The problem with *Seinfeld* is that measuring up is no easy standard." The stars seemed to also be, at least in part, victims of changing trends in television. In 2002, reality show *Fear Factor,* in which contestants ate bugs, was a hit, and sexy spy drama *Alias* was a critical favorite — hardly an environment ripe for masters of the sitcom. Meanwhile, they were appearing constantly, at all hours, in their best-known roles, thanks to syndication. Elaine, George, and Kramer were harder to live down than ever, and that didn't seem to be abating as time passed.

However, Louis-Dreyfus finally "broke" the curse with the 2006 premiere of the solid *The New Adventures of Old Christine,* in which she played a neurotic divorced mom. When she won an Emmy for the role in 2006, she said in her acceptance speech, "I'm not somebody who really believes in curses, but curse this, baby!" The series ran until 2010, long enough to reach syndication — the industry benchmark of true success. She won another Emmy for her role as narcissistic vice president Selina Meyer on HBO's *Veep* in 2012, going on to win two more Emmy Awards for that performance.

She declined opportunities during interviews to whine about the difficulties of having played a famous character, and instead used her *Seinfeld* clout to her advantage, securing producing credits on both *Old Christine* and *Veep.* She saw it as critical to guaranteeing authority over her projects and using her extensive experience.

Of course, there was one cast member

who managed to bring a curse upon himself, and it was a doozy.

The Laugh Factory on sunset boulevard in Los Angeles had hosted almost every major comic in America since opening in 1979: At one time or another, Tim Allen, Roseanne Barr, George Carlin, Kathy Griffin, Bob Hope, Andy Kaufman, Jay Leno, Howie Mandel, Richard Pryor, Paul Reiser, and Jerry Seinfeld had all stepped onto its stage, in front of its distinctive sunset logo, to attempt a night of making audiences laugh.

It's here that we see Kramer — that is, Michael Richards — all lanky body and wiry hair, pacing the stage and screaming: "Shut up! Fifty years ago we'd have you upside down with a fucking fork in your ass. You can talk, you can talk, you can talk. You're brave now, motherfucker. He's a nigger, he's a nigger, he's a nigger. A nigger, look, there's a nigger!" It's here, on a cell phone video that millions saw online in the days after Richards's 2006 comedy-club meltdown, that you can hear audience members gasping. Now Richards mocks not only the two African American men with whom he was originally sparring but also his entire audience: "Ooh, ooh. All right, you see, this shocks you, what's buried beneath you stupid motherfuckers."

"That was uncalled for!" a voice yells back.

"That was uncalled for? It's uncalled for you to interrupt my ass, you cheap motherfucker! I don't know, I don't know, I don't know. They're going to arrest me for calling a black man a nigger."

The voice again: "That was uncalled for, you motherfucking cracker-ass motherfucker."

"Cracker ass? You calling me 'cracker ass,' nigger?"

"It's not funny, that's why you're a reject, never had no shows, never had no movies, *Seinfeld,* that's it."

The vicious tirade became one of the Internet age's first major scandals perpetuated by cell phone camera, video-driven gossip site TMZ, and YouTube. Millions saw Richards's rant and were disillusioned by the sight of one of America's favorite sitcom characters spewing such vicious words.

The club banned all future use of the word *nigger.* Less than a month later, Damon Wayans paid a $320 fine, $20 for each use, and was banned from the Laugh Factory for three months. Richards had returned to the club the night after the debacle and did his scheduled set (no finable offenses this time). But as word of the confrontation spread, he would stop doing comedy altogether. Seinfeld, though he'd always admired Richards as a comedic genius, was forced to release his own statement on the issue, saying he was "sick" over what had happened. "I'm sure Michael is also sick over this horrible, horrible mistake," Seinfeld said in his statement. "It is so extremely offensive. I feel terrible for all the people who have been hurt." At first Richards declined to comment beyond expressing his regret.

Seinfeld was booked to appear on *Late Night with David Letterman* that week — to promote the release of the seventh season of *Seinfeld* on DVD — and requested Richards appear with him via satellite to apologize publicly. "He's someone that I love, and I know how shattered he is" about the incident, Seinfeld told Letterman.

Richards appeared beamed in from Los Angeles, looking tired and washed-out in a black button-down shirt against a stark, gray backdrop, his trademark hair slicked back. "I lost my temper onstage," Richards said in the appearance, adding, "I said some pretty nasty things to some Afro-Americans. . . . You know, I'm really busted up over this and I'm very, very sorry." When a few audience members — either confused by the serious tone on the usually comedic show, or struck by the retro term *Afro-Americans* — giggled, Richards said, "I'm hearing your audience laugh and I'm not even sure that this is where I should be addressing the situation."

Still, he continued to ramble: "I'm deeply, deeply sorry. And I'll get to the force field of this hostility, why it's there, why the rage is in any of us, why the trash takes place, whether or not it's between me and a couple of hecklers in the audience or between this country and another nation, the rage . . ." Finally, he concluded, "I'm not a racist. That's what's so insane about this."

As racists embraced Richards as their truth teller, he became radioactive waste to Hollywood, impossible to cast — there was little hope of recovery after an "N-word" incident. "Once the word comes out of your mouth and you don't happen to be African American, then you have a whole lot of explaining," said fellow stand-up Paul Rodriguez, who was at the Laugh Factory during the performance. "Freedom of speech has its limitations and I think Michael Richards found those limitations." Publicist Michael Levine told the *Today* show: "I've never seen anything like this in my life. I think it's a career ruiner for him. . . . It's going to be a long road back for him, if at all."

Jason Alexander was guest-starring on a black family sitcom produced by comedian Chris Rock, *Everybody Hates Chris,* when the controversy was unfolding. He worried about his former costar, who he thought was struggling with "anger issues." The day after the news broke, Alexander discussed the incident with *Chris* cocreator Ali LeRoi. "I don't know what to tell you," Alexander later recalled telling LeRoi. "I've talked to Mike. I know he is devastated."

"I know exactly what happened," said LeRoi, who is black. "I get it. Let's offer him a part on the show."

"I can't imagine Michael's in a place where he could physically do it," Alexander said. "But even if you called him and made that gesture, it would be an amazing thing." Alexander was correct; the deal never worked out. A 2007 episode contained a minor joke at Richards's expense, with Rock as the narrator saying, "Because I was planning on cutting school, I was acting guiltier than Michael Richards at an NAACP convention."

Even the "real" Kramer experienced some blowback from the incident, from fans who couldn't discern the difference between Kenny Kramer and the man who played Cosmo Kramer. He got hate e-mail calling him a "racist piece of shit" and worse. Seinfeldia was not immune to controversy.

In 2012, Jerry Seinfeld began a true cultural renaissance when he launched a web series, *Comedians in Cars Getting Coffee*. The first season included ten episodes, each featuring a different comedian in conversation with Seinfeld over coffee. (The "cars" came in when Jerry picked them up in one of his extensive collection of vintage automobiles.) The series was a hit for the new millennium, racking up 10 million viewers per episode.

The first season's finale brought Richards back into the public eye for the first time since his meltdown. Here, he atoned more than he had in the six years that had passed. "I think I worked selfishly and not selflessly," he told Seinfeld. "I should've been working selflessly that evening. I busted up after that event. It was a selfish response. I took it too personally, and I should've said, 'You're absolutely right, I'm not funny.'" Then he added, to Seinfeld, "Thanks for sticking by me. It meant a lot to me. Inside, it still kicks me around a bit."

■ ■ ■ ■

When Jason Alexander first heard Larry David's idea to reunite the *Seinfeld* cast on *Curb Your Enthusiasm,* he balked. Why should HBO get such a golden goose? The cast could make gazillions on a *Seinfeld* movie — it was all anyone asked them about in interviews, besides the damn "*Seinfeld* curse." Now they were just going to give it away, and not even to the network that made the show in the first place? Not to mention the question of whether they could pull it off. They were eleven years older, it was eleven years later, and they hadn't worked as a group since. Would it really be up to their standards?

Then again, they'd be in David's hands. Alexander talked to Louis-Dreyfus about it, and they decided: For Larry, they'd do it.

And as they discussed the idea, it seemed so natural that they couldn't resist it. Jerry and Larry, working together, their desks facing each other, just like the olden days. As they began to shoot what would become a string of 2009 episodes of *Curb Your Enthusiasm* — directed by former *Seinfeld* writer Jeff Schaffer — it looked and felt just like the olden days.

The meta-plot setup was simple: Larry would agree to get the gang back together for a *Seinfeld* reunion on NBC — a gracious nod to their home network — in an effort to give estranged wife Cheryl, an actress, a part on the show as George's wife.

In the resulting episodes, they all gather for table reads, rehearsals, and a taping in front of a live, laughing studio audience, a jarring departure from *Curb*'s quiet, single-camera approach. The first scene they shot was the faux table read. They returned to their old space at the CBS Radford lot, where the old sets for Monk's Café and Jerry's apartment had been reassembled. Even the people who would have been at the table read in 1998 reappeared to play themselves — director Andy Ackerman, crew members, Castle Rock and NBC executives. It was the closest thing to time travel any of them would ever experience. The series finale shoot felt like it had happened five minutes earlier, not eleven years.

As they prepare the show within the show, we get glimpses of what the *Seinfeld* characters have been up to in the ten years since the show ended: Jerry donated sperm so Elaine could have a daughter. George got rich off his invention of the iToilet, an app that helps you find the nearest decent public restroom anywhere in the world; but he lost all his money by investing it with Bernie Madoff. His ex-wife, played by Larry's on-screen ex Cheryl, kept her half because she pulled out of Madoff's investments when she saw him on the street wearing a quilted jacket that bothered her.

As they discuss all of this in Jerry's old, familiar living room set, fake cameras surround them. Real cameras surround the fake cameras. As the faux *Seinfeld* scene unfolded before him, Schaffer realized he had a note on the scene, and started to walk out onto the set to tell David and the actors, just like he would have during a rehearsal when he was twenty-five years old. Berg grabbed him and held him back: "No, idiot," he said, "we're shooting." Right. This wasn't the real show. This was on camera, pretending to be a show — which, all together, was the show.

The ultimate *Seinfeld* reunion came to us with every backstage mechanism in view. The construct sucked the potential cheesiness out of the exercise and enabled the producers to show us only the good parts — because, of course, they wrote *only the good parts*. In a move typical of both *Seinfeld* and *Curb,* the plots that show up in the show-within-the-show come from — you guessed it — earlier episodes of the show. This is Larry's "real life" material. Jerry gives a little girl's doll a haircut, just as Larry once did in an episode, to disastrous effect. Kramer hires a prostitute so he can use the carpool lane, just as Larry once did on-screen. They also get some classically *Seinfeld* observational-humor lines for the modern era, as when Elaine checks her phone while talking to Jerry in his apartment, and Jerry fumes, "Oh, you're gonna do the BlackBerry head-down thing on me now?"

Curb plots also swirl around the actors playing themselves. Julia blames Larry for a ring-stain left on a valuable wood coffee table during a party at her house, and Larry determines to find the real culprit. "Larry David, Wood Detective," Jerry chides under questioning. Larry upsets Jason by referring to his new book, *Acting Without Acting,* as a "pamphlet."

The most fun comes from the two separate worlds of *Curb* and *Seinfeld,* each one as real as the other, colliding. Larry's friend Leon appearing nonplussed by the appearance of Elaine and Jerry, together again on the set of Jerry's apartment: "Now who are these two right here?" Larry offering to play George — who was, after all, based on him

401

— and succeeding in showing us how great Jason Alexander is by comparison.

Behind the scenes of *Curb* itself, David did panic the day he had to fake playing George. He called Alexander that morning, frantic. "I don't know how to do George! You have to come down and give me line readings!" Alexander went to the set and directed Larry in how to play Jason playing George, who is Larry. Even at that, David argued with some of Alexander's interpretations. (As Jerry explains to Larry during the episode, he does not belong on-screen with them. Pointing to himself, Jerry proclaims, "Icon!" Pointing at Larry, he yells, "Nocon!") In the end, Larry storms off in a jealous rage as Cheryl and Jason flirt — and even quits before the show is done, in a nod to his departure from *Seinfeld* two seasons before its finale.

As the reunion episodes wrap up, Larry gets what he wanted: all of the plot strands coming together. That, and a reunion with Cheryl. She shows up at his place proffering iced coffee and asking to watch the show together, having been replaced by an actress named Virginia (played by Elisabeth Shue, for some reason not playing herself). When Cheryl leaves her sweating coffee cup on Larry's wood table, however, he realizes:

She's the one who ruined Julia's table! Of course, he can't enjoy the romantic moment and leave that unnoted. He can't believe that she doesn't respect the sanctity of wood! And that, not a romantic embrace (no hugging!), ends the season and the *Seinfeld* reunion.

The reunion did allow for a bit of a redo on *Seinfeld*'s reviled finale. There was no talk of prison sentences or trials, only riffs on what the characters would get up to in the world of cell phones, Ponzi schemes, and IVF. There were even some direct admissions, as when Jerry says, "We already screwed up one finale."

This time, critics agreed. *Seinfeld* had mastered the perfect sendoff at last, as only *Seinfeld* could: by playing itself on another show, by blurring fiction and reality beyond conception. And by being, simply, funny.

15

SEINFELDIA

Chela Holton got a text from her partner, John: her picture, he cryptically claimed, was "all over New York." She was sitting in her office near Los Angeles International Airport, at a motorcycle company where she worked as an accountant. She wracked her brain to figure out what his mysterious message could possibly mean. She lived in the suburb of Monrovia, California, with John and his teenage son and daughter. She spent most of her time working or commuting an hour each way along the crammed L.A. freeways, wearing jeans and motorcycle T-shirts. There was no reason for her picture to show up in any public way on the other side of the country.

That is, except for that *one* reason. That had to be it.

She wouldn't know for sure until he calmed down enough to send her a more thorough, explanatory e-mail that included photos of her photo, which was, indeed, plastered on a building in New York City. It was that picture she had posed for twenty years before, in 1993, when she was twenty-two. She and John had, in fact, been looking for a decent copy of it since she'd told him about it in the early months of their courtship, eight years earlier.

Luckily, you wouldn't necessarily realize it was her, even if you knew her. In her everyday life, she had smooth, dark hair past her shoulders, pretty blue eyes, and well-tended eyebrows; in this old photo, her hair and eyebrows were unkempt, her eyes cast down. Once you knew it was her, you could see it. But even a friend wouldn't immediately say, "Hey, there's Chela Holton."

If that friend knew anything about *Seinfeld,* however, he or she *would* say, "Hey, there's *Rochelle Rochelle.*"

That was the one thing Holton had done that could cause her photo to show up in New York City — and cause a sensation that reached from there to Monrovia and beyond. She had "played" the star of a fictional moody, dramatic film called *Rochelle Rochelle* on a prop movie poster that showed up for a few seconds in a few episodes of a sitcom in the 1990s. That sitcom just happened to have such a lasting cultural effect that she never knew when those few seconds of screen time might make her, or at least her image from twenty years ago, famous again. And again. And again.

Jason Shelowitz had been watching *Seinfeld* since adolescence, but at thirty-four he still recorded the daily reruns on two different channels so his DVR stayed full of episodes. He never wanted to find himself short. He needed to watch at least five episodes per week.

For every life situation, he could find a *Seinfeld* parallel, but he tried to note them aloud only occasionally — to save his reputation and his loved ones' sanity. With like-minded people, such as his cousin and his cousin's fiancée, he particularly liked to recall all the fictional movie titles referenced throughout the show's run: *Prognosis Negative, Chunnel, Sack Lunch.*

Shelowitz — who had the buzz cut, perfectly tended facial stubble, and shy smile of a teen idol — was a well-known street artist (going by the handle JayShells) in New York City, where his most famous project was placing street signs quoting rap lyrics near the places that inspired them. (For example, Big Daddy Kane's line: "158 Lewis Avenue between Lafayette and Van

Buren, that was back durin' the days of hangin' on my Bed-Stuy block." Rappers are often quite specific with their directions.) So for Shelowitz, declaring his love for *Seinfeld* in a big, public way wasn't as elusive an idea as for the average fan.

Once when watching the fourth-season episode "The Movie," it hit Shelowitz: *Rochelle Rochelle,* "a young girl's strange, erotic journey from Milan to Minsk" — the fictional film all four *Seinfeld* characters end up watching after trying to see the equally fictional *Checkmate.* He caught a glimpse of the *Rochelle Rochelle* movie poster in a theater scene, and he paused his DVR on the moody, black-and-white image of a beautiful young woman with mussy long hair and impeccable bone structure. He could re-create the poster and hang it at a vacant movie theater near him that had been closed for a few years on the east side of Manhattan, on Second Avenue at Sixty-Fourth Street. It would look as if *Rochelle Rochelle* were actually playing. He wondered how many people passing by would think it was a real film, how many others would get the joke. He liked the idea of "talking" to fellow fans through his art.

He snapped a photo of his TV screen with the DVR paused on the poster, then grabbed a similar screenshot from a You-Tube version of the episode. Getting a clear-enough version of the model's face — the main feature of the poster — proved the most challenging part of the project. Finally, he got enough detail to allow him to fill in the rest with Photoshop. For the final touch, he added copy across the bottom — usually several lines of credits on a real movie poster — using the text from a *"Rochelle Rochelle"* description on the WikiSein website that catalogs every *Seinfeld* data point. *"Rochelle Rochelle* is a film referenced many times during the series. It is most likely based on the 1974 erotic film *Emmanuelle.* Like other films referenced by the show, it is never shown, but characters are portrayed watching it." Shelowitz's copy ends with a shout-out to the show's creators: "Thank you, Jerry Seinfeld and Larry David!"

At a cost to Shelowitz of about $100 each, he made two posters. On the day before Thanksgiving in 2013, he took advantage of the unseasonably warm, fifty-two-degree weather; he had to act fast because the huge, vinyl decals he was using for the posters wouldn't stick at below fifty. He put them up outside the movie theater, on either side of the closed and locked doors, as if it were playing there.

Online, Shelowitz posted photos of himself putting the posters up, and he signed the posters at the bottom with his street-artist name, JayShells. Fans cheered and shared on Twitter: "Made me miss *Seinfeld* even more!" one said. Websites such as *Gothamist, The A.V. Club, New York* magazine, and *Refinery29* covered it with glee. "*Seinfeld* Fans, Get Ready to Freak Out," one headline said.

Shelowitz hadn't realized there were so many fans as preoccupied with *Seinfeld* as he was. But soon he found out, as e-mails poured in asking about buying copies of his posters. Because the format was so expensive, he agreed to sell them (after checking with a copyright lawyer) to make back some of his investment in the project. He sold several copies, mostly to comedy writers in California and New York. In New York, he even hand-delivered a few.

Then, a few weeks after he'd put up the posters, he got an e-mail from a guy who claimed to be the partner of the woman who "played" Rochelle. The guy explained that his partner had been an extra on the show in a few episodes and was now an accountant; they lived in California with their two kids. He had managed to track Shelowitz down online. And they would love a copy of the poster.

Shelowitz wrote back, saying that if he could prove his partner was Rochelle, the poster was his for free. The guy — John — sent back four photos of his wife, clearly Rochelle in the present day.

Holton was working as an extra in 1993 in Los Angeles when she was hired to pose for a fake movie poster on *Seinfeld.* She was among three young women who were asked to show up on the set ready to be photographed. They had to bring their own wardrobe, a summery dress. Holton didn't have anything she deemed appropriate, so she borrowed a sundress from a neighbor.

One of the three girls didn't show up, leaving two for producers to choose from. They chose Holton. They gave her a little attention from hair and makeup beyond the standard treatment for extras, then brought her to a small, parklike area outside the *Seinfeld* soundstage. She was surprised at how efficient and serious things were on the *Seinfeld* set. It felt different — more professional — from the sitcom sets she was used to as an extra.

After a few hours shooting her walking around, looking forlorn, and carrying a suitcase on this overcast afternoon, the crew stopped and sent Holton to change. She'd also serve as an extra in a bar scene in the same episode, wearing different clothes and with her hair pulled up, her back to the camera. By the time she was done shooting for the day, she saw the *Rochelle Rochelle* poster for the first time, a cropped, black-and-white image of her from the waist up, looking down. All she could think about was her untweezed eyebrows, so large.

Producers told Holton to call the studio office a week later to get a copy of the poster to have as her own, but when she did, she was told they couldn't give out studio property.

She never got a copy, but she saw the image show up several more times again throughout the series. For instance, when George is renting it at the video store as he runs into his ex, Susan, and her new girlfriend, the movie poster appears on the VHS cover.

Like most of America, Holton regularly tuned in for reruns after the show ended in 1998. Every once in a while, there was a glimpse of her image again. Her two stepchildren learned of her moment in the spotlight when John, after years of searching for a copy of the poster, made his own version from a screenshot of the show and

411

hung it above his desk at home. It was, however, blurry, and even more so when blown up to poster size. He set up a Google alert so he'd know any time *Rochelle Rochelle* was mentioned on the Internet. Thanks to Shelowitz's project showing up online, he was able to replace his original attempt at a poster with Shelowitz's better version at last.

Holton couldn't believe how strange it felt to see her twenty-year-old photo resurfacing in such a public way. When she heard someone had stolen the posters Shelowitz originally hung in New York, she was even more confused: Why would people want such a thing? She wanted it only because it was *her*. And whenever she caught the episode, she barely felt a connection to that girl in the poster. Rochelle had become her own character with her own identity separate from Holton. Chela was a stepmom and accountant, not a young girl on an "erotic journey from Milan to Minsk."

Holton rarely mentioned her involvement with *Seinfeld* to anyone outside her family. At the motorcycle company where she worked, one of her young coworkers was so obsessed with *Seinfeld* that his office mates banned him from further show references. They even instituted a *Seinfeld* jar, where he had to put a dollar each time he broke the ban. Holton never told him that every day at work, he saw *Rochelle Rochelle.*

She liked keeping her little secret.

Two decades after *Seinfeld*'s finale, the show is intruding on the real world more than ever, with portals into Seinfeldia popping up everywhere. Jason Shelowitz caused an online sensation, made a few bucks, and connected with the "real" Rochelle with his *Rochelle Rochelle* posters. NextMovie.com put together its own take on *Seinfeld*'s fictional films, casting them with modern actors and mocking up posters for them: Jason Bateman and Tina Fey in *Sack Lunch,* Hugh Jackman in the David Cronenberg–directed *Prognosis Negative,* and Channing Tatum and Jason Statham in *Death Blow.* Artist Rinee Shah turned her drawings featuring food references from *Seinfeld* into an online business called "Seinfood." The Tom's Restaurant façade, pretzels ("These pretzels are making me thirsty"), bear claws ("You're the bear claw in the garbage bag of my life"), and black-and-white cookies were among the subjects of her works, which she sold to Internet shoppers around the world. Washington, DC, rapper Wale, born just five years before *Seinfeld* premiered, drew inspiration from the show for his *Mixtape About Nothing* in 2008 — which included riffs on the theme song and a meditation on Michael Richards's racist outburst. His 2015 album, *The Album About Nothing,* on which Seinfeld himself made a cameo appearance, went to No. 1 in its first week on the *Billboard* 200 chart.

Seinfeldia has its own art, its own music. And it has, more than anything, lots and lots and lots of its own media. Bloggers abound in Seinfeldia, chronicling its every detail, poring over its stars and its stories, and even documenting anti-*Seinfeld* sentiment. Several blogs are dedicated to binge-watching *Seinfeld* from start to finish, their writers ranking its episodes or narrating their experiences as first-time viewers or sharing what it's like to learn English via subtitled versions across the world. Others recap *Seinfeld* the way they do shows that are currently airing. One programmer even built a detail-perfect 3-D version of Jerry's apartment that anyone with an Oculus Rift virtual-reality headset can explore.

Canadian *Seinfeld* fan Jason Richards had watched the show since he was a kid in Montreal. At thirty, he still counted *Seinfeld* among his favorite shows of all time; he even had a *Seinfeld*-theme ringtone on his cell. He'd grown from a sweet, gap-toothed kid who didn't understand all the jokes on *Seinfeld* into a tawny-skinned, clean-cut TV producer with a cynical, strange sense of humor, who appreciated *Seinfeld* far more now, even though it hadn't aired a new episode in fourteen years.

And now *Seinfeld* was about to take over his life.

It began in 2012 when, years after he'd moved to Toronto, friends started talking about, e-mailing about, retweeting, and Facebooking about a new Twitter account called SeinfeldToday. The account imagined *Seinfeld* plots in the modern world, as if the show never went off the air. "George finds a rare gun from his dad's war days. Kramer talks him into selling it on eBay for $200. It shows up on *Pawn Stars* for $50,000." "Jerry gets paranoid about his girlfriend's past when her iPhone automatically connects to the wi-fi at Newman's apartment." "Elaine's BF notices she has no Instagrams with black people. She awkwardly tries to take pics w/black co-workers to prove she's not racist." It went on and on: Kramer meets a new girlfriend on Craigslist who turns out to be a hooker, Elaine tries JDate; Jerry buys a smart car. Over and over, Richards's friends forwarded these tweets to him because they knew he loved *Seinfeld* so much.

Richards followed SeinfeldToday on Twitter at first, like the thousands of others going Internet-crazy for the idea. But the more he read its tweets, the less funny it felt to him. The whole operation seemed kind of . . . smug, like someone claiming to be tweeting as Shakespeare or Hemingway. Who were these people, anyway? He checked out the handle's Twitter bio, which revealed that the masterminds were a senior editor at *BuzzFeed,* Jack Moore, and a New York writer and comedian, Josh Gondelman. Here these guys thought they'd just pick up where some true comic geniuses left off, and in 140 characters or less? It started to bug Richards.

But what could he do about it, besides unfollow the account, or spew disapproval back at it? At first, he figured he'd just ignore it. But still many of his friends kept retweeting it, showing it to him, reading it to him, and tagging him about it online. He couldn't take it anymore.

Then he thought: What if SeinfeldToday faced competition on its own turf — from an ignorant, insane, taunting, anonymous presence? SeinfeldToday didn't make Richards laugh anymore, but what *did* amuse him was the idea of countering Gondelman and Moore's polished plot pitches with lunacy, the idea of a crazy person putting himself in the same position as successful BuzzFeed editors and comedians. If the Internet gave everyone a voice, why shouldn't that include a deranged person who thought he was as clever as Gondelman and Moore — and, by the transitive property, as clever as *Seinfeld* creators Larry David and Jerry Seinfeld?

On a slow afternoon in January 2013 at the Toronto-based TV network where he worked, Richards sent his first tweet as Seinfeld2000, aka "Seinfeld Current Day": "Jerry use internet and Elaine start using internet."

Gondelman and Moore didn't expect to inspire such ire — or even such a large following — with their little Twitter joke.

Gondelman made his name as a stand-up comedian in New York City with a sort of hipster George Costanza vibe, all cool self-deprecation. While watching *Seinfeld* reruns one day, he noted how many of its episodes would be rendered obsolete by modern technology. A large portion of its plots would collapse if Jerry, Elaine, George, and

Kramer could text. They'd find one another at movie theaters and pick each other up at airports without a hitch. Then again, texting would create so many more of the kinds of social problems *Seinfeld* specialized in: dating, etiquette, secrets, lies. Gondelman's friend Moore had the brainstorm that brought it all together: They could start a Twitter feed to pontificate on how *Seinfeld* would be different if it were set in "modern" times.

The approach played well because it was so simple. As the account's Twitter tagline explained: "What if *Seinfeld* were still on the air?" Because *Seinfeld*'s characters were so well-defined, they could transport to any time and place and behave predictably. If the Elaine of the '90s broke up with a guy just because he was bad at breaking up, she'd also break up with a guy circa 2013 because he didn't punctuate his texts. If women's smallest gestures flummoxed '90s George, a Facebook "like" could drive him to days of obsession.

After Gondelman and Moore set up the SeinfeldToday account in December 2012, they picked up more than 75,000 followers their first day. Within a week, they had hundreds of thousands. *Seinfeld*'s George Costanza himself, actor Jason Alexander, retweeted a news story about the feed. Director and actor Jon Favreau, who appeared on the show in one of his earliest roles, tweeted about them. *Time* magazine named them to its list of 140 best Twitter feeds of 2013.

But Seinfeld2000 wasn't alone in his disapproval. Slate.com's Jeremy Stahl wrote: "In contrast to the sitcom that gave it life, SeinfeldToday is not *about* tedium and banality: It is merely tedious and banal. SeinfeldToday supposedly imagines what the show would be like if it were still on the air — but all it does is appropriate the show's characters and hand them iPhones plus a knowledge of the last fifteen years of popular culture." Sam Biddle of *Valleywag* told Stahl the feed was nothing more than a "lazy take on the novelty" of *Seinfeld* characters existing in the present. "Jerry Seinfeld . . . WITH AN IPHONE? Elaine . . . TRIES ONLINE DATING? George . . . LOSES HIS KINDLE? It's just a combination of nouns."

Seinfeld2000 gained a legitimate following tapping into this sentiment of annoyance, though his fan base remained a fraction of SeinfeldToday's. Seinfeld2000 had a definite acquired-taste quality — "an almost insurmountable barrier of entry," as its earliest press coverage said — as a parody of a parody written in what appeared to be its own special version of broken English, full of misspellings, pop culture allusions, and clumsy constructions. Followers were awfully close to being sucked into a cultural black hole via one too many cycles of meta-joke.

Seinfeld2000's works included existential musings: "You need to really take a minute and be honest with youre self about how you would actualy feel if 'senfeld' on TV today." And awful wordplay: "Jery in TV aisel of Best buy, 152-Inch Sony Plasma TV tip over and fall on him. Staff lift it off him. But what if TV was still on Seinfeld?"

Richards chose the odd voice by instinct, but he soon developed a rationale for it: a mediocre 1996 movie starring Michael Keaton called *Multiplicity*. In it, a harried father and businessman clones himself so he can get to everything on his to-do list, only to find that once he makes too many "copies" of himself, the "quality" degrades. Richards saw Seinfeld2000 as a copy of a copy, and thought the bad diction also lent his character a bit of pathos. He *tried* to compete with smooth BuzzFeed guys, but couldn't pull it off.

Because of the character's strangeness and

because Richards had chosen to remain anonymous, devoted followers couldn't help but feel there was a deeper point here. Was this part of a phenomenon known as "Weird Twitter," a public art project using the form of Twitter to make a statement? A sane person, a smart person, sending up the idea of parody accounts, and even the Internet as a whole? Or was it just exactly what it seemed to be, an insane person obsessed with SeinfeldToday, no more, no less?

Who or whatever it was, it had a considerable fan base: 7,000 people followed the account by 2013, and more than 61,000 by late 2014.

Richards refused to reveal that he was behind the account, taking a sort of Banksy approach to Internet memedom. The anonymity fanned his fans' ardent flames. Hints to his possible identity began circulating online: He was identified as a male by May 2013. He was around thirty, read Kafka, and listened to Daft Punk, some bloggers had discovered.

Richards was shocked that anyone cared that much. He was surprised anyone other than his parents, friends, and girlfriend followed the crazy feed.

The targets of Seinfeld2000's ire, meanwhile, took his existence as flattery. Besides which, Moore had by now parlayed the account into a writing gig for a new Fox sitcom and moved to Los Angeles. Gondelman went on to a staff writing job at HBO's *Last Week Tonight with John Oliver.* They were doing just fine, thanks.

While SeinfeldToday remained way ahead in the race for followers, hitting 787,000 by late 2014, Seinfeld2000 developed a cool factor, counting *Girls* creator and star Lena Dunham and Vampire Weekend front man Ezra Koenig among its fans. When Richards did an "Ask Me Anything" Q&A on the sharing site Reddit — which allows fans to ask celebrities questions in a real-time chat — almost all of the questioners attempted to mimic the broken, misspelled Seinfeld2000 voice, a sure form of flattery.

From there, things started to get weird. No, really this time.

To drive traffic to the Seinfeld2000 feed, Richards launched a dizzying number of spin-off projects large and small. Small: a YouTube video of the *Seinfeld* theme slowed down 1,200 percent. Large: a 16,000-word e-book, *The Apple Store.* In this opus, fiction and reality merge more than David and Seinfeld could ever have dreamed. Seinfeld2000 calls Jerry out on his endless conquest of women under thirty: Jerry meets actress Amanda Seyfried when he's so down on his luck that he's hitchhiking back to New York after getting kicked off Carrot Top's Kings of Prop Comedy Tour. But he still Googles her age to make sure she's young enough to bed. Seinfeld2000 makes Kramer a raging racist, spewing the kind of vitriol Michael Richards uttered in his infamous YouTube moment. Seinfeld2000 also makes it very clear that George plotted Susan's murder and must pay for it.

After the book, Seinfeld2000 got a gig writing for *Vice* magazine and interviewing musicians in character. He launched a YouTube channel. He made connections, and many of them were to talented people who wanted to work with this enigmatic web presence.

Richards's next major project was a collaboration with Pippin Barr, a respected New Zealand game artist with a heavy résumé: He taught at the Institute of Digital Games at the University of Malta, had a PhD in video game values, and had collaborated with performance artist Marina Abramović on a series of video games.

The resulting game, released in May 2014, reflected both of its avant-garde creators' aesthetics. Though it provides no concrete way to "win," it awards dollar amounts every time you manage to flip a mint into a moving open body cavity. You get a finite number of tries, then you're done; your only reward is a message that however much "money" you won will be donated to the Human Fund, George's fake charity from the show. Blocking the path between the player (either "Jerry" or "Kramer," who we see as photo cutouts) and the body are various obstructions off of which the mint may bounce: George and Elaine glide through, the doctors and their equipment slide back and forth, and pop star Miley Cyrus — for modernity! — flies through on a wrecking ball.

Richards never imagined his little Twitter outburst against SeinfeldToday would go this far. By this time, he figured, he would have unfollowed Seinfeld2000 if he weren't Seinfeld2000. He revealed his identity in a *New York Times* piece announcing the Junior Mint game. He had gone mainstream. He was getting a little sick of himself, or at least a little worried that others were getting sick of him. But cool collaborations kept presenting themselves. In July 2014, he got sucked in again, working with a developer who was a fan of Seinfeld2000 to launch a free *Seinfeld* emoji app.

He often considered shutting the Twitter feed down and going out on top, just like *Seinfeld* had. Someone tweeted to him that he had grown into the very sort of sellout he'd created the account to mock. That hurt. And would he want to keep doing this, only to end up a fifty-year-old man obsessed with his follower numbers?

But for the moment, he decided to keep going, with possible collaborations on live shows in New York and Australia on the horizon; ideas included a live *Sein-Quest2000,* a Tony Robbins–style presentation, and a "new" episode of *Seinfeld* written in the Seinfeld2000 voice. He was even considering moving to Los Angeles to pursue a career in Hollywood.

Meanwhile, Richards, as Seinfeld2000, hadn't forgotten his original mission: mocking SeinfeldToday. When he was vacationing in Los Angeles in October 2013, he caught wind of a radio interview Larry David had done in which the host asked David how he felt about SeinfeldToday. ESPN New York's Michael Kay read David one of the tweets: "Jerry's blind date shows up drunk and heckles the screen during *12 Years a Slave.* Kramer creates an app that gives you ideas for other apps." After a second's pause, David said, "Nah . . . I could guarantee you that show would not get on the air. . . . That does not pass the funny test."

Richards couldn't contain his glee. So he didn't. He time-coded the snippet of the interview in which David addresses SeinfeldToday and asked his followers — since he was traveling — if someone could put it on SoundCloud, a service that makes it easy to share audio files online. Once it was there, Richards tweeted the clip. It was picked up around the blogosphere. Sure, it would have likely made it onto some writers' radars eventually, but, as Richards said, he "produced it a little bit."

A few months later, during a Reddit "Ask Me Anything," Jerry Seinfeld expounded on his and David's dislike for the SeinfeldToday phenomenon. "Oh this is a very painful subject," he wrote. "As you can probably imagine, over the nine years of doing the show, Larry David and I sat through hundreds of ideas that people wanted to do on the show. And most of the ideas are not good. Which I saw Larry say the other day on some show, somebody asked him the same question and he said, 'I know you think it's funny, but it's really hard.' The ideas that Larry and I would respond to, I don't even know, they just need to be very unique. It's just a lot harder than it seems to come up with."

Richards, for his part, insisted that as Seinfeld2000 gathered steam, his hatred for SeinfeldToday dissipated. He simply couldn't resist a poke now and then when it presented itself. With this particular poke, he'd accomplished the ultimate: He had brought Seinfeldia to the feet of Larry David and Jerry Seinfeld, and asked them to pronounce judgment. Their disapproval only showed that Seinfeldia was a force far beyond their control by this point — even if its denizens would *always* welcome a visit from them, and would commence an appropriate level of freak-out if it ever happened.

On January 13, 2014, at about 10:30 A.M., it happened. George Costanza and Jerry Seinfeld walked into Tom's Restaurant. Cameras were rolling, which is why passersby who happened to catch the pair strolling into the Upper West Side diner knew it was George and Jerry, not Jason Alexander and Jerry Seinfeld. Alexander's Costanza-esque puffy red jacket and faded jeans provided further evidence. Alexander was also once again balding, a natural trait the actor had used some *Seinfeld* money to reverse in the elapsed time; the removal of his toupee only further confirmed that he was acting as George. The fact that it was Tom's Restaurant — the exterior body double for the fictional Monk's Café — and not a Monk's Café set indicated that something was a little . . . off. Then again, the real and fictional worlds of *Seinfeld* had swirled and mixed and mushed so much in the sixteen years since *Seinfeld* signed off that no one knew what to think anymore.

"Just George and Jerry casually walking into their corner coffee shop," one observer, Ali Philippides, tweeted. Online speculation ranged from mundane — maybe Alexander was shooting a second episode of Seinfeld's *Comedians in Cars Getting Coffee* — to what in Seinfeldia seemed as fantastical as it could get — a *Seinfeld* movie, or, better yet, a return of *Seinfeld* to television! The intrigue thickened when the New York website *Gothamist* posted a blurry video of Larry David leaving the scene later that afternoon, pursued by a pack of photographers and camera operators.

Soon, news arrived that placed the shoot right in the middle of those speculations: The two were filming a commercial set to run during the Super Bowl a few weeks later.

The ninety-second spot, which ran during the game's halftime break to promote *Comedians in Cars,* had George and Jerry trading old, *Seinfeld*-style banter as if they were hitting Tom's during that very game's halftime. "I can't believe the Super Bowl is in New York," George complains, referring to the city's hosting duties that year.

The two, it emerges, have been banished from the annual Super Bowl party of their friends, the Wassersteins, due to George's "over-cheer" two years before. The extended version online plays like George is a guest on Jerry's show. Jerry picks him up in a pea-green, 1976 Pacer, "a total disaster from initial concept to final execution," as the voice-over explains, equating the car with his friend. Seinfeld goes on to describe George as "my best friend from almost every single day of the 1990s." That famous TOM'S RESTAURANT sign gets a full camera shot, including the TOM'S.

The Seinfeld spot was the Super Bowl's most re-watched commercial of the game, according to statistics released by the digital video recorder company TiVo. It beat out more "modern" phenomena such as a Ford Fusion ad featuring actor James Franco and a spot for Beats headphones featuring Ellen DeGeneres dancing with anthropomorphic bears and wolves.

Seinfeld's stars still held the keys to Seinfeldia and could stroll in and out as they pleased, causing mass hysteria among its citizens with every appearance. But they are merely royalty: They are figureheads we will continue to celebrate long after their on-screen demise. They are not necessary to keeping the land running day-to-day. And that is the very secret to its magic; this land is of the people, by the people, and for the people, a monarchy no more.

For inhabitants of Seinfeldia, building and rebuilding it, keeping it alive with their every new idea and keystroke, it's not so simple to leave. Just ask Larry David, who tried to extricate himself several times and found himself pulled back in every time — to write a reviled finale episode, to write a reunion into his own show, to shoot a Super Bowl spot. Every year more young fans are learning of this place, of its strange language and customs. Who knows what they may come up with next?

ACKNOWLEDGMENTS

Seinfeldia is full of colorful, funny, smart characters to whom I am forever indebted. Those who shared their experiences with me for this book did so generously, thoroughly, and often hilariously. Thanks especially to director Tom Cherones and the show's writers who spoke with me, answered my weirdly detailed questions on demand ("What kind of car did you drive in 1993?"), shared tremendous photos with me, and helped me get in touch with their colleagues: Alec Berg, Jennifer Crittenden, Spike Feresten, Tom Gammill, Gregg Kavet, David Mandel, Bill Masters, Peter Mehlman, Dan O'Keefe, Max Pross, Andy Robin, Jeff Schaffer, and Fred Stoller, you are excellent people. Thank you to Jeremiah Bosgang, Adam Rainbolt, and Rick Lipps for sharing tales from some of the most interesting peripheries of Seinfeldia, and for having awesomely Seinfeldian names. Chela

Holton, Monica Shapiro, Kenny Kramer, (decidedly noncrazy) Joe Davola, John Peterman, Jason Shelowitz, Larry Thomas, and Jonathan Wolff, your stories made this book special. Anthony Tobia, Sabine Sebastian, Greg Miller, William Irwin, Jazmine Hughes, Kelli Marshall, Josh Gondelman, and Jason Richards get extra props for keeping Seinfeldia alive in the 2010s and beyond.

My early readers, Erin Carlson and Heather Wood Rudúlph, saved my sanity. So did Kathryn Sanders, my right-hand woman throughout researching this book. So did A. Jesse Jiryu Davis, of course, who has made me a better writer and human being since the second I met him. Much, much love to Carter Covington and Patrick Sean Smith, also known as my West Coast office (and occasional infirmary); and to Dave Freiberg and Bill O'Meara, my Chicago office. Thanks for the support, listening, lunches, drinks, and cushy assignments that allowed me to pay my bills, Andi Bartz, Melissa Collom, Allison Hantschel, A. K. Whitney, and Kim Potts.

Superagent Laurie Abkemeier can't be thanked enough. Neither can Jon Karp and the team at Simon & Schuster, who made my literary dreams come true, then handed me this idea.

Love, as always, to my family, who taught me to appreciate weirdness and humor.

SOURCE NOTES

"*Seinfeld* is something I learned to do": Jerry Seinfeld, Julia Louis-Dreyfus, Michael Richards, and Jason Alexander, *Sein Off* (New York: Harper Perennial, 1998), 11.

Chapter 1: The Origin Story

ventured into a Korean deli: Chris Smith, "Jerry Seinfeld: Making Something Out of Nothing," *New York,* April 6, 1998.

Catch a Rising Star: James Kaplan, "Angry Middle-Aged Man," *The New Yorker,* Jan. 19, 2004.

Lee's Market: Matthew Kassel, "Korean Deli Where *Seinfeld* Was Conceived Has Closed," *New York Observer,* June 12, 2014.

Korean jelly: "How It Began" documentary extra, *Seinfeld,* seasons 1 & 2 (Culver

City, CA): Sony Pictures Home Entertainment, 2004), DVD.

first become friends in the bar of Catch a Rising Star: Jerry Seinfeld, Reddit AMA, Jan. 6, 2014: https://www.reddit.com/comments/1ujvrg/jerry_seinfeld_here_i_will_give_you_an_answe

"actually typed something out": "How It Began."

"This . . . is what the show should be": Ibid.

after their comedy sets at the Improv: Ibid.

worried about filling an entire ninety minutes: Ibid.

"two guys talking": Ibid.

shared a car, a TV, and one pair of black slacks: Anne E. Kornblut, "Cashing In," *Daily News* (New York), Jan. 27, 1996.

funny at age eight: Ron Givens, "Funny, Didn't Look Like Him," *Daily News* (New York), Nov. 23, 1997.

spent his childhood watching: Seinfeld, Reddit AMA.

Kal Signfeld Signs: Givens, "Funny, Didn't Look Like Him."

At Birch Lane Elementary School: Jerry Oppenheimer, *Seinfeld* (New York: HarperCollins, 2002), 26.

he grew obsessed: Ron Givens, "Not Part of Wild Bunch During Turbulent Period in U.S., Jerry Went His Own Way," *Daily*

News (New York), Nov. 24, 1997.

Julius Caesar: Oppenheimer, *Seinfeld,* 51.

geometry class as training for comedy: Jerry Seinfeld, interview by Larry Wilde, *On Comedy,* Laugh.com, July 24, 2001.

acted in school productions: Oppenheimer, *Seinfeld,* 91–4.

eavesdropped: Seinfeld, Reddit AMA.

graduated in 1976 as an honor student: Seinfeld, interview by Larry Wilde.

His first appearance: Tod Caviness, "Get Your Laugh On!," *Orlando Sentinel,* Jan. 3, 2013.

practiced his routine with a bar of soap: Jerry Seinfeld, interview by Judd Apatow, *Club Comedy,* Syosset High School radio station, circa 1984 (exact date unknown); republished online by the *New York Times,* May 27, 2007, http://www.nytimes.com/2007/05/27/magazine/27apatow-t.html?pagewanted=all.

Comedian Elayne Boosler: Oppenheimer, *Seinfeld,* 119.

four years: Seinfeld, interview by Larry Wilde.

After three episodes: Scott Williams, "Jerry Gets the Last Laugh," *Daily News* (New York), Nov. 25, 1997.

"Funny is the world I live in": Jerry Seinfeld, interview by Peter Lauria. *BuzzFeed*

Brews, BuzzFeed.com, Feb. 3, 2014: https://www.youtube.com/watch?v=7RxKMvX7LRA.

"the Olympics": Seinfeld, interview by Larry Wilde.

JERRY SEINFELD OF MASSAPEQUA: Oppenheimer, *Seinfeld,* 188.

"the difference between thinking you're a comedian": Mark Goodman and Michael A. Lipton, "A Bittersweet Goodbye," *People,* May 25, 1992.

In 1988: Oppenheimer, *Seinfeld,* 236.

doing up to three hundred appearances: Chris Smith, "City Slicker," *New York,* Feb. 3, 1992.

"which means I sucked": Kaplan, "Angry Middle-Aged Man."

putting himself on trial: Jim Windolf, "Master of the Domain," *New York Observer,* Sept. 16, 1996.

"a combination of Bozo and Einstein": Kaplan, "Angry Middle-Aged Man."

affiliates . . . refused to air it: Dennis Perrin, "*Fridays:* The *SNL* Ripoff That Nearly Surpassed the Original," *Splitsider,* Jan. 31, 2012, http:// splitsider.com/2012/01/fridays-the-snl-ripoff-that-nearly-surpassed-the-original/.

Fiat convertible: Deirdre Dolan, *Curb Your Enthusiasm: The Book* (New York: Gotham

Books, 2006), 109.

In David's one season: Tom Shales, "*SNL* in the '80s," *Washington Post,* Nov. 12, 2005.

Prognosis Negative: Kaplan, "Angry Middle-Aged Man."

William Morris: George Shapiro, interview by Bill Dana and Jenni Matz, *Archive of American Television,* Feb. 12, 2007.

The Steve Allen Show: Allan Neuwirth, *They'll Never Put That on the Air* (New York: Allworth Press, 2006), 251.

told NBC executives: "How It Began."

November 2, 1988: "Notes About Nothing," *Seinfeld,* seasons 1 & 2.

to have his days free: "How It Began."

5:15 P.M.: Smith, "Jerry Seinfeld: Making Something Out of Nothing."

"What would you like to do in television?": "How It Began."

recent investment . . . from Columbia: Shapiro, interview by Bill Dana and Jenni Matz.

They weren't sure: "How It Began."

"He's expressive": Lawrence Christon, "Laughing on Empty," *Los Angeles Times,* Jan. 17, 1989.

Shapiro asked a staffer: Oppenheimer, *Seinfeld,* 243.

making disco jewelry: John Tierney, "With the Help of 'Seinfeld,' Legend in His Own Time," *New York Times,* Jan. 18, 1996.

Bic clear-barrel pens: Jerry Seinfeld, interview by Jenny Woodward, *New York Times,* Dec. 20, 2012, http://www.nytimes.com/video/magazine/ 100000001965963/jerry-seinfeld-how-to-write-a-joke-.html.

Seinfeld worried: "How It Began."

wanted to use Kramer's real name: "Kramer vs. Kramer: Kenny to Cosmo," *Seinfeld,* season 3 (Culver City, CA: Sony Pictures Home Entertainment, 2004), DVD.

with yet another shrug: "How It Began."

Stage actor Nathan Lane: Bradford Evans, "The Lost Roles of *Seinfeld,*" *Splitsider,* April 14, 2011, http://splitsider.com/2011/04/ the-lost-roles-of-seinfeld/.

Top Gun costar Anthony Edwards: "Jason + Larry = George," *Seinfeld,* season 5 (Culver City, CA: Sony Pictures Home Entertainment, 2005), DVD.

Robert Schimmel: Mike Flaherty, "A Comic's Trip," *Entertainment Weekly,* Nov. 5, 1999.

Rob Reiner had seen Jason Alexander: Jason Alexander, interview by Amy Harrington, *Archive of American Television,* May 10, 2013.

Seinfeld had noticed: "Jason + Larry = George."

McDonald's McDLT: Alexander, interview by Amy Harrington.

young George Burns: Alan Bunce, " 'Everything's Relative': Fast-Paced Gags Keep the Show's Laugh Track Puffing," *Christian Science Monitor,* Sept. 28, 1987.

"I thought there'd be more plumes": Alexander, interview by Amy Harrington.

invited to read for the *Seinfeld* part: "How It Began."

a few pages of the script: "Jason + Larry = George."

Woody Allen prototype: Alexander, interview by Amy Harrington.

That's the guy: "Jason + Larry = George."

About a week: Alexander, interview by Amy Harrington.

"complete waste of time": "Jason + Larry = George."

"Not so obviously Woody": Alexander, interview by Amy Harrington.

David could see the chemistry: "Jason + Larry = George."

By the time he landed: Alexander, interview by Amy Harrington.

yoga: "Michael Richards," *People,* May 14, 1998.

thousand pounds of dirt: "Kramer vs. Kramer: Kenny to Cosmo."

Seinfeld knew Richards's work: Michael Richards, interview by Jerry Seinfeld, "It's Bubbly Time, Jerry," *Comedians in Cars Getting Coffee,* September 27, 2012: http://comediansincarsgettingcoffee.com/michael-richards-its-bubbly-time-jerry.

Tony Shalhoub and character actor Larry Hankin: Evans, "The Lost Roles of *Seinfeld.*"

"the mysterious hand of the universe": Richards, interview by Jerry Seinfeld.

Richards had to read for the producers: "How It Began."

"Well, if you want *funny*": Warren Littlefield, *Top of the Rock* (New York: Anchor Books, 2013), 74.

"So, Mr. Experience": "How It Began."

pages contained few to no behavioral cues: Alexander, interview by Amy Harrington.

first test came: Stephen Battaglio, "The Biz: The Research Memo That Almost Killed *Seinfeld,*" *TV Guide,* June 27, 2014.

"Who will want to see": David Zurawik, "The world according to *Seinfeld,*" *Baltimore Sun,* May 3, 1998.

"I'm not from New York": Neuwirth, *They'll*

Never Put That on the Air, 227.

about four hundred households: Battaglio, "The Biz."

In the first week of May: Littlefield, *Top of the Rock,* 78.

"You can't get too excited": Battaglio, "The Biz."

"Jerry Seinfeld, who was familiar to about a quarter of the viewers": Littlefield, *Top of the Rock,* 77.

"the oversexed head": NBC, "NBC Announces New Season's Prime Time Schedule," press release, May 16, 1989, Rick Ludwin Collection, Miami University Libraries, Oxford, OH.

"aimless wandering": Kathryn Baker, "Seinfeld Plays Himself in Sitcom," Associated Press, July 5, 1989.

network's rights to *The Seinfeld Chronicles* neared expiration: Battaglio, "The Biz."

Bob Hope special: Littlefield, *Top of the Rock,* 83.

"lacked estrogen": Elizabeth Kolbert, "A Visit with: Julia Louis-Dreyfus," *New York Times,* June 3, 1993.

Patricia Heaton . . . Megan Mullally . . . Rosie O'Donnell: Evans, "The Lost Roles of *Seinfeld.*"

She joined at twenty-one: Jonny Black, "Julia Louis-Dreyfus Facts: 21 Things You (Probably) Don't Know About the 'Veep' Star," Moviefone.com, Aug. 29, 2014, http://news.moviefone.com/2014/08/29/julia-louis-dreyfus-facts/.

youngest female cast member: Megh Wright, "Saturday Night's Children: Julia Louis-Dreyfus (1982–85)," *Splitsider,* Dec. 18, 2012, http:// splitsider.com/2012/12/ saturday-nights-children-julia-louis-dreyfus-1982-1985/.

shocked to find a cutthroat atmosphere: Julia Louis-Dreyfus, interview by Dave Davies, *Fresh Air,* NPR, May 3, 2012.

New York sensibility: Margot Dougherty, "Laughing Out Loud with Julia Louis-Dreyfus," *More,* April 2013.

Lucille Ball, Mary Tyler Moore: Daniel Fienberg, "Julia Louis-Dreyfus Talks Emmys, 'Veep,' and the New Nicole Holofcener Film," *Hitfix,* Aug. 8, 2012, http://www.hitfix.com/the-fien-print/ julia-louis-dreyfus-talks-emmys-veep-and-obscenities.

Preston Sturges's funny, sexy heroines: John Patterson, "Julia Louis-Dreyfus: Bucking the Seinfeld 'Curse,' " *Guardian,* June 15, 2012, http://www.theguardian.com/tv-and-radio/2012/jun/15/ julia-louis-dreyfus-veep-iannucci.

parents wouldn't allow her: Kolbert, "A Visit with: Julia Louis-Dreyfus."

left Northwestern before graduating: Jenny Hontz, "On the Wild Side," *Northwestern,* Fall 2014.

eating cereal: Scott Feinberg, "Julia Louis-Dreyfus, Queen of Frazzled Single Women, on Taking Her Act to the Big Screen," *Hollywood Reporter,* Dec. 11, 2013.

sat on a sofa: "Queen of the Castle: The Elaine Benes Story," *Seinfeld,* season 7 (Culver City, CA): Sony Pictures Home Entertainment, 2006), DVD.

figured this thing would get canceled: Patterson, "Julia Louis-Dreyfus: Bucking the Seinfeld 'Curse.' "

cowboy boots: "Queen of the Castle: The Elaine Benes Story."

came from her upbringing: Kolbert, "A Visit with: Julia Louis-Dreyfus."

good enough to worry Alexander: Alexander, interview by Amy Harrington.

Thelonious Monk poster: Smith, "Jerry

Seinfeld: Making Something Out of Nothing."

crunched on cereal: Larry David, interview by Jerry Seinfeld, "Larry Eats a Pancake, *Comedians in Cars Getting Coffee,* July 19, 2012: http://comediansincarsgettingcoffee .com/larry-david-larry-eats-a-pancake.

holding on to most of *Cheers'* audience: Steve Weinstein, " 'The Simpsons' Jumps Into the Top 10," *Los Angeles Times,* June 6, 1990.

later recalled Fox rejecting the idea: "Kramer vs. Kramer: Kenny to Cosmo."

Preston Beckman: Littlefield, *Top of the Rock,* 87.

"brisk funniness": Ken Tucker, "White House Showcase, Jerry Seinfeld Sitcom," *Inquirer,* July 5, 1989.

"This Jerry Seinfeld": Tom Shales, "He's a Stand-Up Kind of Guy," *Philadelphia Daily News,* May 31, 1990.

fifth season in first place: Lee Winfrey, " 'Roseanne' Tops Season's Ratings," *Inquirer,* April 18, 1990.

reminded him of when: Dolan, *Curb Your Enthusiasm: The Book,* 108.

"I'm going to get a Lexus": Ibid., 50.

January 16, 1991: "Notes About Nothing."

Chapter 4: The Cult Hit

"Some of the writers": Glenn Collins, "How Does Seinfeld Define Comedy? Reluctantly," *New York Times,* Sept. 29, 1991.

Littlefield loved the Elaine-Jerry dynamic: "Notes About Nothing."

As the grad students later recalled: Blake Bailey, *A Tragic Honesty: The Life and Work of Richard Yates* (New York: Picador, 2004), iTunes e-book, 675.

a butcher knife from Jerry's apartment: "Inside Looks: 'The Jacket,' " *Seinfeld,* seasons 1 & 2.

"please help me": Alexander, interview by Amy Harrington.

James Hong expressed his confusion: "Unforgettable Characters," *People,* May 14, 1998.

"Like real life": Kit Boss, "Simply Seinfeld," *Seattle Times,* June 28, 1991.

"*Seinfeld* doesn't feel like sitcom television": Smith, "City Slicker."

"No hugging, no learning": Kaplan, "Angry Middle-Aged Man."

"All hits are flukes": Betsy Frank, "Cable Hits: Myth or Reality," *Multi-channel News,* Feb. 26, 2001.

run up a deficit: Chris Heath, "The End of 'Seinfeld,' " *Rolling Stone,* May 28, 1998.

speed off in his Porsche: Smith, "City
Slicker."

finished the 1990–91 season: Jonathan
Storm, "Crunching TV's Numbers," *Inquirer,* April 17, 1991.

Jason Alexander's sense of indignation:
Alexander, interview by Amy Harrington.

Louis-Dreyfus was routinely voicing:
"Queen of the Castle: The Elaine Benes
Story."

Chapter 5: The Production

script is supposed to end: Alexander, interview by Amy Harrington.

knew nothing about sports: "Jason + Larry
= George."

"How are you getting all these girls?": Alexander, interview by Amy Harrington.

"this little twinkle": "Jason + Larry =
George."

army draftee: Tom O'Neill, "Michael Richards," *US Weekly,* May 1997.

in on the joke: Jeff Labrecque, "What Really
Happened the Night Andy Kaufman
Melted Down on Live TV," *Entertainment
Weekly,* Aug. 5, 2013.

compared to Jacques Tati: O'Neill, "Michael
Richards."

"His act is": David Bellos, *Jacques Tati*

(New York: Random House, 2012), 63.

requested a preshow announcement: "Kramer vs. Kramer: Kenny to Cosmo."

"subtle, powerful reinvention": Alexander, interview by Amy Harrington.

doorjamb: "Kramer vs. Kramer: Kenny to Cosmo."

"to be grotesque about it": Alexander, interview by Amy Harrington.

didn't feel like they knew him: "Kramer vs. Kramer: Kenny to Cosmo."

ambushed by paparazzi: O'Neill, "Michael Richards."

"thousands of American girls": Edward Marshall, "The Gibson Girl Analyzed by Her Originator," *New York Times,* Nov. 20, 1910.

model and inspiration: Stacy Schiff, "Otherwise Engaged," *New York Times,* March 19, 2000.

East Seventy-Third Street: Karen Adams, "Irene Langhorne Gibson: From Hollins Girl to Gibson Girl," *Hollins Magazine* (Hollins University, Roanoke, VA), Spring 2013.

"sexy modified Gibson girl coif": Lisa Schwarzbaum, *Entertainment Weekly Seinfeld Companion* (New York: Warner Books, 1993), 11.

"Oh my God": Kolbert, "A Visit with: Julia

Louis-Dreyfus."

"I have an idea": "Scenes from the Round-table," *Seinfeld,* season 9 (Culver City, CA: Sony Pictures Home Entertainment, 2007), DVD.

"Sometimes it's like": David Wharton, "Humor on the Hot Seat," *Los Angeles Times,* Nov. 30, 1995.

"TV's funniest": Smith, "City Slicker."

"*Seinfeld* shows why": Francis Davis, "Recognition Humor," *Atlantic,* December 1992.

"the most intriguing showdown": Tom Jicha, "Networks Force a Series Showdown," *Sun Sentinel,* June 4, 1992.

"They tell us": Scott D. Pierce, " 'Home Improvement' vs. 'Seinfeld,' " *Deseret News,* Aug. 19, 1992.

1988 Toyota: Bill Zehme, "Jerry & George & Kramer & Elaine," *Rolling Stone,* July 8–22, 1993, Issue #660/61.

Lexus: Nancy Mills, "*Seinfeld*'s Kramer," *Los Angeles Times,* Sept. 6, 1993.

sprinkling a few fall leaves: Smith, "City Slicker."

men yelling: Zehme, "Jerry & George & Kramer & Elaine."

"blow off": Alexander, interview by Amy Harrington.

"*Seinfeld* wasn't showing signs": Daniel

Cerone, "*Seinfeld* Is Suddenly Something," *Los Angeles Times,* March 4, 1993.

"Thanks for quitting *Cheers*": Shapiro, interview by Bill Dana and Jenni Matz.

"I don't want to be": "How It Began."

57 percent: Cerone, "*Seinfeld* Is Suddenly Something."

Chapter 6: The Writers

6.4 million fans: Jennifer Block, "What?," *Ms.,* August/September 2000.

Chapter 7: The Bizarros

Balaban later said: Bob Balaban, Reddit AMA, Oct. 21, 2014: https://www.reddit.com/r/IAmA/comments/2jw6ps/bob_balaban_here_im_doing_the_best_i_can_ama/.

made an appearance at the NBC up-front: Littlefield, *Top of the Rock,* 220.

O'Hurley often hung out: Meghan Keneally, " 'Seinfeld' Star John O'Hurley Shares 5 Surprises That Came with Being Elaine's Boss," ABC News online, July 1, 2014.

filed for bankruptcy: Leslie Kaufman, "Company Killer or Retail Guru?," *New York Times,* April 2, 1999.

more than thirty years: Deniz Rosenberger, "A Chat with Michael Zoulis, Owner of Tom's Restaurant," *Spectrum,* March 26, 2014.

"I am struck by how seriously": John Updike, *Odd Jobs: Essays and Criticism* (New York: Random House, 1991), 60.

"panhandlers" and "squeegee men": Alison Mitchell, "Giuliani Zeroing In on Crime Issue," *New York Times,* Sept. 20, 1993.

"I'm impressed with the detail": Ira Berkow, "On the Set with: The 'Seinfeld' Steinbrenner," *New York Times,* March 28, 1996.

"All sarcasm": John Leonard, "The New York Canon: TV," *New York,* April 7, 2008.

Penny Arcade: "On Saving the Soul of New York City and Yourself," Greenwich Village Society for Historic Preservation blog, April 30, 2014, http://gvshp.org/blog/2014/04/30/ on-saving-the-soul-of-new-york-city-and-yourself/.

Chapter 8: The *Seinfeld* Nation

only competition was *Seinfeld:* Jesse Kornbluth, "Who Needs America Online?," *New York Times Magazine,* Dec. 24, 1995.

450,000: Frank Rose, "Keyword: Context," *Wired,* December 1996.

more loyal to shows: Grant Tinker, *Tinker in Television* (New York: Simon & Schuster, 1994), 180.

"Kmart": Jerry Useem, "Another Boss, Another Revolution," *Fortune,* April 5, 2004.

Friends had ripped off their show: Roger Friedman, "Did *Friends* Rip Off *Seinfeld*? Creators Say Yes," Fox News, May 19, 2003: http://www.foxnews.com/story/2003/05/19/ did-friends-rip-off-seinfeld-creators-say-yes.html.

"I just did a *Seinfeld*": Littlefield, *Top of the Rock,* 169.

This is a Shakespearean soap opera: Ibid., 176.

"*Seinfeld* had different rules": Ibid., 189.

"Paul Reiser, like Jerry Seinfeld": Ibid., 121.

In 1996: Elizabeth Lesly, "Seinfeld," *Businessweek,* June 2, 1997.

$200 million: Janet Lowe, *Jack Welch Speaks* (Hoboken, NJ: John Wiley & Sons, 2008), 14.

11.4 percent: Ken Auletta, *Three Blind Mice* (New York: Vintage, 1992), 81.

more than $1 million: Lesly, "Seinfeld."

bought himself a Porsche: John DeBellis, "My Trip to San Diego with Larry David," 920spot.com, Feb. 25, 2013, http://

920spot.com/2013/02/25/my-trip-to-san-diego-with-larry-david/.

Stanley Kubrick: Michael Herr, "The Real Stanley Kubrick," *Vanity Fair,* August 1999.

Ann Landers . . . Phyllis Diller . . . Dave Barry: Tom Gilatto, "Much Ado About Nothing," *People,* Jan. 12, 1998.

Louis-Dreyfus served alongside: Army Archerd, "Hillary Packs 'Em In at Bev Hills Appearances," *Variety,* Oct. 30, 1994.

Alexander became friends: Jason Alexander, interview by Val Zavala, *L!ve Talks Los Angeles,* Jan. 25, 2012.

"I'm going to really bite him": Andy Ackerman, interview by Jenni Matz, *Archive of American Television,* Nov. 13, 2007.

"the best years of my life": Jerry Stiller, interview by Gary J. Rutkowski, *Archive of American Television,* Dec. 12, 2005.

"sweetest man": Ackerman, interview by Jenni Matz.

"I can't do that": Alexander, interview by Amy Harrington.

"Don't forget to drag it": Stiller, interview by Gary J. Rutkowski.

"stand in the middle": Alexander, interview by Amy Harrington.

"can't be anything but Jewish": Naomi Pfefferman, "After George," *Jewish Journal,*

Oct. 19, 2000.

"Jewish family": Stiller, interview by Gary J. Rutkowski.

former New York Police Department detective: "Barney Martin, TV Father of *Seinfeld,* Dead at 82," Associated Press, March 24, 2005.

youthful affair with James Dean: Michael A. Lipton, "An Affair to Remember," *People,* June 24, 1996.

$1.6 million: Mark Morrison, "Seinfeld Peaks," *Salina Journal* (Kansas), Sept. 19, 1993.

possible Oscar host: Lacey Rose, "Jerry Seinfeld on Why He May Never Go Back to TV," *Hollywood Reporter,* Aug. 21, 2013.

showed up on set: "The Breakthrough Season," *Seinfeld,* season 4 (Culver City, CA: Sony Pictures Home Entertainment, 2005), DVD.

Seinfeld met seventeen-year-old: Karen S. Schneider, "The Game of Love," *People,* March 28, 1994.

her very own public spat: Tom Gilatto, "Two Against the World," *People,* March 29, 1993.

Louis-Dreyfus later said: Zehme, "Jerry & George & Kramer & Elaine."

"Call me a hopeless Puritan": David Lavery and Sara Lewis Dunne, *Seinfeld, Master of*

Its Domain (New York and London: Continuum International Publishing Group, 2008), 2.

"*Seinfeld* is the worst": Maureen Dowd, "Yada Yada Yuppies," *New York Times,* May 14, 1997.

When Florida high school student: "Touched by a *Seinfeld,*" *People,* May 14, 1998.

Seinfeld loved filming: Seinfeld, Reddit AMA.

HoneyBaked hams: Ackerman, interview by Jenni Matz.

"Oh, you're the Marble Rye Lady": "Unforgettable Characters."

Chapter 9: The Show About Something

Nine advertisers: Ashley Fetters, "Masturbation on TV," *Atlantic,* Nov. 19, 2012.

a script in 1990: Mike Ryan, "The Lost Episode of *Seinfeld* That No One Has Ever Seen," *Screencrush,* July 9, 2014, http://screencrush157.com/seinfeld-the-bet/.

"We've got a great arc": Littlefield, *Top of the Rock,* 100.

threatening to join the circus: Dan Jewel, "George's Girl," *People,* March 25, 1996.

"it's hard to figure out where to go": Littlefield, *Top of the Rock,* 100.

"It would have been dishonest": Windolf, "Master of the Domain."

"too self-hatingly Jewish": Tom Shales, "So Long, *Seinfeld," Washington Post,* April 16, 1998.

Stanford University Jewish Studies symposium: Natalie Weinstein, "Is *Seinfeld* Jewish?," *j.* (San Francisco), May 24, 1996.

Rabbi Jonathan Pearl: Rebecca Seagall and Peter Ephross, "Critics Call Show 'Self-Hating,' " *j.* (San Francisco), May 8, 1998.

didn't disagree: Alexander, interview by Amy Harrington.

"the enemy": Peter Bogdanovich, "Seinfeld Battles Actor Danny Hoch," *New York Observer,* March 9, 1998.

"Jerry Seinfeld is sending you something": Kathy Griffin, *Official Book Club Selection* (New York: Ballantine, 2009), 118.

"If you ever need any help": Ackerman, interview by Jenni Matz.

"Either it's going to be wonderful": Jay Rayner, "Wing and a Prayer," *Guardian,* July 10, 2005.

Bizarro first appeared: "Bizarro," DC Comics website, accessed Oct. 1, 2015, http://www.dccomics.com/characters/bizarro.

"I was certainly inspired": Mike Conroy, *500 Comic Book Villains* (London: Collins & Brown, 2004), 244.

"It felt like it shifted": Littlefield, *Top of the Rock,* 292.

he obsessed over: Ackerman, interview by Jenni Matz.

$550,000 per thirty-second ad spot: Degen Pener and Jessica Shaw, "Seined and Sealed," *Entertainment Weekly,* May 23, 1997.

$40 million: Michael Fleming, " 'Blackout' Awakens at Miramax; Hammer Hit," *Variety,* Dec. 4, 1996.

$500,000 per episode: Marcus Errico, "Seinfeld's Co-Stars Want Equal Pay," *E!,* Jan. 14, 1997.

"I want to leave": Jason Alexander, interviewed by Charlie Rose, *Charlie Rose,* April 27, 1998; posted on CharlieRose.com as part of *Seinfeld* archive compilation, Aug. 27, 2014, available at http://charlierose.com/watch/60438669.

"Having raised the bar": Phil Gallo, "Review: 'Seinfeld,' " *Variety,* Nov. 5, 1997.

At the show Christmas party: Seinfeld et al., *Sein Off,* 51.

Chapter 11: The End

$1 billion in profits: Lesly, "Seinfeld."

$200 million of that from *Seinfeld:* "Forever Seinfeld," *People,* May 14, 1998.

"People only want to know": Littlefield, *Top of the Rock,* 295.

"For me, this is all about timing": Bill Carter, "Seinfeld Says It's All Over, and It's No Joke for NBC," *New York Times,* Dec. 26, 1997.

"It seemed artistically right": "Scenes from the Roundtable."

Warner Brothers could ask: Hal Boedeker, "CBS Chief: 'ER' can fetch more than $10 million," *Orlando Sentinel,* Jan. 13, 1998.

$2 million: Bill Carter, "The Thursday Night Massacre," *New York Times Magazine,* Sept. 20, 1998.

"an idiot clown": David B. Caruso, "Immortalized by 'Seinfeld,' the Soup Nazi Returns to NYC," Associated Press, July 20, 2010.

WABC-AM's Babita Hariani: Scott Williams, " 'Soup Nazi' Seins Off with On-Air Tantrum," *Daily News* (New York), Dec. 30, 1997.

"Five million bucks a week?": David Bauder, "Is He Crazy?," Associated Press, Jan. 16, 1998.

largest single deal: Joe Schlosser, "WNYW Pays $300,000 for 'Nothing,' " *Broadcasting & Cable,* Mar. 23, 1998, 10.

$2 million: Stuart Elliott, "Commercial-Time Rates for Last 'Seinfeld' Should Break Records," *New York Times,* Feb. 11, 1998.

"We think it's all a trick": Jorge Fitz-Gibbon, Kevin McCoy, and Douglas Feiden, "Fans in Sitcom Shock," *Daily News* (New York), Dec. 27, 1997.

Manuel Mirabal wrote to NBC: "NBC Apologizes for 'Seinfeld' Episode on the Puerto Rican Day Parade," *New York Times,* May 9, 1998.

spent a month: Seinfeld et al., *Sein Off,* 47.

"Where could I send them": Ibid.,103.

"A Tough Nut to Crack": Jen Carlson, "*Seinfeld* Finale Aired 15 Years Ago," *Gothamist,* May 14, 2014.

confidentiality agreement: Chris Heath, "The End of 'Seinfeld,' " *Rolling Stone,* May 28, 1998.

ink that could not be copied: "The Last Lap," *Seinfeld,* season 9.

"You're going to hear me": Heath, "The End of 'Seinfeld.' "

For the first time since the first episode: Seinfeld et al., *Sein Off,* 47.

As David and Seinfeld stood on the sidelines: Heath, "The End of 'Seinfeld.' "

a logistical nightmare: Ackerman, interview by Jenni Matz.

"How does Kramer function": Seinfeld et al., *Sein Off,* 107.

"For the rest of our lives": Alexander, interview by Amy Harrington.

"Because you don't hear that enough": Seinfeld et al., *Sein Off,* 163.

Ackerman had a hard time leaving: Ackerman, interview by Jenni Matz.

"racist": Carlos Rovira and Leslie Feinberg, "Protesters Tell NBC, 'Seinfeld': Racism Is No Laughing Matter," *Workers World,* May 28, 1998.

"unconscionable insult": "NBC Apologizes for 'Seinfeld' Episode on the Puerto Rican Day Parade."

Maxim magazine had rented: George Rush, Virginia Breen, and Michelle Caruso, "Party's Not Over," *Daily News* (New York), April 9, 1998.

"Talk about sour grapes": Ken Tucker, "Seinfeld," *Entertainment Weekly,* May 29, 1998.

"The ludicrously humorless": Ron Rosenbaum, "The Final Seinfeld: I Told You

So!," *New York Observer,* May 25, 1998.

"The hilarious final episode": Caryn James, " 'Seinfeld' Goes Out in Self-Referential Style," *New York Times,* May 15, 1998.

able to rush him to the hospital faster: Michelle Caruso, "Wail of Sirens Heralds Crooner's Last Hours," *Daily News* (New York), May 16, 1998.

proffered a Tiffany diamond ring: Tom Gilatto, "Jerry Engaged? Get Out," *People,* Nov. 22, 1999.

"I was manipulated, misled": Neal Travis, "His Latest Engagement," *New York Post,* Nov. 9, 1999.

vacationing together: "Jerry Engaged? Get Out."

picketers once again gathered: Tom Shales, "Jerry Seinfeld, Warmed Over on Broadway," *Washington Post,* Aug. 11, 1998.

Chapter 12: Seinfeldia Emerges

Bank of America sold KLBK: Lavery and Dunne, *Seinfeld, Master of Its Domain,* 195.

$500 million minority stake: Bill Carter, "Fox Will Sign Up 12 New Stations," *New York Times,* May 24, 1994.

Seinfeld started beating: Windolf, "Master of the Domain."

462

For the second-season episode "The Revenge": David Sims, "*Seinfeld:* 'The Revenge,' " *A.V. Club,* July 8, 2010, http:// www.avclub.com/tvclub/ seinfeld-the-statuethe-heart-attackthe-revenge-42851.

the crew reshot Randolph's scenes: David Sims, "*Seinfeld:* 'The Handicap Spot,' " *A.V. Club,* Jan. 20, 2011, http:// www.avclub.com/tvclub/ seinfeld-the-handicap-spotthe-junior-mintthe-smell-50267.

most successful show ever in syndication: Sony Pictures Television, "Sony Pictures Television's *Seinfeld* Earns an Unprecedented Fifth Cycle in Syndication," press release, Nov. 18, 2013, available at http:// www.prnewswire.com/news-releases/sony-pictures-televisions-seinfeld-earns-an-unprecedented-fifth-cycle-in-syndication-232391521.html.

more than $3 billion: Adam Sherwin, "Seinfeld Is Laughing All the Way to the Bank," *Independent* (UK), April 3, 2013.

WUTV in Buffalo: Alan Pergament, "In a Reversal, 'Seinfeld' Returns to Rightful Spot at 10:30 P.M. on WUTV," *Buffalo News,* Sept. 25, 2014.

Richards went to Bali: Richards, interview by Jerry Seinfeld.

peak of $75 million: Susan Fornoff, "J. Peterman is back," *SFGate,* June 12, 2004, http://www.sfgate.com/homeandgarden/article/J-Peterman-is-back-This-time-the-catalog-king-2714289.php.

filed for Chapter 11: Mark Graham Brown, *Winning Score* (New York: Productivity Press, 2000), 6.

Eric Cantor threw Festivus fund-raisers: Chris Frates, "OWS Protests Cantor's Festivus Fundraiser," *National Journal,* Dec. 6, 2011.

Google gave *Seinfeld* fans: James Hibberd, "Google Celebrates Festivus with 'Seinfeld'-Inspired Easter Egg," *Entertainment Weekly,* Dec. 11, 2012.

Atheist activist Chaz Stevens: Tia Mitchell, "Nativity Scene, Festivus Pole, and Atheists . . . but No Satanist Display for the Capitol," in *The Buzz, Tampa Bay Times,* Dec. 19, 2013.

"Is this how PC we've gotten": Asawin Suebsaeng, " 'Seinfeld' Writer Takes on Conservative Outrage over Holiday Festivus Pole Protests," *Mother Jones,* Dec. 12, 2013.

he signed a deal to open soup kiosks: Matt Giles, "Breaking Down the Multi-Billion-

Dollar *Seinfeld* Economy," *Vulture,* June 29, 2014.

thirteen locations: Stephanie Vozza, "9 Wildly Successful Brands Born from TV Fame," *Entrepreneur,* Nov. 22, 2013.

Chapter 14: The Legend of the Curse

"David's anger": Kaplan, "Angry Middle-Aged Man."

"I find his character": Jerry Seinfeld. Reddit AMA.

"the most absurd": Scott Raab, "An Extremely Awkward Encounter with Larry David," Esquire.com, Sept. 18, 2009: http://www.esquire.com/entertainment/ movies/a5955/ larry-david-interview-0709/.

$320 fine: Tony Pierce, "Black Man Yells 'Nigger' in Hollywood, Gets Banned," *LAist,* Dec. 7, 2006, http://laist.com/ 2006/ 12/07/ black_man_yells_nigger_in_holly-wood_gets_banned.php.

"I'm sure Michael is": Paul Farhi, " 'Seinfeld' Comic Richards Apologizes for Racial Rant," *Washington Post,* Nov. 1, 2006.

"He's someone that I love": " 'Seinfeld' Star Michael Richards Apologizes on Letter-

man for Racial Slurs," Fox News, Nov.
21, 2006: http://www.foxnews.com/story/
2006/11/21/ seinfeld-star-michael-
richards-apologizes-on-letterman-for-
racial-slurs.html.

"Once the word comes out of your mouth":
"Richards Says Anger, Not Racism,
Sparked Tirade," Associated Press, Nov.
22, 2006.

Jason Alexander was guest-starring: Alexander, interview by Amy Harrington.

10 million viewers: Bill Carter, "Still Riffing
Over Coffee Cups, Seinfeld Renews a Web
Series," *New York Times,* Jan. 6, 2013.

"I think I worked selfishly": Richards,
interview by Jerry Seinfeld.

When Jason Alexander first heard Larry David's idea: Alexander, interview by Amy
Harrington.

Chapter 15: *Seinfeldia*

"Just George and Jerry": retrieved from
ClubAliP Twitter, Jan. 13, 2014, 10:39
A.M., https://twitter.com/clubalip/status/
422769902291009536.

INTERVIEW LIST

Pippin Barr, via e-mail, June 2, 2014.
Alec Berg and Jeff Schaffer, in Los Angeles, Jan. 16, 2014.
Matt Bergstein, Evan Chinoy, Emily Donati, and Jerry Kallarakkal, in Brooklyn, July 5, 2014.
Jeremiah Bosgang, via phone, April 18, 2014.
Tom Cherones, Los Angeles, Jan. 14, 2014.
Jennifer Crittenden, Los Angeles, Jan. 14, 2014.
Joe Davola, via phone, Feb. 12, 2014.
Spike Feresten, via phone, July 1, 2014.
Tom Gammill and Max Pross, Los Angeles, Jan. 14, 2014.
Lee Garlington, via phone, March 27, 2014.
Josh Gondelman, via phone, May 25, 2014.
Chela Holton, via phone, Aug. 4, 2014.
Jazmine Hughes, via phone, June 4, 2014.
William Irwin, via phone, June 10, 2014.
Gregg Kavet, Los Angeles, Jan. 13, 2014.

Steve Koren, via phone, Jan. 29, 2014.
Kenny Kramer, via phone, June 9, 2014.
Mike Lacher, via phone, May 27, 2014.
Carol Leifer, Los Angeles, March 11, 2014.
Rick Lipps, via phone, June 10, 2014.
David Mandel, Los Angeles, Jan. 15, 2014.
Bill Masters, Los Angeles, March 7, 2014.
Peter Mehlman, Los Angeles, Jan. 13, 2014.
Greg Miller, via phone, June 6, 2014.
Dan O'Keefe, Los Angeles, March 10, 2014.
John Peterman, via phone, Oct. 11, 2013.
Adam Rainbolt, via phone, July 17, 2014.
Jason Richards, via phone, June 5, 2014.
Andy Robin, via phone, Feb. 10, 2014.
Rinee Shah, via phone, July 2, 2014.
Monica Yates Shapiro, via phone, July 29, 2014.
Jason Shelowitz, via phone, June 16, 2014.
David Sims, via phone, June 13, 2014.
Fred Stoller, Los Angeles, Jan. 14, 2014.
Larry Thomas, via phone, June 6, 2014.
Jonathan Wolff, via phone, July 29, 2013.

ABOUT THE AUTHOR

Jennifer Keishin Armstrong is the author of *Mary and Lou and Rhoda and Ted,* a history of *The Mary Tyler Moore Show.* She writes about pop culture for several publications, including the *New York Times Book Review, Fast Company, New York*'s *Vulture, BBC Culture, Entertainment Weekly,* and others. She grew up in Homer Glen, Illinois, and now lives in New York City. Visit her online at JenniferKArmstrong.com.

The employees of Thorndike Press hope you have enjoyed this Large Print book. All our Thorndike, Wheeler, and Kennebec Large Print titles are designed for easy reading, and all our books are made to last. Other Thorndike Press Large Print books are available at your library, through selected bookstores, or directly from us.

For information about titles, please call:
  (800) 223-1244

or visit our Web site at:
  http://gale.cengage.com/thorndike

To share your comments, please write:
  Publisher
  Thorndike Press
  10 Water St., Suite 310
  Waterville, ME 04901